The Death of Cuchulain

THE CORNELL YEATS

Plays: *The Death of Cuchulain,* edited by Phillip L. Marcus

The Death of Cuchulain

MANUSCRIPT MATERIALS INCLUDING
THE AUTHOR'S FINAL TEXT

BY W. B. YEATS

EDITED BY
PHILLIP L. MARCUS

CORNELL UNIVERSITY PRESS
ITHACA AND LONDON

THIS BOOK HAS BEEN PUBLISHED WITH THE AID OF A GRANT FROM THE HULL MEMORIAL PUBLICATION FUND OF CORNELL UNIVERSITY.

First published 1982 by Cornell University Press.
Published in the United Kingdom by Cornell University Press Ltd.,
Ely House, 37 Dover Street, London W1X 4HQ.

Library of Congress Cataloging in Publication Data

Yeats, William Butler, 1865-1939.
The death of Cuchulain.

(The Cornell Yeats)
1. Yeats, William Butler, 1865-1939—Manuscripts—Facsimiles. I. Marcus, Phillip L., 1941- II. Title. III. Series: Yeats, William Butler, 1965-1939. Cornell Yeats.
PR5904.D28 1981 822'.8 80-25851
ISBN 0-8014-1379-6

Printed in the United States of America

The paper in this book is acid-free, and meets the guidelines for permanence and durability of the Committee on Production Guidelines for Book Longevity of the Council on Library Resources.

THE CORNELL YEATS

The volumes in this series will present the manuscripts of W. B. Yeats's poems (all extant versions), plays (complete insofar as possible), and other materials (including selected occult writings) from the rich archives preserved in the collections of Senator Michael B. Yeats, the National Library of Ireland, and elsewhere. The primary goal of the editors is to achieve the greatest possible fidelity in transcription. Photographic facsimiles will be used extensively to supplement the texts.

The series will include some important unpublished works of high literary quality, and individually and as a whole the volumes will help to illuminate Yeats's creative process. They will be essential reference works for scholars who wish to establish definitive texts of the published works. They will contain many passages of biographical interest as well as passages that will be helpful in interpreting other works by Yeats. The emphasis throughout, however, will be on the documents themselves, and critical analysis will be limited to discussion of their significance in relation to the published texts; the editors assume that publication of the documents will stimulate critical studies as a matter of course.

THE YEATS EDITORIAL BOARD

Contents

Preface

. . . art / Is but a vision of reality—"Ego Dominus Tuus"

It is always fascinating to observe the process of manipulation and discovery by which an author's vision manifests itself in a work of literature: hence the appeal of "manuscript" studies. This generic appeal is enhanced in the case of *The Death of Cuchulain* (1938–39) by the fact that it was one of W. B. Yeats's very last works, in the composition of which there was the urgency of imminent death. (He himself had once written of Synge's *Deirdre,* "The thought that this was Synge's reverie over death, his own death, made all poignant."[1]) The vision that emerged in the play concerned the significance of death itself, both for the one who dies and for the world left behind. The extant manuscript materials give no indication that Yeats had any major difficulties in discovering his stance concerning that most crucial of questions; composition of the play seems to have proceeded rather smoothly (by Yeatsian standards), and there was nothing comparable to the major shifts in development revealed in the history of such plays as *The Shadowy Waters, The Countess Cathleen, Deirdre,* and *The Player Queen*. It is possible, of course, that now-lost documents from the earliest stages of composition would reveal great struggles to clarify and embody the meditations upon death out of which the play must have begun, but what remains attests less to struggle than to achievement. The unpublished materials do show changes in intention and contain valuable and interesting passages not found in the printed versions. They offer potential illumination of what is after all one of the most enigmatic of Yeats's plays and of the great works of his final period.

My work on the manuscript materials is indebted to pioneering studies of Yeats's manuscripts by Curtis Bradford, Jon Stallworthy, Michael Sidnell, George P. Mayhew, and David R. Clark, and also to the distinguished Cornell Wordsworth series edited by Stephen Parrish.

In addition to the members of the Yeats Editorial Board, individuals who have aided me in various ways include Barry B. Adams, Douglas N. Archibald, Elisabeth Cluer, Michael Colacurcio, Ellen Doeble, Narayan Hegde, Thomas D. Hill, Michael Horniman of A. P. Watt & Son, Kathryn Hume, John V. Kelleher, John Kelly, Ellen Kline, Richard Londraville, W. W. Lyman, Robert O'Driscoll, Virginia Rohan, Yvette Rubio, Michael Sidnell, Sandra Siegel, Joan Winterkorn, Senator Michael B. Yeats and Mrs. Grainne Yeats, and the staff of Cornell University Press. Senator Michael B. Yeats and

[1] *Memoirs,* ed. Denis Donoghue (London: Macmillan, 1972), p. 239.

Miss Anne Yeats generously gave me permission to examine and reproduce the unpublished materials included in this volume. Sarah J. Marcus was a continual source of encouragement and also helped prepare the typescript. My parents, Ben and Virginia Marcus, have contributed more than any acknowledgment could express.

I have found the staffs of the many libraries with which I have had dealings remarkably helpful. In this regard I must mention especially Patrick Henchy of the National Library of Ireland, Ann Hyde of the University of Kansas, David Farmer of the University of Texas, and Nora Niland of the Sligo County Library and Museum. Thanks are due also to the Henry E. Huntington Library and Art Gallery, the National Library of Scotland, the Newberry Library, the Carl H. Pforzheimer Library, the Providence Public Library, and the libraries of the following institutions: Boston College, Brown University, the University of California at Berkeley, the University of California at Los Angeles, Cambridge University, City College of the City University of New York, Colby College, Columbia University, Cornell University, Harvard University, the University of Illinois, Indiana University, the University of Iowa, Kenyon College, McMaster University, the University of Michigan, Mills College, the University of Minnesota, the University of Missouri, Northwestern University, Ohio State University, the University of Pennsylvania, the University of Reading, Seton Hall University, Sonoma State College, Southern Illinois University, Stanford University, the State University of New York at Buffalo, Temple University, the University of Toronto, Trinity College, Dublin, the University of Victoria, Wellesley College, Wesleyan University, the University of Wisconsin at Madison, the University of Wisconsin at Milwaukee, and Yale University.

Financial support for my research on this project was provided by Cornell University and the Penrose Fund of the American Philosophical Society.

I wish to thank John H. Sutherland, editor of the *Colby Library Quarterly,* and Maurice Harmon, editor of the *Irish University Review,* for permission to use in my Introduction material that appeared in a different form in their journals; and the Trustees of the National Library of Ireland, for permission to reproduce in facsimile the *Death of Cuchulain* manuscripts held by the Library.

P.L.M.

Ithaca, New York

The Death of Cuchulain

Introduction

Although *The Death of Cuchulain* was Yeats's last play, his interest in the legend of Cuchulain's death can be traced back to the early decades of his career. In 1892 he published a poem entitled "The Death of Cuchulain," based on an Irish folktale from Jeremiah Curtin's *Myths and Folk-lore of Ireland*. In a note to this poem he commented that "the bardic tale of the death of Cuchullin is very different."[1] Yeats might have encountered the "bardic" version in Whitley Stokes's translation, published in 1877;[2] he definitely knew Standish O'Grady's account in the famous *History of Ireland* (1878–80), for in a letter of 1895 or 1896 he wrote O'Grady that "the story from the laying on of the spell till the death, as you tell it in the 'History,' is not less than any epic tale in the world."[3] In an 1895 review, Yeats placed the story "among the greatest things of all legendary literature."[4] Its impression upon him was no doubt strengthened by Lady Gregory's rendering of it; she herself recalled that "it was only when I had read him one day in London my chapter the 'Death of Cuchulain' that he came to look on me as a fellow writer."[5]

In the early years of the twentieth century Yeats began writing plays about incidents in Cuchulain's career: *On Baile's Strand* and *The Green Helmet*. They were to form part of a "cycle" of plays dealing with the legendary hero. In 1915 Yeats wrote to John Quinn that "all my mythological people have come alive again and I want to complete my heroic cycle."[6] His first Noh-influenced play, *At the Hawk's Well*, dealt with Cuchulain, and in 1916 he said he hoped "to write another of the same sort and so complete a dramatic celebration of the life of Cuchulain planned long ago."[7] In his next Cuchulain play, *The Only Jealousy of Emer*, he picked up the story where he had left off in *On Baile's Strand* and brought Cuchulain (who had apparently died at the end of the earlier play) back to life, thus preparing the way for another play based on the "bardic" version of the death. However, more than twenty years were to pass before that play would actually be written.

In a 1937 letter Yeats told his wife, George, "I think of writing a long Noh play on the death of Cuchulain."[8] Presumably the story of Cuchulain's death held a renewed

[1]*The Variorum Edition of the Poems of W. B. Yeats*, ed. Peter Allt and Russell K. Alspach (1957; rpt. New York: Macmillan, 1973), p. 799.

[2]"*Aided Conculaind*," *Revue Celtique*, 3 (1877): 175–185.

[3]Letter (datable from internal evidence), University of Kansas Library.

[4]"The Story of Early Gaelic Literature," *The Bookman*, June 1895, p. 86.

[5]Lady Augusta Gregory, *Seventy Years*, ed. Colin Smythe (Gerrards Cross: Colin Smythe, 1974), p. 390.

[6]*The Letters of W. B. Yeats*, ed. Allan Wade (London: Rupert Hart-Davis, 1954), p. 595; see also p. 488. Yeats referred to the idea of a cycle or "series" as early as 1901; see *W. B. Yeats and T. Sturge Moore: Their Correspondence 1901–1937*, ed. Ursula Bridge (New York: Oxford University Press, 1953), p. 2.

[7]*Essays and Introductions* (New York: Macmillan, 1961), pp. 221–222.

[8]Letter of October 13 (datable 1937 from internal evidence).

interest for him as he reached the end of his own life. He began work on the play in 1938, informing Edith Heald on October 2: "I am in the middle of a play about Cuchulain s death. It is necessary to wind up my plays on that theme," and on the twenty-fourth writing her that he was "just emerging from the fatigue that follows over work, partly caused by difficulty in constructing my little play *The Death of Cuchulain.*"[9] On the thirty-first he wrote Dorothy Wellesley, "I think I shall have a play to show you."[10] By November 5 he was able to inform Mrs. Yeats that "the prose draft of my play seems finished except for a kind of prologue."[11] Late in November he left for France, and by December 1 he was writing from Cap Martin.[12] Dorothy Wellesley took a villa nearby, and on her first visit to him, "Almost his first words were: 'I want to read you my new play'. And this he did. In spite of the confusion of a much corrected manuscript, he read with great fire."[13] Chronology in her account is somewhat vague, but this reading presumably took place sometime in December. On December 19 he wrote Edith Heald that he had "tired my self finishing the play" and on the twenty-fourth he added a postscript to a letter to F. R. Higgins informing him that "I have almost finished my *Death of Cuchulain.*"[14] In a letter of January 1, 1939, he referred to "Cuchulain Comforted" as "a kind of sequel."[15] Preparation of a legible copy of his corrected typescript was going on as late as January 22.[16] He died six days later, and so never saw proofs or printed text.

Shortly after Yeats's death, Mrs. Yeats gave Dorothy Wellesley "the original MS. with a typed version."[17] The manuscript referred to may well be that now in the National Library of Ireland (MS 8772#1), for on one of its pages ($P13^r$) there is a short note signed "Dorothy Wellesley."[18] That manuscript is primarily a poetic version, but mixed in with it are some pages of prose draft. The play was written on looseleaf paper held in a ring binder; when removed from the binder the leaves were easily confused. In fact, Dorothy Wellesley's note queries the appropriate position in the verse draft of what is actually a page of prose draft. (A page of manuscript which is actually a holograph insertion in a typescript has also been mixed in with this material, but there is no indication of who placed it there.) Dorothy Wellesley's "typed version" would then be one of the five now in the National Library. Of these, one (NLI MS 8772#6) has holograph revisions by Yeats. Another (NLI MS 8772#7), with the same text as the preceding, seems to have been corrected correspondingly by Mrs. Yeats.[19] It

[9]Letters to Edith Shackleton Heald, Harvard University Library. See also *Letters,* ed. Wade, p. 917.

[10]Letter, Humanities Research Center, University of Texas.

[11]Letter of November 5 (datable 1938 from internal evidence).

[12]*Letters,* ed. Wade, p. 918.

[13]*Letters on Poetry from W. B. Yeats to Dorothy Wellesley* (1940; rpt. London: Oxford University Press, 1964), p. 192.

[14]Letters, Harvard University Library and the Humanities Research Center, University of Texas.

[15]*Letters,* ed. Wade, p. 922.

[16]See p. 167.

[17]*Letters on Poetry,* p. 192.

[18]The manuscript would presumably have been returned to Mrs. Yeats and then donated by her, along with the manuscripts of many of Yeats's other plays, to the National Library; National Library records indicate that Mrs. Yeats was the donor of the *Death of Cuchulain* materials now in the Library's possession.

[19]See pp. 167–168.

is this latter which is dated "corrected Jan 22 · 1939." The other typescripts are later than these. In the National Library's collection of manuscripts of the *Last Poems* there are two leaves with drafts of the lyric on their versos. Senator Michael Yeats's collection includes two further pages of prose draft, two pages of verse draft, and a page of the lyric, as well as another late typescript.

Documents missing from the body of known manuscript material include the bulk of the prose draft or drafts and any prose scenarios there may have been, at least one typescript stage, and possibly a fair copy of the extant verse draft made to facilitate preparation of the typescripts. It is conceivable that Mrs. Yeats and Dorothy Wellesley together went through all the materials, Dorothy Wellesley making at that time the note referred to above, and that Mrs. Yeats then gave her *other* items: perhaps the prose-draft material and the missing typescript. This would explain why those items are not with the rest of the documents.[20] In either case, the contents of the typescript or typescripts and of the fair copy, if there was one, can be reconstructed (except of course for passages that may have been added to them during the process of copying or revision and then cancelled) by comparison of the extant documents preceding and following them chronologically in the evolution of the play; so this loss is not a serious one, and except at its earliest stages the process of composition is well represented in the surviving material.

About the absent materials from the genesis of the play one can only speculate, basing those speculations upon what is known of Yeats's general practice. There may have been a brief statement of an "idea for a play." When Yeats had decided upon his subject, he must have reread, or at least looked over, Lady Gregory's account in *Cuchulain of Muirthemne*; possibly he looked up or recalled other versions.[21] He may have made notes about the relevant events. Then there would almost certainly have been one or more scenarios, the significance of which in Yeats's process of composition has been described by Curtis Bradford:

> These are always written in prose and are usually very roughly written. Yeats had a visionary mind, and his scenarios record visions of a dramatic action, sometimes intense visions. Yeats sees in his mind's eye, as it were, a dramatic action unfolding before him in a theater. . . . Just as Yeats's subjects for poems sometimes do not fully anticipate the poems that will develop out of them, so too his scenarios do not always accurately forecast the play. . . . When Yeats had trouble with a play, he would start again by writing new scenarios. . . . A successful scenario states the theme of the play, begins to develop the principal characters, outlines the action, suggests the staging, and sometimes begins to develop the dialogue.[22]

[20]Whatever materials Dorothy Wellesley had she apparently disposed of during her lifetime, for there is no specific reference to them in her will or the various codicils to it and her executors report no knowledge of such papers being left at her death (letter of April 14, 1975, from the firm of Withers, London, U.K.; letter of May 24, 1975, from Miss Elisabeth Cluer).

[21]Lady Gregory's book was referred to directly in the manuscripts; see PV16^{r}.

[22]Curtis Bradford, *Yeats at Work* (Carbondale and Edwardsville: Southern Illinois University Press, 1965), pp. 171–172.

In the scenario he would already be moving away from his donnée. In the traditional legend (as Lady Gregory gave it in Chapters 19 and 20 of *Cuchulain of Muirthemne*), years of battle-victories had made Cuchulain many enemies, chief among them Queen Maeve of Connaught, Erc, son of Cairbre Niafer, Lugaid, son of Curoi, and the three daughters of the enchanter Calatin. Cuchulain's own people tried to shield him from the machinations of these enemies until Conall Caernach and his forces could come to the rescue; but one of the evil daughters, taking upon herself the form of Cuchulain's mistress Niamh, tricked him into going out to fight alone. Sensing that his "time [was] at an end," he would not be swayed by the importunities of his friends and his wife Emer, or the intervention of the Morrigu, a war-goddess, who "did not like Cuchulain to go out and to get his death in the battle." Mortally wounded by Lugaid, Cuchulain strapped himself to a pillar-stone in order to die on his feet. Conall avenged his death and brought Emer her husband's head and those of his slayers. After lamenting him, she died herself and they were buried together; his spirit was seen in his Druid chariot, "singing the music of the Sidhe."

The sources do deal with "fate" and heroic death, but more specific connections with Yeats's thought had to be developed from latent suggestions or imposed upon the vehicle provided by the traditional story. Thus the Old Man has no counterpart in Irish legend, and the sources do not surround Cuchulain with the same figures from his past as does Yeats's play. The latter feature both ties *The Death of Cuchulain* to the other plays in the Cuchulain cycle (in cancelled stage directions for the prologue [PV1 ^{r}] the Old Man even wore "the mask of the old man in the Hawk s well") and contributes to the expression of the play's vision. In a late 1938 letter about his "private philosophy" concerning death, Yeats wrote that "the sensuous image is changed from time to time at predestined moments called *Initiationary Moments*. . . . One sensuous image leads to another because they are never analysed. At *The Critical Moment* they are dissolved by analysis and we enter by free will pure unified experience. When all the sensuous images are dissolved we meet true death."[23] This letter suggests that Yeats structured *The Death of Cuchulain* around a series of "critical moments" in which various "sensuous images" from Cuchulain's past are analyzed and, presumably, dissolved.

After producing a successful scenario, he drafted the play in prose. The prose-draft material that has survived provides no evidence of whether more than one draft was required to produce a prose version that satisfied him and that he could then put into verse. By November 5 he had completed the prose draft except for the prologue. The manuscript materials for the prologue show that Yeats had a great deal of trouble writing it. A second source of difficulty involved the choral lyric. His original intention was to have *two* lyrics, one before the action and one following it—a pattern he had used in a great many of his later plays. This plan persisted through at least one revision and possibly more. Stage directions on the holograph leaf numbered "20" (V20 ^{r}) show that when Yeats wrote that page he still intended to have two lyrics. Furthermore, although those directions were eventually cancelled, in the earliest extant complete typescript the "first" lyric was on a page (apparently taken from an earlier draft) ori-

[23] *Letters,* ed. Wade, pp. 916–917.

ginally numbered "3" and changed to "17." This suggests that the two-lyric structure persisted beyond the manuscript stage.[24] In other plays in which he had used the two-lyric pattern there had been nothing comparable to the Old Man's prologue, and Yeats's reason for abandoning the pattern here may have been a feeling that the prologue and the lyric together delayed too long the opening of the action.

A related problem involved the end of the play. When composing the extant verse draft, Yeats had comparatively little trouble with the middle scenes of the play; the manuscript, though filled with revisions, moves relatively smoothly and easily, and there are no textual complexities until after the death of Cuchulain. But at that point, the playwright encountered a new difficulty. His original plan had been to have the Old Man reappear after the hero's death to comment upon that death and to introduce Emer's dance. After some futile revision, he abandoned this plan and gave the speech in question to the Morrigu.

When this draft was in shape, presumably in early December, the play was well on its way toward completion. Except for the placement of the lyric, the basic structure had been established and, while the texture of the verse would still need much polishing, there was already considerable verbal subtlety. For example, Eithne refers to Cuchulain as "about to die" ($V6^r$, l. 13). Later Aoife tells Cuchulain that the reason he cannot understand her is because he is "about to die" ($V11^r$, l. 3). Then, just as the Blind Man is going to cut off Cuchulain's head and we expect him to tell Cuchulain "you are about to die," Cuchulain shifts the emphasis to the imminent freeing of his soul: "I think it [is] about to sing" ($V14^r$, l. 2). The use of "about to" in all three incidents links the episodes and at the same time highlights a difference between the first two and the third, a transmutation of death into song. (The third of these lines later becomes the assertive "I say it is about to sing" [TS6, 15, l. 1], thereby heightening the element of contrast.)

After getting all the parts of his play into at least roughly satisfactory form in manuscript, Yeats was ready to think about typescripts. Either he wrote out a fair copy of the entire verse draft (doing some revision as he went) or he dictated from his manuscript to the typist, who may well have been Mrs. Yeats. In either case, the typescripts would provide him with the opportunity to make whatever further changes he desired.

The earliest surviving complete typescript (TS6) contains Yeats's holograph corrections and revisions throughout. He made many alterations, for purposes of stylistic improvement and fuller expression of the complex vision of the play. When the revision of TS6 was complete, the play had reached final form in all but some minor details.

The manuscript materials for *The Death of Cuchulain* offer an exciting opportunity to observe Yeats's imagination at work at the end of his life, and provide evidence for correction of the printed texts (see pp. 167–182). In addition, as the following pages suggest, they may aid in the interpretation of the finished play. A simple instance involves the prologue. In view of recent assertions by Kathleen Raine and Liam Miller that the dancer referred to by the Old Man in the finished play—"I could have got such

[24]See p. 163.

a dancer once, but she has gone"—was Isadora Duncan, the draft version of the passage (V2D^r, l. 4) is illuminating.[25] Universalizing of specific references is common in the manuscript stages of Yeats's work, and took place here, but the draft leaves no doubt that he had originally been thinking of Ninette de Valois.

The references to the "Song of Sixpence" in the first draft of the Old Man's speech after Cuchulain's death (P15^r, PV16^r) are of interest because of the macabre irony produced by the juxtaposition of childish innocence and severed heads, infantile jingle and literary tragedy; and the connection between the singing blackbirds (a grimly comic version of the Morrigu, who could take the form of a crow) and the song of Cuchulain's bird-soul. They also establish a resonance between the Old Man and Yeats himself at the end of his life. In a very late letter, written when work on *The Death of Cuchulain* was virtually complete, he summed up a lifetime's quest for wisdom: "It seems to me that I have found what I wanted. When I try to put all into a phrase I say, 'Man can embody truth but he cannot know it.' I must embody it in the completion of my life. The abstract is not life and everywhere draws out its contradictions. You can refute Hegel but not the Saint or the Song of Sixpence."[26] The 1937 version of *A Vision* provides a gloss upon this passage and indicates at least one of his sources or "authorities" for the idea: "The whole system is founded upon the belief that the ultimate reality, symbolised as the Sphere, falls in human consciousness, as Nicholas of Cusa was the first to demonstrate, into a series of antinomies."[27] Thus "the sphere . . . can be symbolised but cannot be known."[28] Reality evades the philosophers, bound by logic and the principle of noncontradiction. The passionate faith of the holy man and the non-sense of the nursery are both closer to the truth—grounded in life itself, incarnating the mythic and the timeless, and not dependent upon the ultimately specious order of argument. Nicholas of Cusa is contrasted by Yeats in the "Genealogical Tree of Revolution" with Hegel's view "all things transparent to reason."[29] That the ideas considered in the letter were already in Yeats's mind when he wrote the Old Man's speech is made virtually certain by the following passage:

> Four & twenty black birds — the pie — the six pence —
> the ry & the pocket — nothing to do with each other
> an untrue song & yet immortal. And thats a strange
> [?thing], a very strange thing [P15^r, ll. 6–9]

From a rational point of view, the elements of the Song of Sixpence have "nothing to do with each other"; "untrue" in this sense, they are true at a higher level, and thus immortal. (In "An Indian Monk" Yeats had already referred to "that irrational element

[25] Kathleen Raine, *Death-in-Life and Life-in-Death* (Dublin: Dolmen Press, 1974), pp. 55–56; Liam Miller, *The Noble Drama of W. B. Yeats* (Dublin: Dolmen Press, 1977), pp. 324–325.

[26] *Letters*, ed. Wade, p. 922.

[27] *A Vision* (New York: Macmillan, 1956), p. 187; cf. also *Essays and Introductions*, p. 503. Nicholas's importance to Yeats is discussed by Virginia Moore, *The Unicorn* (New York: Macmillan, 1954), pp. 339–344.

[28] *A Vision*, p. 193.

[29] See A. N. Jeffares, *W. B. Yeats: Man and Poet*, 2nd ed. (London: Routledge and Kegan Paul, 1962), pp. 351–352; and Moore, pp. 340, 342.

which has made 'Sing a Song of Sixpence' immortal."[30]) The nursery rhyme introduces the more inclusive view at the moment of death, when all philosophies receive the ultimate test.

The "little bo peep . . ." reference (PV16^{r}, l. 1) would have had similar symbolic associations. The fact that Yeats abandoned the idea of using any nursery rhyme at this point may have been merely a function of his difficulty in getting the entire section into even roughly satisfactory shape—a difficulty which led to the substitution of a speaker who could not plausibly have spoken such a line. Or it might reflect a recognition that the association was too private to bear sufficient *dramatic* weight. The finished play seems somewhat impoverished without it; but analysis of the typescripts reveals that Yeats did decide to raise the question of "truth" prominently at another point in the play.

Many of Yeats's revisions in the typescript stage involved improvements in style and theatrical viability of the sort familiar to all who have studied his manuscripts and the revisions from one edition of his work to another; but one key passage shows that he was still concerned with that larger thematic problem of "truth." That passage involves the encounter between Cuchulain and Eithne. (The unrevised typescript is printed in boldface; revisions are in roman.)

~~Soldier~~
~~Attendant~~ **~~Your men stand ready.~~**
Servant
Your great horse is bitted. All wait the word.

Cuchullain **I come to give it, but must ask a question.**
This woman, wild with grief, declares that she
Out of pure treachery has told me lies
That should have brought my death. What can I do?
How can I save her from her own wild words?

Servant
~~Soldier~~
~~Attendant~~ **Is her confession true?**

I make the truth
~~nothing is true~~ ~~I make the~~
Cuchullain **~~No, most untrue.~~** ~~What can be true~~ ∧
I say
~~But that~~ she brings
~~She has but brought~~ **a message from my wife.**

[TS6, 7, ll. 1–9]

The progression of events in that encounter is obscure and difficult to follow. Eithne, bringing Cuchulain a letter from Emer warning him not to fight until reinforcements arrive, has been put into a trance by his old enemy Maeve and tricked into giving him a

[30]*Essays and Introductions,* p. 434.

conflicting message urging immediate combat. The Morrigu reveals the duplicity to Eithne, but Cuchulain will not accept this story and insists on believing that Eithne herself, desirous of a younger man, planned the scheme to send her aging lover to his death. Eithne is driven wild with rage, not by the accusation, which she denies, but by the thought that Cuchulain has so declined from his former greatness as to forgive where he *imagines* there to be treachery. She will do anything, even denounce herself to Cuchulain's men and meet death at their hands, in order that her shade may greet his "and prove it is no traitor." When Cuchulain's servant comes to summon him to the battle, Cuchulain tells him, falsely, that "This woman, wild with grief, declares that she / Out of pure treachery has told me lies / That should have brought my death." Apparently Cuchulain is trying to protect her by forestalling the false confession she might make after his death. When the servant asks "Is her confession true?" Cuchulain proleptically undercuts it: "No, most untrue. / She has but brought a message from my wife."

This initial "No, most untrue" in the unrevised typescript triggered a series of revisions in which Yeats explored the underlying question of "truth" itself. The order in which he wrote the alternate versions can only be guessed at; as his habit was to put revisions first above the line involved, perhaps "nothing is true" was the earliest. In "No, most untrue" the concept of truth is being used narrowly, in a context of possible lying and deception. "Nothing is true" can also be taken in this sense—that is, "none of what she says is true"—and the continuation "But that she brings a message from my wife" demands such a sense; but isolated in a hemistich, "nothing is true" becomes susceptible of interpretation in a more philosophical sense as a totally pessimistic, Pyrrhonist view of human knowledge and perhaps also of human existence. One of the most characteristic movements of Yeats's thought is from the declarative statement to the interrogative, and such a movement seems to have taken place here. "What can be true," while it could be a rhetorical version of "Nothing is true," calling for the answer "nothing," could also be a genuine question.

In the final stage of revision, the line which had been a sweeping negation becomes a dramatic affirmation. Truth emerges as subjective and personal, its ontological status dependent upon the individual: "I make the truth." The exclamation point in the printed versions is not authorial, and Cuchulain's mood in speaking the line *could* be almost ruminative rather than emphatic; in either case the final affirmation is far more significant than the colorless original version and shows that the old heroic pride, the passing of which Eithne has been lamenting, is not in fact extinguished.

However, while direct affirmation is fully in character for Cuchulain, it is less so for Yeats. The movement of the revisions was apparently from statement through speculation back to statement, but Yeats may well have been dramatizing only part of himself in this final swing of the pendulum. He was strongly attracted to the "subjective" vision implicit in Cuchulain's words, and gave it memorable expression in Part III of "The Tower" and elsewhere, but he felt also that it was a limited and partial view, quite literally a half-truth.[31]

[31]I have presented this argument more fully in " 'I make the truth': Vision and Revision in Yeats's *The Death of Cuchulain,*" *Colby Library Quarterly,* 12 (June 1976): 57–64.

The "Song of Sixpence" and "I make the truth" are both examples of how revision of specific passages affected the expression of the play's overall vision. Structural changes had a similar effect. Yeats's original plan was to have the Old Man (or "Attendant" or "Producer") appear several times in the play. He was to have appeared as the Morrigu to Eithne ($V4^r$) and as Cuchulain's servant ($V7^r$), as well as at the end of the play as commentator upon Cuchulain's death and introducer of Emer's dance. This was in part a simple theatrical convention for reducing the number of actors required to perform the play. But the final appearance as commentator would have produced a very different dramatic tone as well; and perhaps the plan threatened to give him too much prominence. Framing the scenes of Cuchulain's death with such a figure would have made the hero seem subordinate to and less significant than the Old Man. Both characters obviously embody aspects of their creator's own personality, elements of his personal vision; and adjustments in their relative dramatic importance would directly affect the vision of the play as a whole. The final version contains many negative implications; but the negative element would have been even more prominent if the initial strategy had been maintained, for the Old Man's concern with "truth" produces no exaltation in his words, and in recounting the events of Cuchulain's death he shows no passionate involvement.

When the Old Man's black humor and slack prose were replaced by the stately verse of the Morrigu ($V13^v$), the tone of the passage changed markedly. His casualness, his ramblings, and his uncertainties suggest a detachment that at least partially undermines the positive aspects of Cuchulain's death; the new version reinforced those aspects, not only through the return to poetry but also because the Morrigu is a figure definitely sympathetic to Cuchulain.[32]

The evolution of the lyric offers yet another example of the interest of the manuscripts in relation to the final text. Thus the lines "Adored their bodily beauty / And the intellect in their eye" ($PV1^v$, ll. 5–6) in the early drafts make clearer the resonance between the play and "The Statues": the Harlot yearning to clasp the bodies of the Irish epic heroes corresponds to the "boys and girls, pale from the imagined love / Of solitary beds" who pressed their lips to the Phidian statues; and the heroes themselves, like the statues, are repositories of "intellect" in the Neoplatonic sense, an exalted spiritual faculty. That the heroes are less accessible suggests a difference in mood between play and poem. Similarly, the reference to Swift in an early draft of the "second" lyric ($L4^r$, ll. 1–2) corresponds to the Berkeleyan presence behind "We Irish . . ." in "The Statues," each introducing an eighteenth-century figure engaged in fighting the Salamis of the Irish intellect. Other connections between the two works emerged as the lyric evolved.

During the process of composition Yeats wrote and then cancelled a prose passage that deals with a question he transferred to his developing lyric:

[32]The positive nature of their relationship, which has been misunderstood by critics, is supported by the evidence of another change in the manuscripts and has important thematic implications; see Phillip L. Marcus, "Myth and Meaning in Yeats's *The Death of Cuchulain,*" *Irish University Review,* 2 (1972): 133–148.

I think we love & hate all that is real but
now that hes unreal she can ~~give him~~
now that is dead, she ~~can nothing but love. Perhaps~~
give him un mixed love. Perhaps
that is right, perhaps she can hear his soul
sing in its eternal joy [PV16^{v}, ll. 6–9]

The emergence in the prose fragment and the verse drafts of the references to "reality" is of particular interest in relation to some of the most obscure parts of the lyric. The pertinent lines are:

That there are still some living
That do my limbs unclothe
But that the flesh my flesh has gripped
I both adore and loathe [TS6, 17, ll. 13–16]

and

Are those things that men adore and loathe
Their sole reality? [TS6, 18, ll. 1–2]

F. A. C. Wilson has argued that the Harlot means "there are some human beings who still make love to me, but I do not love them with the intensity I feel for the disparate and evasive (and therefore also loathesome) bodies of the Sidhe."[33] The prose fragment, however, supports the opposite reading: the Harlot, though she cannot make physical contact with the dead heroes, feels adoration for them; whereas her feelings toward mortals, whose flesh she can grip, are a mixture of adoration and loathing.

In the fragment "reality" is defined (uncharacteristically for Yeats) in commonsense terms as the phenomenal realm, the fallen world where antinomies are an inescapable part of experience.[34] The verse draft contains three later-cancelled instances of the love-hate antinomy: Aoife says she "hated men / But loved the sword" (V9^{v}, ll. 12–13); Cuchulain tells her "I had loved & hated you . . ." (V10^{r}, l. 12) and refers to "a blind man & a fool bound to each other / By love & hate . . ." (V12^{r}, ll. 2–3). Eithne, Aoife, and possibly the Morrigu and even Emer feel a mixture of love and hatred for Cuchulain. When one dies, as Cuchulain has, one becomes "unreal." The suggestion that he can then be the object of "unmixed love" is somewhat surprising, for presumably even in the Sphere hatred is not absent but rather unimaginably reconciled with its opposite. The basic point may be simply that toward those in the more harmonious state mortals can feel a purer emotion.[35]

Also, the drafts suggest, for some minds there was another "reality" than that of

[33] *W. B. Yeats and Tradition* (1958; rpt. London: Methuen, 1968), pp. 186–187.

[34] Wilson (ibid., p. 163) says he has found no instance in Yeats's work where he does not use "reality" in reference to the "divine world."

[35] See *The Celtic Twilight and a Selection of Early Poems* (New York: New American Library, 1962), p. 85: "It is one of the great troubles of life that we cannot have any unmixed emotions. . . . If we could love

modern Ireland, an ideal conception embodied in heroes such as Cuchulain. In *Wheels and Butterflies* (1934) Yeats says that "In the eighties of the last century Standish O'Grady, his mind full of Homer, retold the story of Cuchulain that he might bring back an heroic ideal."[36] Yeats himself carried on the effort but did not complete his portrait of the hero's career—"I would have attempted the Battle of the Ford and the Death of Cuchulain, had not the mood of Ireland changed." In the next section of the essay he explains the events involved in that change. The split in the Irish Party following the death of Parnell had been a stimulus to Irish writers:

> When Parnell was dragged down, his shattered party gave itself up to nine years' vituperation, and Irish imagination fled the sordid scene. . . . Repelled by what had seemed the *sole reality,* we had turned to romantic dreaming, to the nobility of tradition [italics added].

But then came the ''Cork Realists'' and Joyce, who, instead of ''turning their backs upon the actual Ireland of their day, . . . attacked everything that had made it possible. . . .'' The audience for literature of the other sort dwindled:

> . . . even if there had been no such cause of bitterness, of self-contempt, we could not, considering that every man everywhere is more of his time than of his nation, have long kept the attention of our small public. . . . Only a change in European thought could have made that possible.

Gyres run on, however, and in the psychical research of Sir William Crookes, Yeats discerns "the slow preparation for the greatest, perhaps the most dangerous, revolution in thought Europe has seen since the Renaissance, a revolution that may, perhaps, establish the scientific complement of certain philosophies that in all ancient countries sustained heroic art." This statement is glossed in an unpublished typescript intended for *A Vision,* where it is said of the coming cycle that "its Schools and Universities would combine some Asiatic philosophy with the latest results of that psychical research founded by William Crookes, preparing all to face death without flinching, perhaps even with joy";[37] and in the *Wheels and Butterflies* essay itself:

> Here in Ireland we have come to think of self-sacrifice, when worthy of public honour, as the act of some man at the moment when he is least himself, most completely the crowd. The heroic act, as it descends through tradition,

---

and hate with as good heart as the faeries do, we might grow to be long-lived like them." This essay was first published in 1893. Cf. also the curse on Cuchulain in *At the Hawk's Well,* ll. 174–175: "Never to win a woman's love and keep it; / Or always to mix hatred in the love."

[36] *Wheels and Butterflies,* p. 70; the quotations in the following discussion are all from pp. 70–77. I have examined O'Grady's treatment of Cuchulain and his efforts to "bring back an heroic ideal" in *Standish O'Grady* (Lewisburg, Pa.: Bucknell University Press, 1970).

[37] Quoted by Hazard Adams, *Blake and Yeats: The Contrary Vision* (Ithaca: Cornell University Press, 1955), p. 302; for tragedy as "a joy to the man who dies" see *Essays and Introductions,* p. 523 and *Explorations* (New York: Macmillan, 1962), p. 448.

> is an act done because a man is himself, because, being himself, he can ask nothing of other men but room amid remembered tragedies; a sacrifice of himself to himself, almost, so little may he bargain, of the moment to the moment. . . . So lonely is that ancient act, so great the pathos of its joy, that I have never been able to read without tears a passage in *Sigurd the Volsung* describing how the new-born child lay in the bed and looked 'straight on the sun'; . . .
>
> How could one fail to be moved in the presence of the central mystery of the faith of poets, painters, and athletes? I am carried forty years back and hear a famous old athlete wind up a speech to country lads—'the holy people have above them the communion of saints; we the communion of the *Tuatha de Danaan* of Erin'.

By 1938 Yeats must have decided that the mood of the world, and consequently of Ireland, had changed enough so he could attempt to finish the task of bringing back "the heroic ideal," could write *The Death of Cuchulain*. Indeed, this description of the "heroic act" states the milieu of the play, and "a sacrifice of himself to himself" warns that Cuchulain's rejection of the prudent course of waiting for reinforcements before joining battle should not be judged by canons according to which it can only be a betrayal either of the community or of his own heroic spirit.[38] The "objective," other-centered culture of Christianity was soon to appear in Ireland, but Cuchulain himself had above him "the communion of the *Tuatha de Danaan,*" represented in the play by the Morrigu and corresponding to the "subjective" vision of life which views reality as a "congeries of beings," man's self supreme and the maker of truth.

So the question of the "sole reality" takes one into the heart of Yeats's own attitudes toward the subject of the play. How does it relate to what follows it in the lyric? Connolly was not in Yeats's terms an artist at all, and Pearse's artistic efforts could hardly have pleased him. Furthermore, neither man turned away from political involvement; instead they pursued revolutionary alternatives to the parliamentary nationalism of the Irish Party. And Yeats's statement that "in Ireland we have come to think of self-sacrifice, when worthy of public honour, as the act of some man at the moment when he is least himself" fits perfectly the men of 1916 and probably alludes to them. But at least for Pearse (and the drafts show that Connolly was a second thought) political activism found its inspiration in "romantic dreaming" and "the nobility of tradition." Yeats knew that Pearse was not of his school, but he could discern in O'Grady's idealized Cuchulain a common ancestor and in Pearse's act a sign that the heroic ideal had already become once again a force in Irish life. In fact the answer to the manuscript query "What singer had filled their thought" ($PV16^{v}$, l. 4) could well be O'Grady,

[38]See *Autobiographies* (1955; rpt. London: Macmillan, 1966), p. 465: "We discussed self-realization and self-sacrifice. He said the classic self-realization had failed and yet the victory of Christian self-sacrifice had plunged the world into the Dark Ages. I reminded him of some Norse God, who was hung over an abyss for three days, 'a sacrifice to himself', to show that the two were not incompatible." The concept of sacrificing "to oneself" undoubtedly appealed to Yeats because it permitted the subjective personality-type to subsume the opposing objective impulse.

who by Yeats's own theory that Life imitates Art was at least as much as Yeats the man who sent out "certain men the English shot."[39]

The early version (L3^{v}) is far more "patriotic" than the lyric in its final form. "Pearse & his boys" appear unambiguously as liberators; and the line "the fight that gave us freed[om]" is one of those rare instances in which Yeats, who during his long literary career had frequently been the target of demands that he write in the service of the national cause, sounds like the heir of the Young Irelanders. ("Wherever green is worn" in "Easter 1916" is perhaps the most striking example in his mature published work.[40]) More typical is "The Statues," which makes the highest claims for Ireland—destined, at the next reversal of the gyres, to become the cradle of an ideal civilization—but supports those claims through a philosophical interpretation of history rather than with what he generally called "rhetoric." As the *Death of Cuchulain* lyric evolves, it grows less clear, focusing upon the same incident as the last stanza of "The Statues" but allowing a more negative interpretation of it. No body like Cuchulain's has appeared in the modern world. At the same time Yeats was finishing the play he wrote to Sir William Rothenstein that "some of the best known of the young men who got themselves killed in 1916 had the Irish legendary hero Cuchulain so much in their minds that the Government has celebrated the event with a bad statue."[41] The echo of the manuscript's "Cuchullain was so much in their thought" (L3^{v}, l. 5) provides a direct link between play and letter. Earlier in 1938 Yeats had told Edith Heald in regard to "The Statues" that "Cuchulain is in the last stanza because Pearse and some of his followers had a cult of him. The Government has put a statue of Cuchulain in the rebuilt post office to commemorate this."[42] While it may have been the fact that Rothenstein was an artist which led Yeats to offer him an aesthetic judgment of the statue, the introduction of the negative adjective is another reflection of a difference in mood between poem and play. The Rising had been heroic, and Yeats wanted to feel part of (even creator of) *some* Irish nation; but he must have found it difficult to convince himself for any length of time that the Free State was a suitable realization of his ideal vision.[43] He may well have doubted whether even his own sublime art could make it so.

On the other hand, the lines

> No body like his body
> Has modern woman borne,
> But an old man looking back on life
> Imagines it in scorn [TS6, 17, ll. 9–12]

could be read as a reference to Yeats himself, magnifying the power of the heroic ideal

[39]See *Essays and Introductions,* pp. 511–516.

[40]The most notorious early instance was his poem on the death of Parnell, "*Mourn—And Then Onward!*"; see *Variorum Poems,* pp. 737–738.

[41]*Scattering Branches,* ed. Stephen Gwynn (New York: Macmillan, 1940), p. 52; letter of December 29, 1938.

[42]*Letters,* ed. Wade, p. 911.

[43]The negative vision is present even in an essay like "Ireland, 1921–1931" (*The Spectator,* January 30, 1932, pp. 137–138), where Yeats does find some positive elements in the new state.

by "imagining" Cuchulain in his play in a way that Sheppard's "bad statue" had failed to do, and thus offering at least the prospect of future improvement. (Similarly, in "Blood and the Moon" Yeats had evoked the tower as a symbol of the eighteenth-century Anglo-Irish tradition, in mockery of the modern world but also as an ideal that might shape the *future* nation.) The ambiguity of the final lyric probably reflects Yeats's own uncertainty. He may have "found what he wanted," but the drafts of *The Death of Cuchulain* show us that even at the very end of his life the creative act was for him still an act of exploration.

Transcription Principles and Procedures

Yeats's manuscripts are impossible to transcribe with absolute fidelity. His hand was almost always difficult to read, especially when he was writing for his eye alone and with a carelessness reflecting the excitement of literary creation. He left the endings of many words unfinished or represented by a vague line, formed letters carelessly and inconsistently, was a poor and erratic speller, and punctuated unsystematically. These difficulties are compounded in the case of *The Death of Cuchulain* by the variety of shades of blue and black ink found in the manuscript, which may indicate stages of composition but are sometimes very hard to distinguish from one another.

The photo-facsimiles will enable the interested reader to *see* what Yeats wrote. The task of the editor is to present a transcription in which the often highly obscure documents are *read,* and this inevitably requires a certain amount of interpretive "translation." The principles in accordance with which that process has been carried out and the conventions used in presenting the resultant text are listed below.

1. Where there is no reasonable doubt what word Yeats intended, even though letters may seem to be missing or run together at the end of it, that word is transcribed in full. In many cases, Yeats's actual spelling is difficult or impossible to determine, and in such cases the standard spelling is given. On the other hand, Yeats's spelling is preserved when it is clear, even if it is incorrect. Thus on V9^{r}, l. 12, the last two words are certainly meant to be "ancient" and "stone," though neither is "finished" and in "ancient" virtually no letter after the *a* is clearly formed; so the standard spellings are used. But in the fifth line of the stage directions on V11^{r}, Yeats has unquestionably written "leggs" for "legs," and the misspelled version is given. (He spells the same word correctly in the preceding line, offering a reminder that it is dangerous to use his spelling of a word in one instance to read the "same" word elsewhere or as evidence that he pronounced certain words in certain ways.)

   In *The Death of Cuchulain* the hero's name is a particularly common source of difficulty. Writing it so often, Yeats frequently compressed it and seems to have made no effort to spell it consistently. Also, his *a*'s and *i*'s are often indistinguishable and the usually undotted *i*'s merge with the *n*'s. In the transcriptions the name is given in full wherever anything beyond "Cuchul" is present; and "Cuchulain" and "Cuchullain" (the number of *l*'s usually is distinct) are used as standard spellings. Occasionally the *h* is clearly absent, in which case the name is transcribed as "Cuculain" or "Cucullain."

2. Yeats frequently broke words at unusual points, or broke words not normally divided. Such words are joined in the transcriptions unless the width of the break approximates the spacing Yeats normally left *between* words, indicating that he considered the word in question to be actually two words or one needing hyphenation (though he himself rarely inserted hyphens). Thus on V4^{r}, "fa ce" in l. 4 has been joined, but "To morrow" in l. 5 has not. The facsimiles of course provide the reader the opportunity to check such distinctions.
3. Symbols for illegible words and editorial conjectures:

[?]	a totally unintelligible word
[? ? ?]	several totally unintelligible words
[~~?~~]	a cancelled and totally unintelligible word
[?and]	a conjectural reading (used only when the editor feels more than ordinary uncertainty)
[?by/?of]	equally possible conjectural readings

4. Overwritings are indicated thus: ha $\left\{\begin{matrix}\text{s}\\ \text{ve}\end{matrix}\right.$ = "have" converted to "has."
5. There are throughout the drafts certain obscure marks or blots, which may have been made accidentally. In cases where their significance has not been determined, they are silently omitted.
6. Cancellation of single lines or of words within a line is indicated by horizontal cancellation lines. (These lines are straight even where Yeats's were wavy.) Parallel lines are used to indicate cancellation first of a word or phrase and then of the entire line or a greater portion of it. Where Yeats intended to cancel an entire word but only struck through part of it, the cancellation line in the transcription extends through the entire word. However, even when it seems likely that Yeats meant to cancel an entire phrase or line, no word that he did not at least partially cancel is cancelled in the transcriptions.
7. Cancellation of entire passages is indicated by vertical brackets in the left margin, heavy or thin to indicate ink color. (See item 12, below.) Arrows indicating relocation of words and passages only approximate the originals. Where typographical limitations make it impossible to print a marginal revision in its actual position, it is given immediately below the transcription of the page on which it occurs. Arrows leading from such passages are not reproduced.
8. Yeats's "stet" marks are preserved, as are his underscorings to indicate italics. Caret symbols that Yeats placed just below the line are raised to line level.
9. In the transcriptions of typescript material, minor and obvious typing errors such as strikeovers may not be recorded; but all holograph corrections of typescript are indicated.
10. Problems in the transcription of words and passages are discussed in footnotes keyed to line numbers in the margin of the transcriptions.
11. Spacing and relative position of words and lines approximate the originals insofar as printed type can reproduce handwritten and typescript material.

12. The following typographical conventions have been used to represent various physical features of the texts:

10-point roman	ink, earlier stage (in *The Death of Cuchulain,* blue ink)
8-point roman	ink, later stage (in *The Death of Cuchulain,* black ink)
8-point italic	pencil
heavy ~~cancellation line~~	deletion, earlier stage
thin ~~cancellation line~~	deletion, later stage
boldface	typescript or print

The Death of Cuchulain

MANUSCRIPTS, WITH TRANSCRIPTIONS AND PHOTOGRAPHIC REPRODUCTIONS

The manuscript versions of *The Death of Cuchulain* were written on white wove loose-leaf paper, punched with three holes and having blue horizontal rules and a double red top-margin rule. The paper measures 22.9 cm × 18.0 cm and is watermarked WALKERS / Loose Leaf / MADE IN GT BRITAIN. Yeats used similar paper for early drafts of *Purgatory* and several of the *Last Poems*. The leaves were kept in a ring binder, where they could be re-arranged during the process of composition and from which they could be removed when no longer needed.

Manuscripts

For purposes of analysis, the transcriptions that follow are separated into four groups:

Manuscripts of the prologue
Manuscripts of the central portion of the play
Manuscripts of the end of the play
Manuscripts of the lyric

To facilitate identification I have assigned a letter and number to every leaf of manuscript material. The establishment of a numbering system has been complicated by the fact that most but not all of the leaves were numbered by Yeats himself and that at different stages in the process of composition certain leaves occupied different relative positions in the developing text. The system I have adopted preserves as far as possible Yeats's own numbering and gives at least a general sense of the position or positions occupied by each leaf. A *P* before the number indicates that the leaf was part of the prose draft, *V* indicates verse draft, and *PV* means prose draft probably adapted for use in the verse draft. *L* is used to identify leaves devoted to the composition of the lyric and not clearly part of either prose or verse drafts of the play as a whole. Superscript ^{r} and ^{v} indicate recto and verso of a leaf as used by Yeats. Most of the manuscript leaves are in the National Library of Ireland, where they are arranged by folder number; a few remain in the private collection of Senator Michael B. Yeats. The location of each leaf is given in the list that follows.

PV1	NLI 8772(1)
V2A	NLI 8772(1)
V2B	NLI 8772(1)
V2C	NLI 8772(1)
V2D	NLI 8772(1)
V2O	NLI 8772(1)
V3	NLI 8772(1)
V4	NLI 8772(1)
V5	NLI 8772(1)
V6	NLI 8772(1)
V7	NLI 8772(1)
V8	NLI 8772(1)
V9	NLI 8772(1)
V10	NLI 8772(1)
V11	NLI 8772(1)
V12	NLI 8772(1)
V13	NLI 8772(1)
V11A	MBY
V12A	MBY
P13	NLI 8772(1)
P14	MBY
P15	MBY
PV16	NLI 8772(1)

V14	NLI 8772(1)
L1	NLI 13593(49)
L2	NLI 13593(39)
L3	NLI 8772(2)
L4	MBY

The bracketed line numbers given for each leaf indicate the lines of Yeats's final text (pp. 169–180) to which that leaf corresponds. As that correspondence is generally only approximate at best, a more precise means of reference to particular portions of a leaf is provided by marginal lineation beginning anew on each leaf.

Manuscripts of the Prologue

The surviving elements of the prose draft are in blue ink, and Yeats used the same blue ink in the early stages of writing the extant verse draft. As the prologue was in prose in all versions, it is impossible to be sure whether the earliest material that remains is from the prose draft or the verse draft. It is clear from Yeats's letter of November 5, 1938, that the prologue was the last part of the prose draft to be finished, which suggests that he was experiencing difficulties with it. What probably happened is that when he did satisfy himself with the prose-draft version he simply left it in his loose-leaf binder, where it would become part of the verse draft and undergo further revision.

The earliest extant draft of the prologue was written on two sides of a single leaf (PV1), in a departure from Yeats's general practice of leaving versos available for revision. At the bottom of the verso (which he numbered 2) is an early version of the first eight lines of what is now the concluding lyric. The following stage direction at the top of page 3 (V3^{r}) was presumably intended to conclude the prologue and initiate the action proper:

> The old man puts out the light — sound of drum & ~~penny whistle~~ flute
> ~~light goes up on bare stage~~ when light goes up
> Eithne Inguba is alone on the stage.

The remaining lines of the first part of what is now the concluding lyric are found on the recto of an unnumbered leaf (L3) of the same paper as that used for the entire verse draft. (This leaf is reproduced in a later section, p. 112.) The ink used in both passages from the lyric is a very dark blue or blue-black, a different shade from that used on page 1, on the rest of page 2, and on the leaves (beginning with page 3) on which Yeats wrote out the remainder of the verse version. The lyric passages and the rest of the materials would thus seem to have been written at separate sittings. Again using the lighter blue ink, Yeats cancelled the lines at the bottom of page 2 (PV1^{v}) and on a new leaf numbered 2A (V2A^{r}) wrote a new version of the lines introducing the song:

> The song of the harlot, the song of the beggar man
> Homer s music."   after music from flute & drum
> The street singer a woman sings.

He then began to write out a revision of the two lyric passages, now clearly combined. Part way through the second passage, however, he switched from blue ink to a black ink with a brownish cast. He finished the lines of the lyric, cancelled the stage direction at the top of page 3 and added a replacement, and then went back over the blue portions of 2A making various revisions. He then further corrected pages 1 and 2, using black ink; but he was still unhappy with the prologue and rewrote two particularly troublesome passages on a new leaf (V2B) identified with the symbol Λ. In the second instance the revision itself proved unsatisfactory, and this led to further leaves and quite considerable expansion of the original. He began on page Ⓧ, in this edition V2C, which was continued on an unnumbered leaf (V2D). Two passages from that leaf were revised on the verso of page Ⓧ. A passage concerning Emer and the dance among the severed heads was worked out on the verso of a separate leaf (V2O). Yeats evidently used the verso because he wanted the passage to face the recto of page Ⓧ, which it supplemented. (The verso of page Λ, which presumably immediately preceded page Ⓧ in the loose-leaf binder, contains a partial draft of "The Black Tower.") The new leaf was apparently later transferred to the end of the play and its recto used for a version of what are now lines 212–227 of the lyric.

After bringing the composition of the prologue to this point, Yeats probably produced a now-lost clean copy of it which (with some further revision) would have been used to prepare the earliest typescript. Evidence of other portions of the manuscript suggests that even into the typescript stage he still planned to have the first part of what is now the single final lyric follow the prologue.

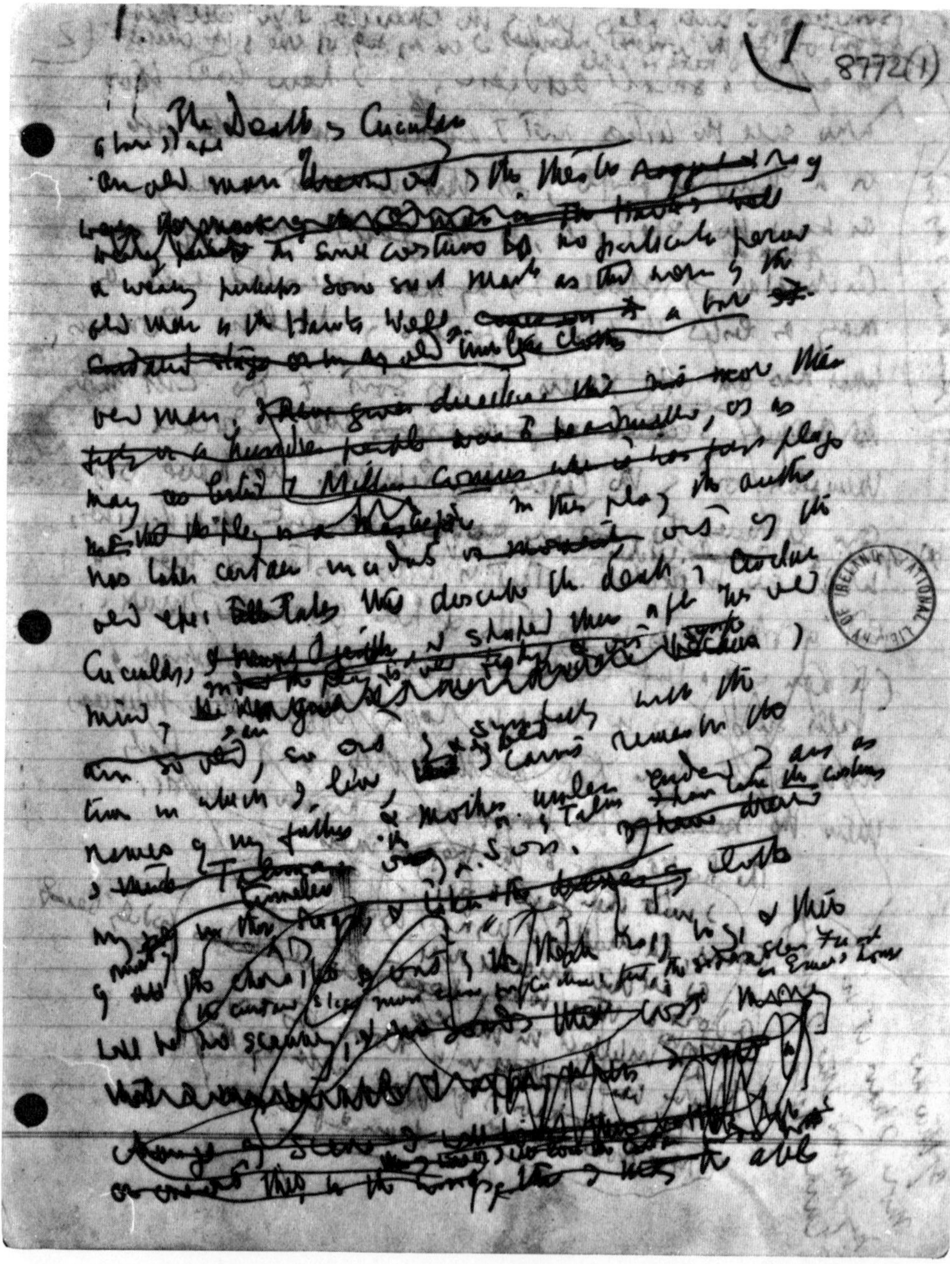

1

The Death of Cuculain

A bare stage

of

An old man ~~dressed out of the theatre~~ ~~ragged &~~ rag
~~wearing the mask of the old man in The Hawk s well~~
~~wearing perhaps~~ in some costume ~~of~~ no particular period
& wearing perhaps some such mask as that worn by the
old man in the Hawks Well ∧ ~~comes on to~~ a bare ~~st~~
~~curtained stage~~ ~~or in any old timeless clothes~~
[Old Man. ~~I have given directions that not more~~ than
~~fifty or a hundred people were to be admitted~~, or as
many ~~as listened to Miltons Comus when it was first~~ played
~~Not that the play is a masterpece~~ In this play the author]
has taken certain incidents ~~or moments~~, out of the
old epic ~~tells~~ tales that discribe the death of ~~Cuchul~~
Cuculain, ~~& brought to gether,~~ & shaped them after his old

~~Indeed the play is old fashioned & out of sympa~~

mind. ~~He has given it to me to produce because~~ I

I am

~~am so old~~, so out of sympathy with the

& so old

time in which I live, ~~that~~ I cannot remember the
names of my father & mother unless endeed I am as

the or of Talma ~~I~~ have taken the costumes

[I ~~think Talma s only~~ ∧ son. ~~I have dressed~~

timeless

my self in these ∧ rags, & taken the ~~dresses of~~ cloths

most of

of ~~all~~ the characters [?&] out of the theatre ragg bag, & there

the curtained stage must serve for Cuchulain s tent, the side of Sleve Fuad

will be no scenery, & no sounds that cost money & Emer s house
~~that I may be able to afford~~ when I want a
change of scene I will touch this button here

~~then I will~~ or I will lower the curtain under [?]

or one out there, in the wings ∧ , that I may be able]

---

14 The period after "mind" is in black ink.
18 The period after "son" is in black ink.
24 The punctuation in this line is conjectural.

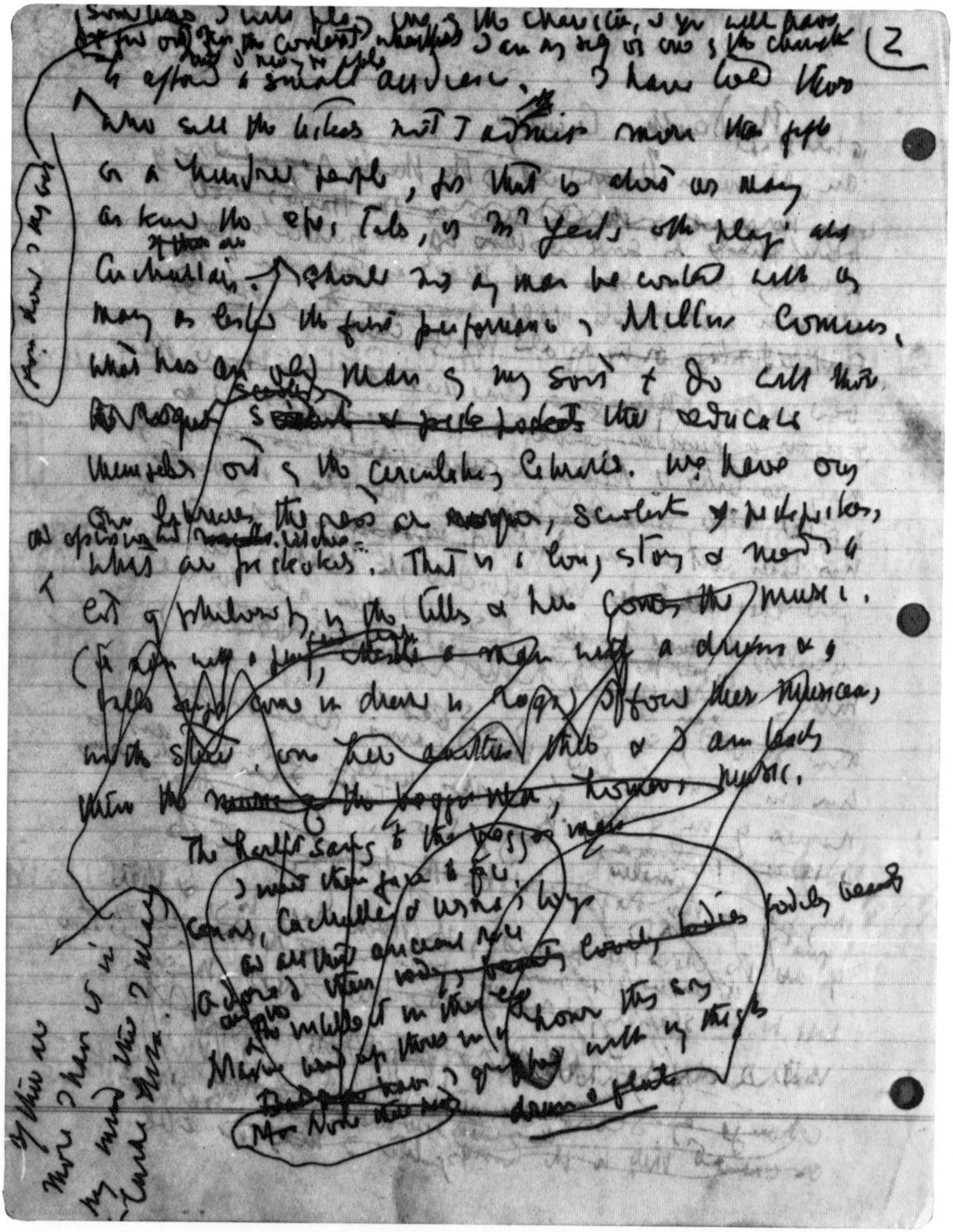

Sometimes I will play one of the characters, & you will have 2
or
to find out from the context whether I am my self or one of the characters
that I may be able
^to afford a small audience. ~~^~~ I have told those
who sell the tickets not to admit more than fifty
or a hundred people, for that is about as many
as know the epic tales, or Mr Yeat s other plays about
~~If there~~ are
Cuchullain. Should not any man be content with as
many as listened the first performance of Miltons Comus.
What has an old man of my sort to do with those
~~sciolists~~
~~the rogues sciolists & pick pockets~~ that educate
themselves out of the circulating libraries. We have our
own libraries the rest are ~~rogues,~~ sciolists ~~&~~ pickpockets,
and opinionated ~~rascals,~~ bitches
^What are pickokets. That is a long story & needs a
lot of philosophy in the telling & here comes the music.
~~flut~~ flute
(a man with a ~~penny whistle~~ a man with a drum & a

ballad singer come in dressed in rags) I found these musiceans
in the street, one here another there & I am teaching
them the music of the beggar man, homer s music.
The harlot sang to the beggar man
I meet them face to face
Conal, Cuchullain & Usna's boys
And all that ancient race
Adored their ~~body s beauty~~ ~~lovely bodies~~ bodily beauty
And the
^ ~~The~~ intellect in their eye
Maeve used up three in an hour they say
~~But none have~~ I gripped with my thighs
[?~~Mo~~] None there have
drum & flute

---

from [?hood] I may [?wear]

If there are
more I have it in
my mind that I may
curse him.

The first passage below the rule is from the top of the left margin; it is marked for insertion in the revisions above l. 1, after "out." The second passage is from the lower left margin, and is marked for insertion in l. 5, after "Cuchullain."

1 The caret after "audience" was written in blue ink, cancelled in black.

17–24 These lines and the stage directions were written in dark blue ink, then cancelled in the same (lighter) blue ink used in the verse draft as a whole. In l. 21, "body s beauty" was cancelled in the lighter blue, and "~~lovely bodies~~ bodily beauty" written in it.

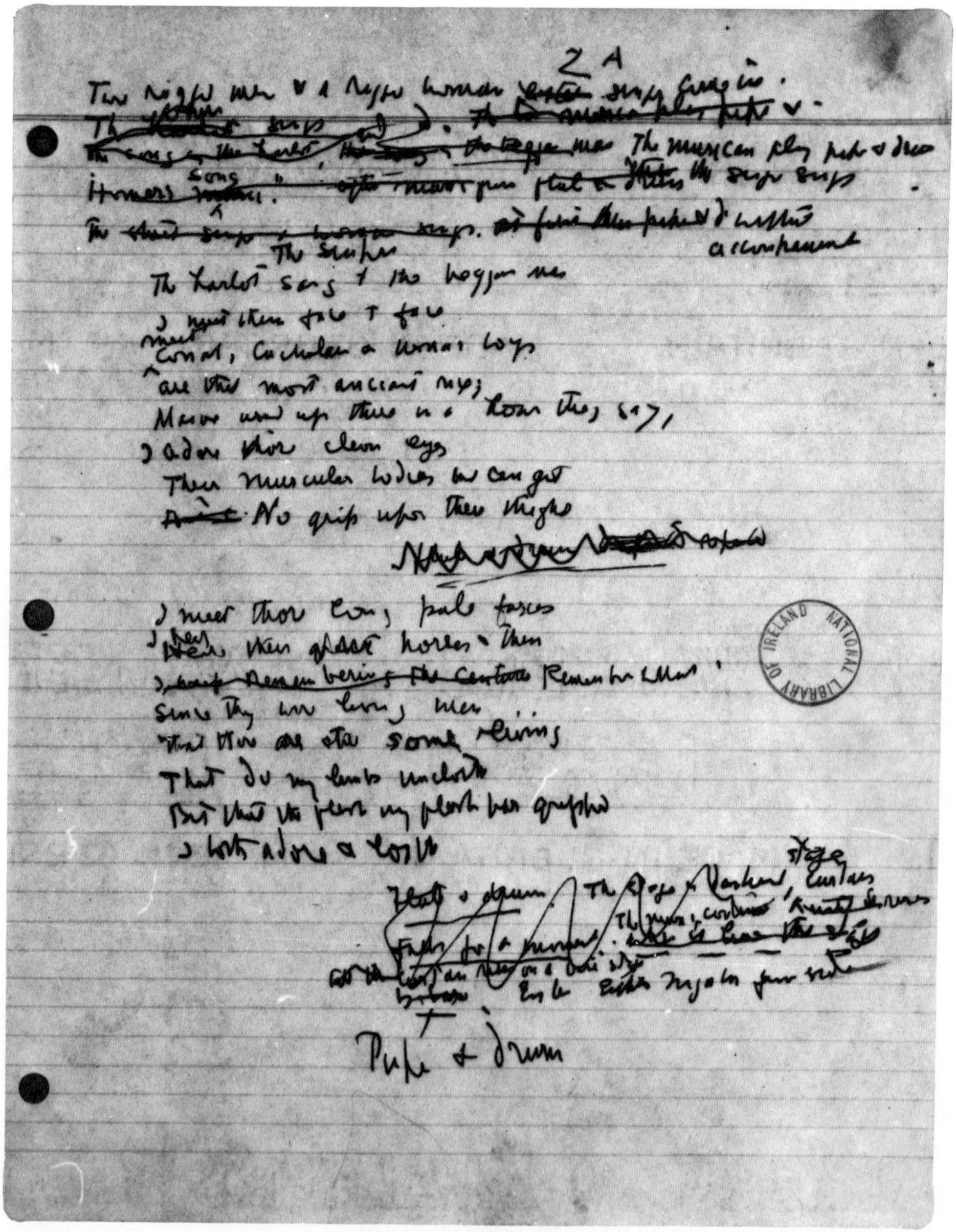
2 A

The harlot sang to the beggar man
I meet them face to face
Conal, Cuchulain & Usnas boys
All that most ancient race;
Maeve had three in an hour they say,
I adore those clean eyes
Their muscular bodies but can get
No grip upon their thighs

I meet those long pale faces
I hear their ghostly horses & them
Remember what
Since they were living men
That there are still some living
That do my limbs unclothe
But that the flesh my flesh has gripped
I both adore & loathe

Pipe & drum

2 A

Two ragged men & a ragged woman ~~enter~~ singer come in.

woman
~~The harlot sings~~ ~~and~~ [?&] ~~The two musicians play pipe~~ &
~~The song of the harlot~~, ~~the song of the beggar~~ man The musicians play pipe & drum
song then the singer sings
~~Homer s music.~~ " ~~after music~~ from ~~flute & drum~~
^

The ~~street singer a woman sings~~. ~~At first~~ [?] ~~pipe &~~ d without
The singer accompaniment

1 The harlot sang to the beggar man
2 I meet them face to face
Meet
3 ^ Conal, Cuchulain & Usna s boys
4 All that most ancient race;
5 Maeve used up three in a hour they say,
6 I Adore those clever eyes
7 Their muscular bodies but can get
8 ~~But c~~ No grip upon their thighs

~~flute & drum defeated repeated~~

9 I meet those long pale fasces
I hear
10 Hear their ~~great~~ horses & then
11 ~~I weep remembering the centuries~~ Remember what
12 Since they were living men
13 That there are still some living
14 That do my limbs uncloth
15 But that the flesh my flesh has gripped
16 I both adore & loath

stage
Flute & drum. The stage is darkened, ^ curtain
The music continues ~~until it~~ rises
Falls for a moment. ~~When it [?] the stage~~
till the curtan rises on a bare stage
~~is bare.~~ Enter Eithne Inguba from side
^

Pipe & drum

---

13 "some" was written first in blue ink, then gone over in black. It was apparently at this point in his revision of the verse draft that Yeats began using black ink, so that the corrections in black on PV1 were made after this.

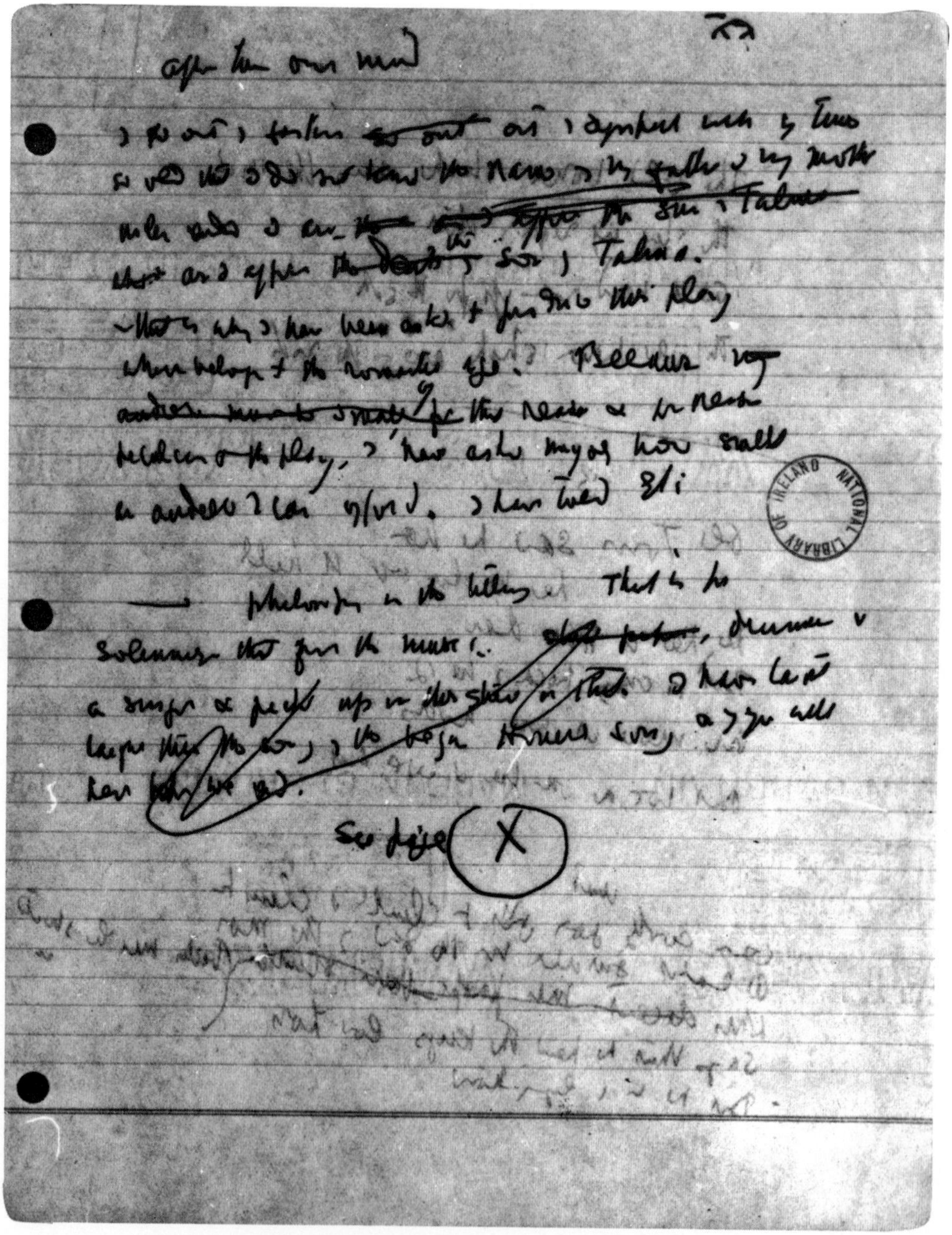
after his own mind
See page (X)

after his own mind

I ~~so~~ out of fashion ~~so out~~ out of sympathy with my time
so old that I do not know the name of my father or my mother
unless endeed I am ~~the as I affirm the sun of Talma~~
the
~~who~~ as I affirm ~~the death of~~ son of Talma.
—that is why I have been asked to produce this play
which belongs to the romantic age. Because ~~my~~
of
~~audience must be small for~~ this reason & for reasons
peculiar to the play, I have asked myself how small
an audience I can afford. I have told Etc

—— philosophy in the telling. That is [?for]
solemnize that from the music. ~~Street piper,~~ drummer &
a singer & picked up in this street or that. I have taught
taught them the song of the begar Homers song as you will
hear before we end.

See page (X)

The first passage is a revision of ll. 14–24 of PV1[r] and l. 1 of PV1[v]; the second revises PV1[v], ll. 12ff. The verso of this leaf contains a partial draft of "The Black Tower," not reproduced in this edition.

2 "am" probably omitted after "I."

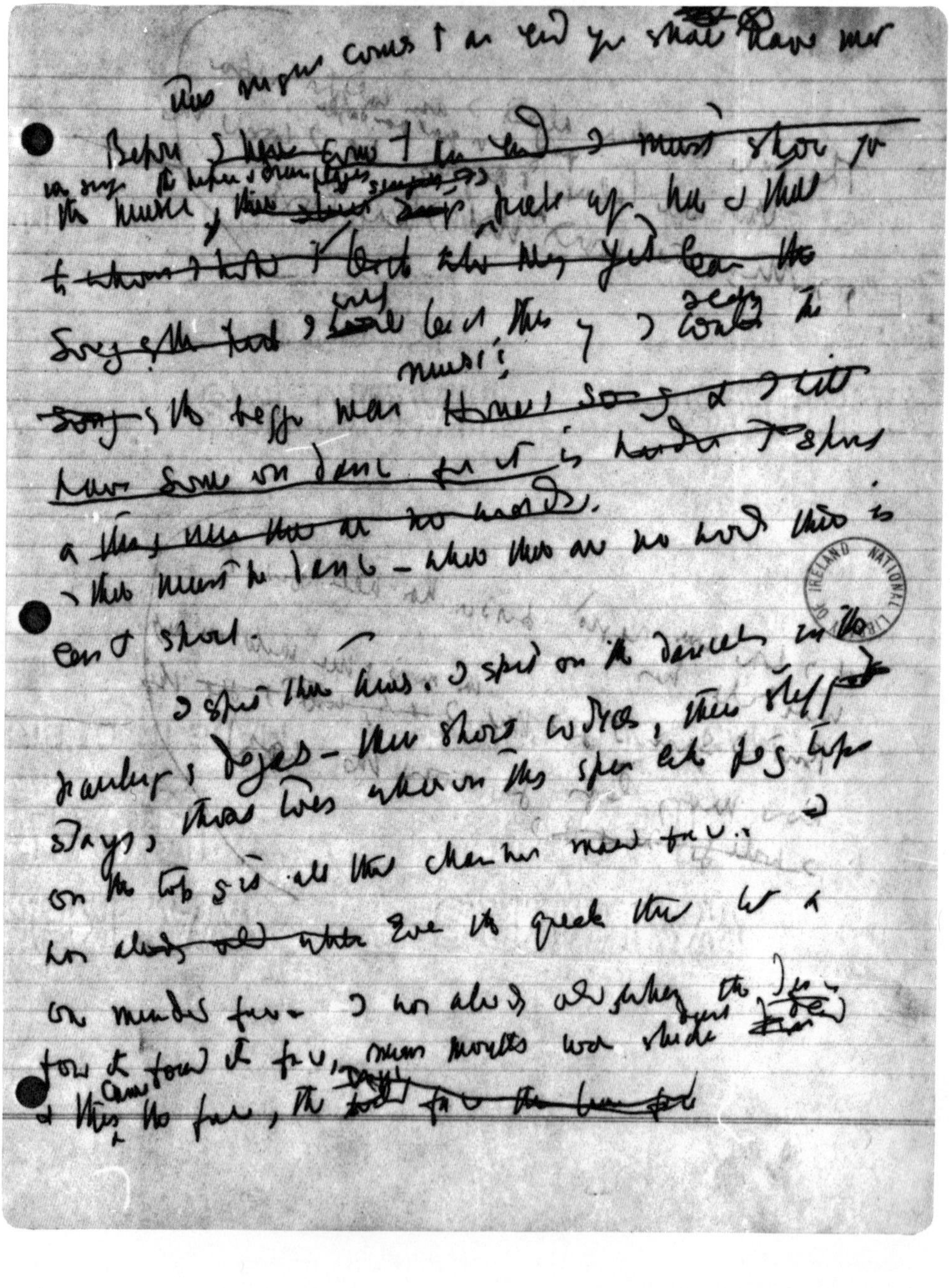

~~(X)~~ (X)

this night comes to an end you shall have met
Before ~~I have come to an end I must show you~~
the singer the piper & drum player
~~singers, I~~ I
the music, ~~three street~~ ~~singers~~∧ pick up here & there
~~to whom I hoped to teach~~ ~~who may yet learn the~~
will I can
~~Song of the harl~~ I ~~would~~ teach them if I could the
music,
~~song~~ of the beggar man ~~Homer s song & I will~~
~~have some one dance for it~~ is ~~harder to~~ spoil
a ~~thing when there are no words.~~
— there must be dance — where there are no words there is
less to spoil.
I spit three times. I spit on the dancers in the
paintings of degas — their short bodices, their stiff[~~?~~]
stays, those toes where on they spin like peg tops
on the top of it all that chamber maid face. I
was ~~already old when~~ [?Even] the greek [? ?] a
one minded face. I was already old when the dance
dumb ~~dead~~
found its found its face, [?mens] mouths were stricken [?~~dum~~]
came ~~tragic~~
& then ∧ the face, the ~~wild~~ ~~face the true face~~

This passage was written to replace the second revision on V2B^r; it is continued on V2D^r. In several places Yeats used what seems to be a darker black ink: in l. 2, the insertion mark, which is written over a comma; the lines cancelling "three street singers"; and all the revisions above the line; in l. 4, "will"; and in l. 5, "music" and the line cancelling the first "song."

15 There may be a comma after "old."

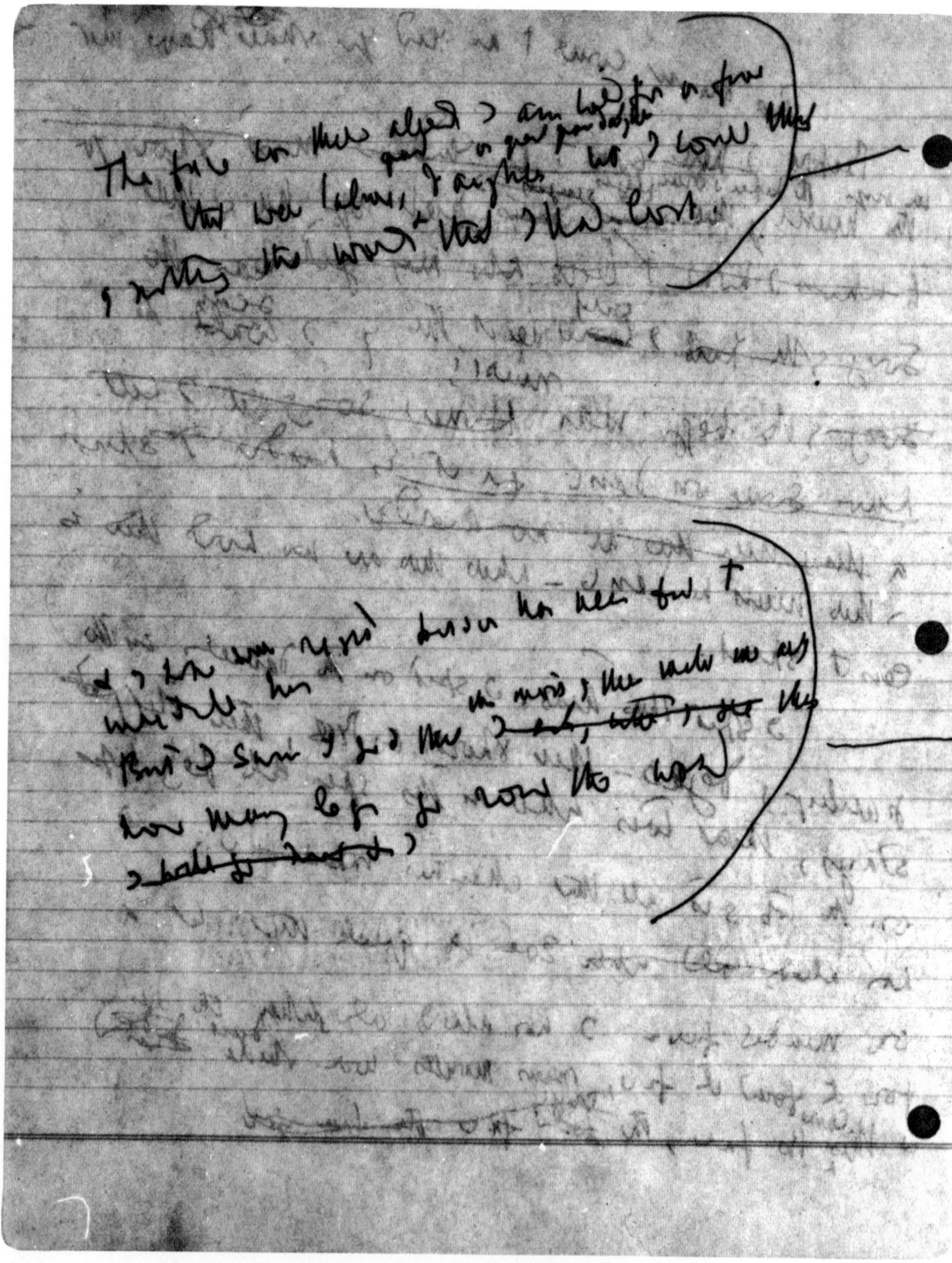

The face was there already I am told, four or five
grand or great grandaughters
that were Talma s daughters but I could think
^
of nothing the words that I had lost.

& I hope some right person has been found to
imitate her
the most of them make me ask
But I swear to god that ~~I ask, when I see~~ them
how many legs go round the world
I ~~will go now [?&]~~ I

Revisions of V2D^{r}, ll. 2ff, 13ff. In l. 2, the insertion mark and the revisions above the line were written in the darker black ink.

3 "but" probably omitted after "nothing."

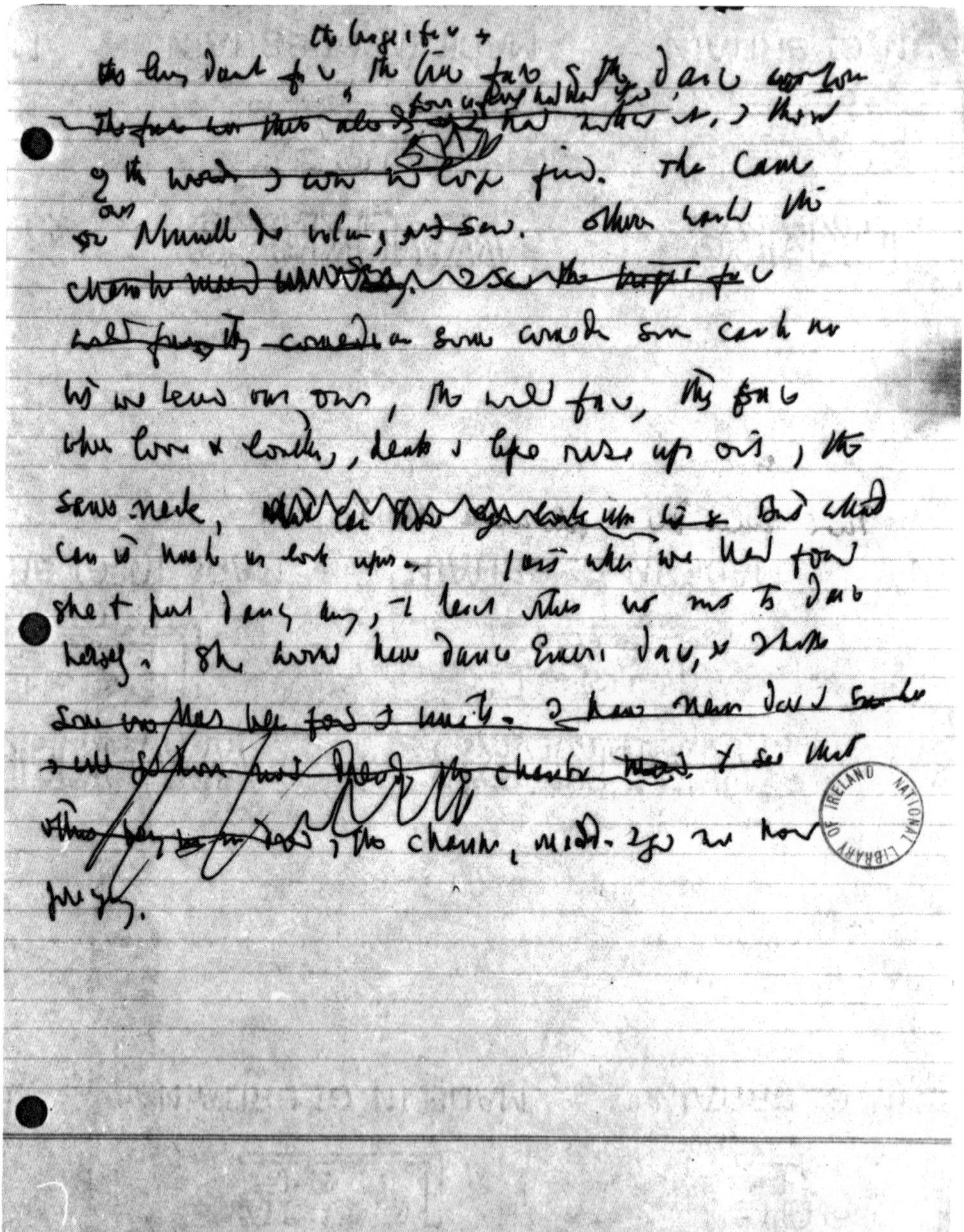
NATIONAL LIBRARY OF IRELAND

the tragic face ~~of~~
the long dark face ∧ the true face of the dance ~~was~~ born
four or five had had it, I
~~The face was there already & I had noticed~~ it, I thought
∧
of the ~~words I could no longer~~ find. Then came
own
ou Ninnette de valois; [?~~&~~] ~~I saw.~~ Others wanted the
~~saw~~
~~chamber maid but I why. I saw the tragic face~~
~~wild face~~ [?~~they~~] ~~comedian~~ some comedian some [? ?]
{f
but we loved our own, the wild face, the {sace
where love & loathing, death & life rise up out of the
same neck. ~~What can those eyes look upon but s~~ But what
can it make us look upon. Just when we had found
she to put dancing away, to teach others but not to dance
herself. She would have dance Emer s dance, & I hope
~~some one has been found to imitate. I have never dared to see her~~
~~I will go home now dreading the chamber maid, to see~~ that
~~others being in in dred~~ of the chamber maid s eyes [?no hood]
[?].

A continuation of V2C^r.
10 "her" probably omitted after "found."
11 "decided" or "chose" probably omitted after "she."
13 "her" probably omitted after "imitate."

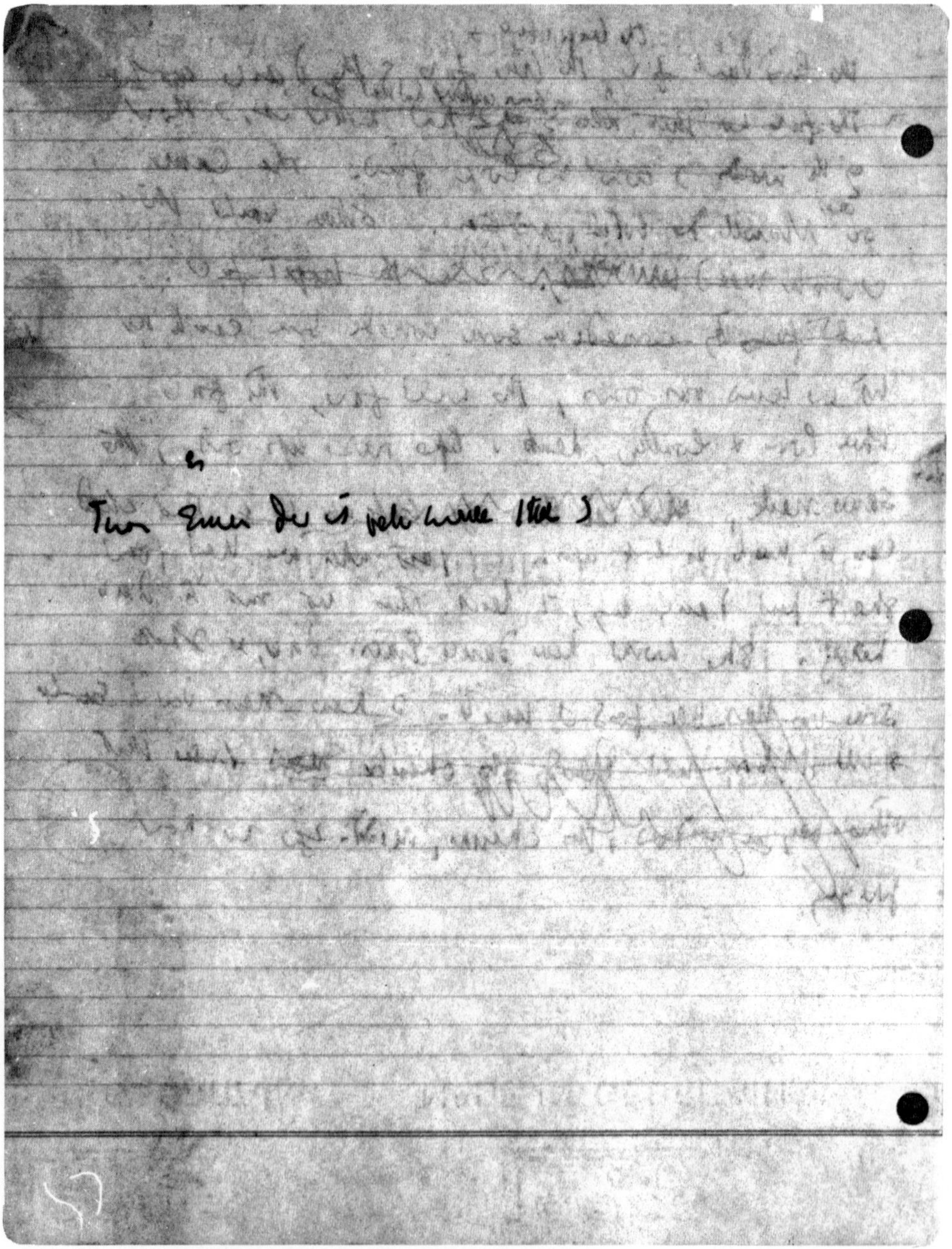

E
Twas Emer did it better women than I

This line is not really part of the verse draft; it was written when Yeats was revising TS6, 6A. See TS6, 6B, l. 6.

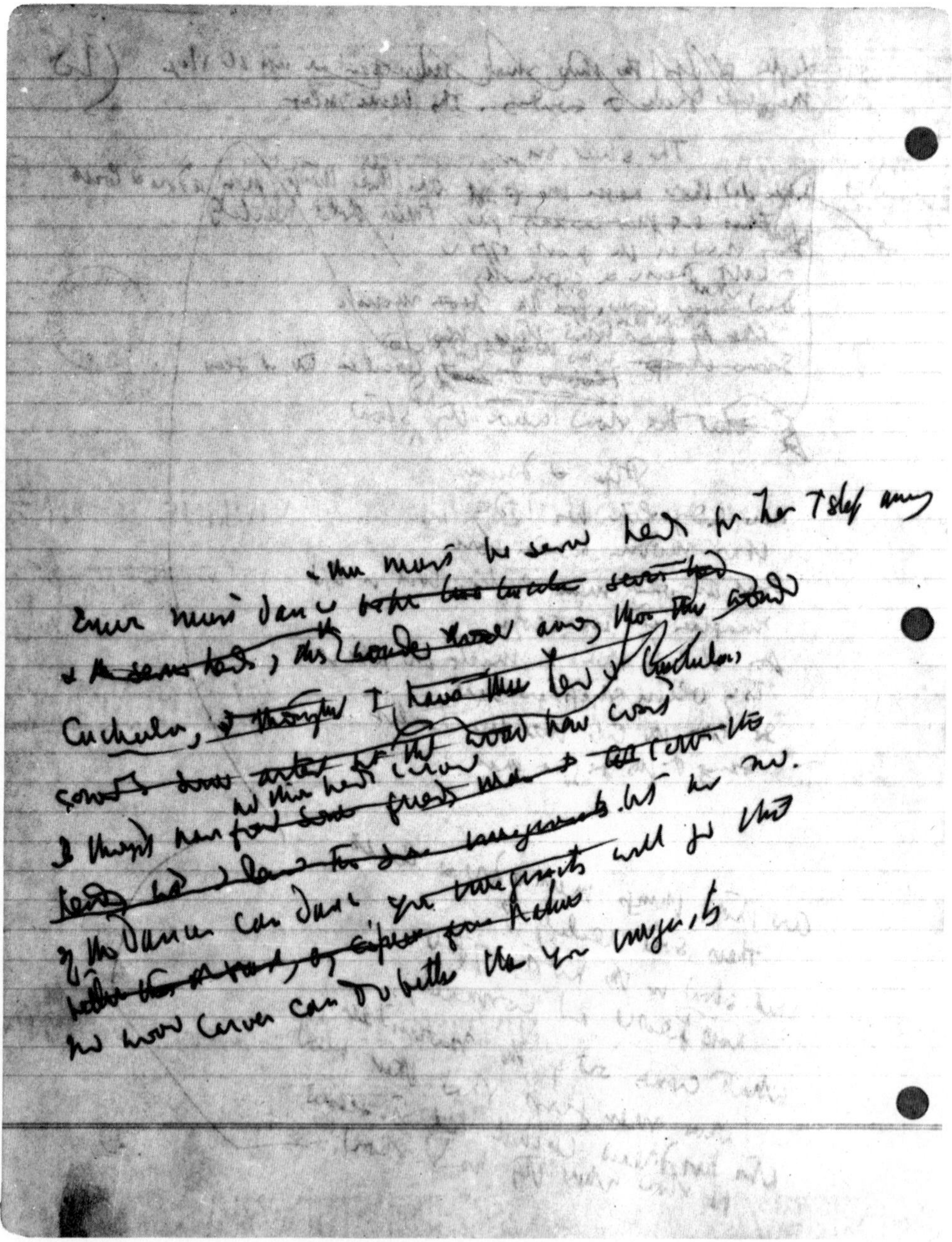

& there must be severed heads for her to step among
Emer must dance ~~before Cuc Cuchulains severed head~~
~~th~~
& ~~the severed heads of those wounded would~~ among ~~those that wounded~~
~~Cuchulain, I thought to have their head & Cuchulain s~~
~~carved by some artist but that would have~~ cost
had those heads carved
I thought have ~~found some friendly man to car carve~~ the
~~heads but I leave for your imagination.~~ but no no.
If the dancer can dance, ~~your imagination~~ will do that
~~better than a brush, or copies from nature~~
no wood carver can do better than your imagination

A revision of V2Cʳ, ll. 5ff.
5 "to" probably omitted after "thought."

Manuscripts of the Central Portion of the Play

The bulk of the extant material for this portion of the play is a verse draft, presenting the action from the entrance of Eithne to Cuchulain's death; it occupies leaves 3 to 13 as numbered by Yeats. This verse version he worked up from his prose draft, two leaves of which (numbered 13 and 14) survive. On the whole, composition seems to have proceeded smoothly, though the draft is filled with revisions and in at least two instances (V11A, V12A) he resorted to unnumbered supplementary leaves. The original drafting and revisions were done in blue ink; later revisions, in black ink, were apparently coeval with those in the prologue.

The materials are transcribed in the following order:

a. The verse draft proper (leaves V3–V13)
b. The supplementary leaves (V11A, V12A)
c. The leaves of prose draft (P13, P14)

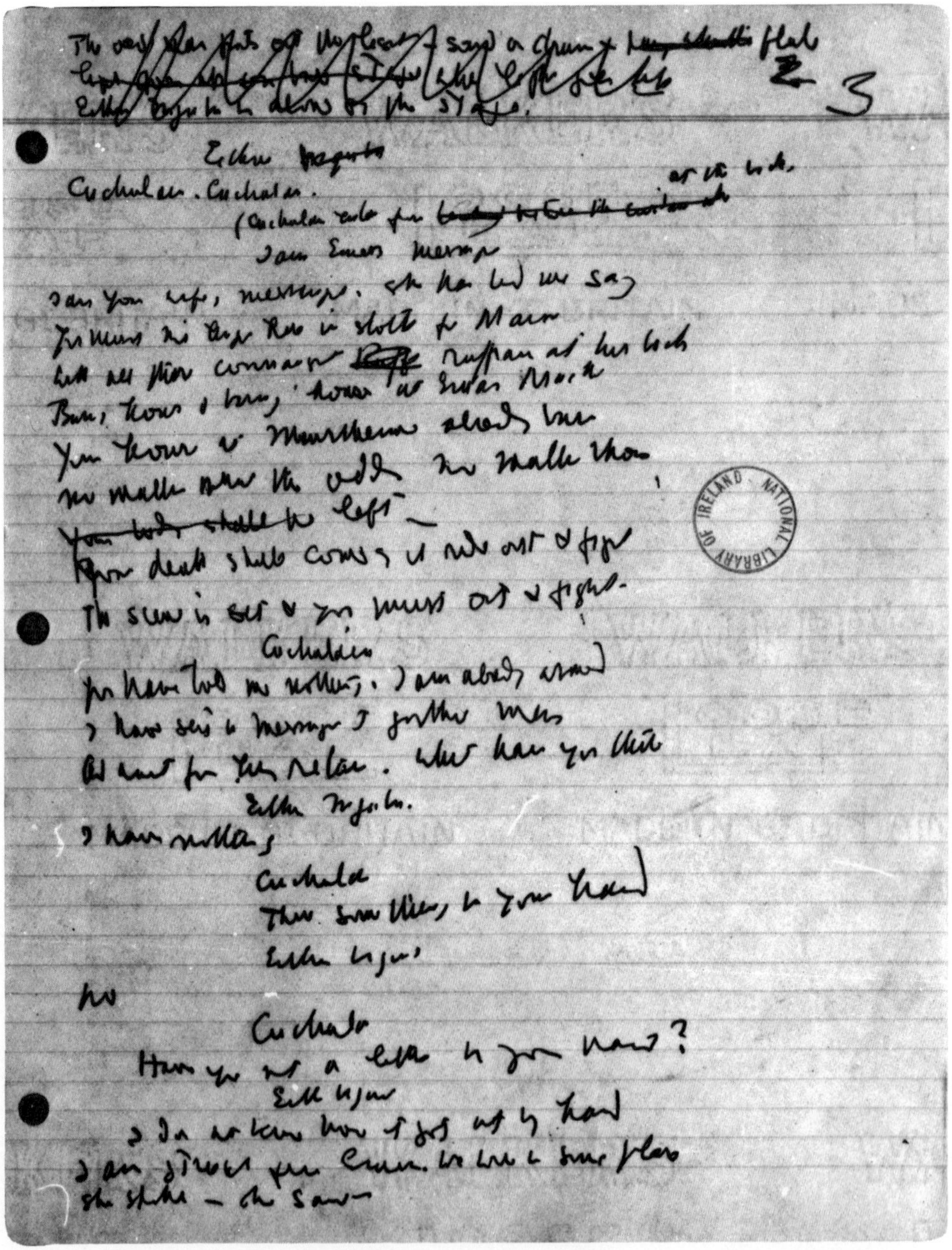
Eithne Inguba

Cuchulain. Cuchulain.

(Cuchulain enters from [illegible] at the back.

I am Emer's messenger

I am your wife's messenger. She has bid me say

You must [illegible] for Maeve

With all those Connacht ruffians at her back

Burns houses & barns, [illegible] Muirthemne

You know [illegible] Muirthemne [illegible]

No matter what the odds no matter though

Your death should come you must ride out & fight

The scene is set & you must out & fight.

Cuchulain

You have told me nothing. I am already armed

I have sent a messenger to gather men

And wait for them [illegible]. What have you there

Eithne Inguba.

I have nothing

Cuchulain

There is something in your hand

Eithne Inguba

No

Cuchulain

Have you not a letter in your hand?

Eithne Inguba

I do not know how it got into my hand

I am straight from Emer. We were in some place

She spoke — she saw —

The old man puts out the light — sound of drum & ~~penny whistle~~ flute

2
2
2
3

~~light goes up on bare stage~~ when light goes up
Eithne Inguba is alone on the stage.

Eithne ~~Inguba~~
Cuchulain. Cuchulain.
at the back.
(Cuchulain enters from [?~~behind~~] ~~between the curtains wh~~
I am Emers messenger
I am your wife s messenger. She has bid me say
You must not linger here in sloth for Maeve
With all those Connaught ~~Ruff~~ ruffians at her back
Burns hous & [?barns] houses at Eman Macha
Your house at Muirthemne already burns
No matter what the odds no matter though
~~Your body shall be~~ left
Your death shall come of it ride out & fight
The scene is set & you must out & fight.
Cuchulain
You have told me nothing. I am already armed
I have sent a messenger to gather men
And wait for his return. What have your there
Eithne Inguba.
I have nothing
Cuchulain
There some thing in your hand
Eithne Inguba
No
Cuchulain
Have you not a letter in your hand?
Eithn Inguba
I do not know how it got into my hand
I am straight from Emer. We were in some place
She spoke — she saw —

14 "is" probably omitted after "There."

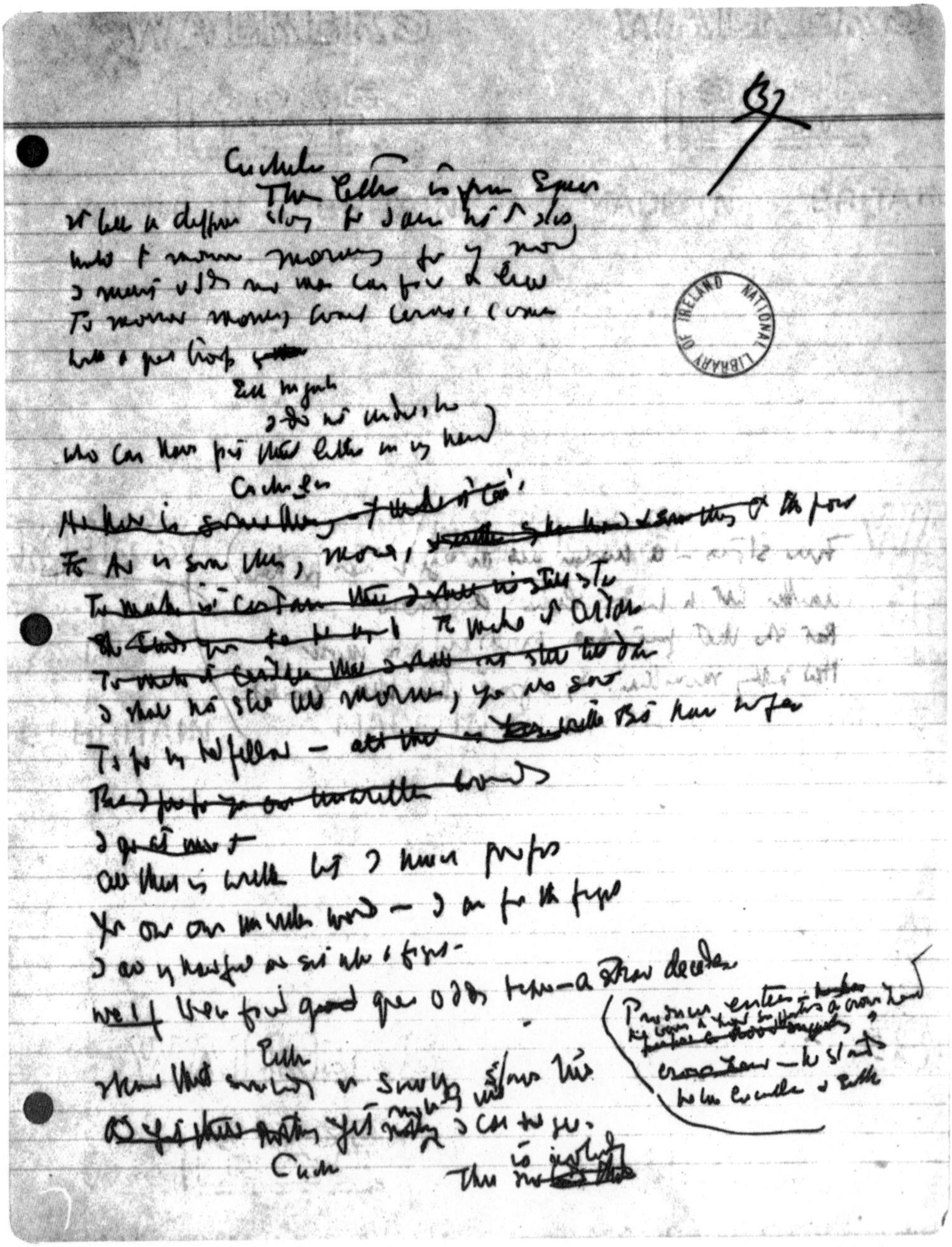

{ 4
{ 3

Cuchulain

1 This letter is from Emer
2 It tells a different story for I am not to stir
3 Until to morrow morning for if now
4 I must odds no man can face & live
5 To morrow morning Conal Carnac comes
6 With a great troop ~~of men~~

Eithn Inguba

I do not understand
7 Who can have put that letter in my hand

Cuchulain

8 ~~And here is some thing — to make it cer~~
9 ~~To~~ And is some thing more, ~~& written by her hand & some thing to~~ the point
10 ~~To make it certain that I shall not ~~still~~ stir~~
11 She ~~sends you to be my~~ b To make it certain
12 ~~To make it certain that I shall not stir till dawn~~
13 I shall not stir till morning you are sent
14 To be my bedfellow — ~~all that is here written~~ But have no fear
15 ~~But I prefer your own unwritten words~~
16 I ~~go at once~~ to
17 All that is written but I much prefer
18 Your own own unwritten words — I am for the fight
19 I and my handful are set upon a fight
20 ~~We ll~~ We ve faced [?~~good~~] great odds before — a straw decides.

Eithne

21 I know that somebody or something stands here
nobody that
22 ~~And yet there nothing~~ Yet ~~nothing~~ I can [?~~see~~] see.
^

Cuch

is nobody
There ~~no body there~~

Producer enters — ~~he has~~
he wears a hood suggesting a crows head
~~perhaps a hood suggesting~~ a
~~crows head~~ — he stands
between Cucullain & Eithne

The passage below the rule is from the right margin (intended as a stage direction between ll. 20 and 21).
4 "face" probably omitted after "must."

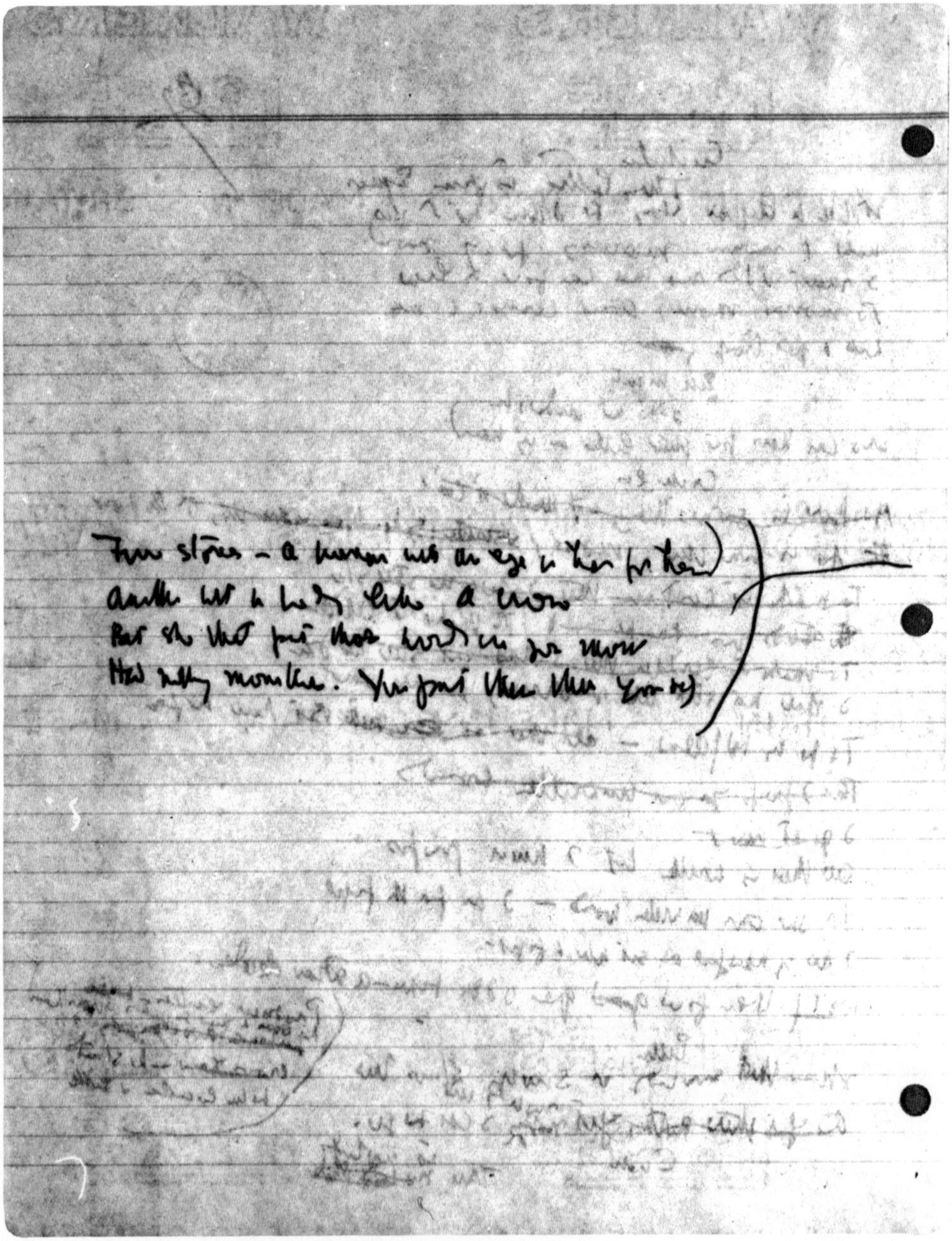

Fine stories — a woman with an eye in her for head
Another with a body like a crow
But she that put those words in your mouth
Had nothing monstrous. You put them there yourself

A revision of ll. 8–9 of V5^{r}.

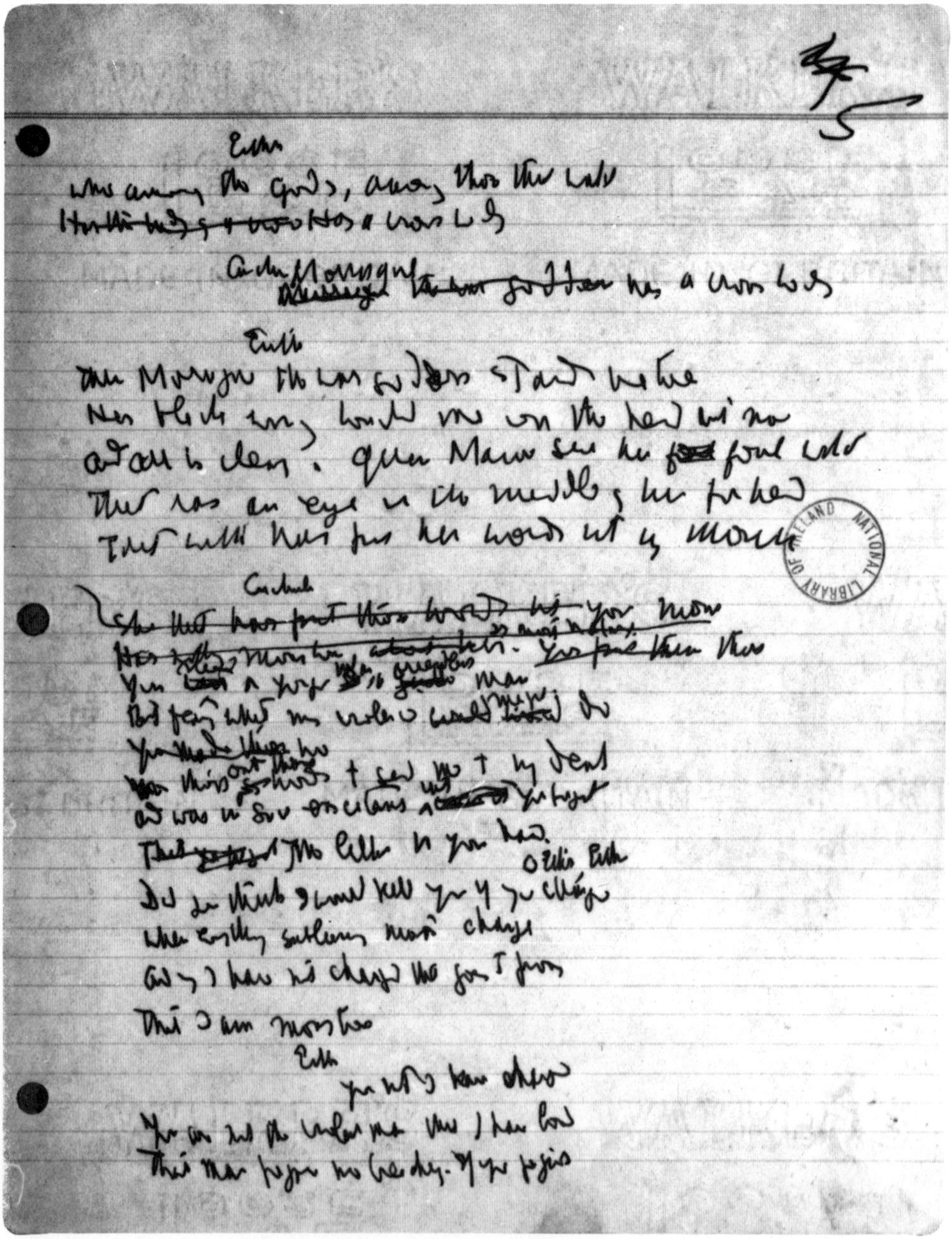

~~4~~
5

Eithne
1 Who among the Gods, among those that watch
2 ~~Has the body of a crow~~ Has a crows body
Cuchu
Morrague
~~Morrigu the war goddess~~ has a crows body
Eithne
{d
3 Then Morrigue the war god{ess stands between
4 Her black wing touched me on the head but now
5 And all is clear. Queen Maeve sent her ~~foul~~ foul witch
6 That has an eye in the middle of her forhead
7 That witch has put her words into my mouth
Cuchulain
8 ~~She that has put those words into~~ your mouth
~~is most natural~~.
9 ~~Has nothing monstrous about her~~. ~~You put them~~ there
need man, friendlier
10 You ~~want~~ a younger ~~&~~ a ~~gentler~~ man
∧
might
11 But fearing what my violence ~~could~~ ~~would~~ do
12 ~~You made these~~ wo
out those
13 [?~~You~~] thought ~~of~~ words to send me to my death
that
14 And were in such excitement ∧ ~~over it~~ you forgot
15 ~~That you forgot~~ The letter in your hand.
O Ethne, Eithne
16 Did you think I would kill you if you changed
17 When everything sublunary must change
18 And if I have not changed that goes to prove
19 That I am monstrous
Eithne
You not I have changed
20 You are not the violent man that I have loved
21 That man forgave no treachery. If you forgive

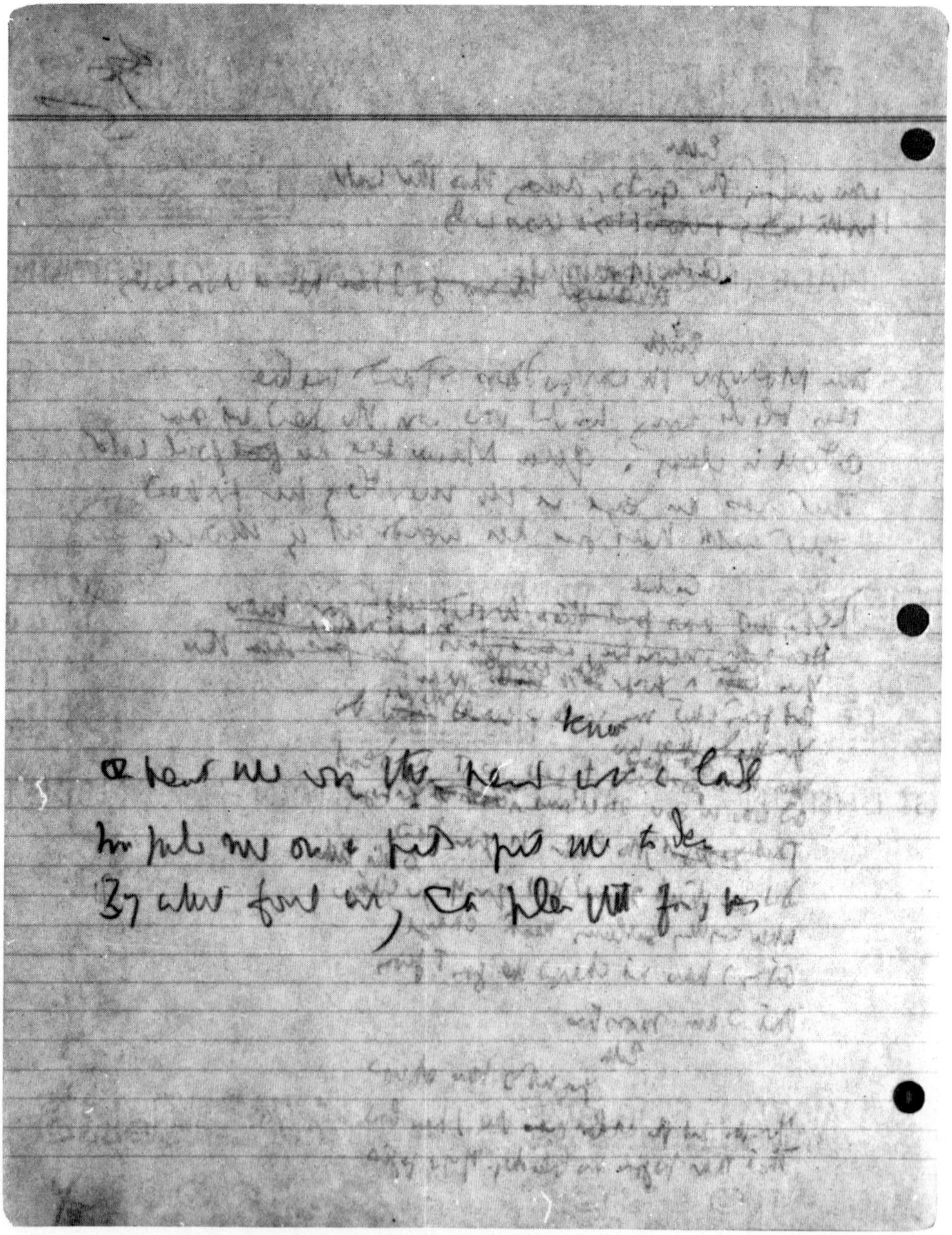

knives
Or beat me on the head with a ladle
Impale me on a spit put me to death
By what foul way can please their fancy best

A revision of V6r, ll. 17–20.

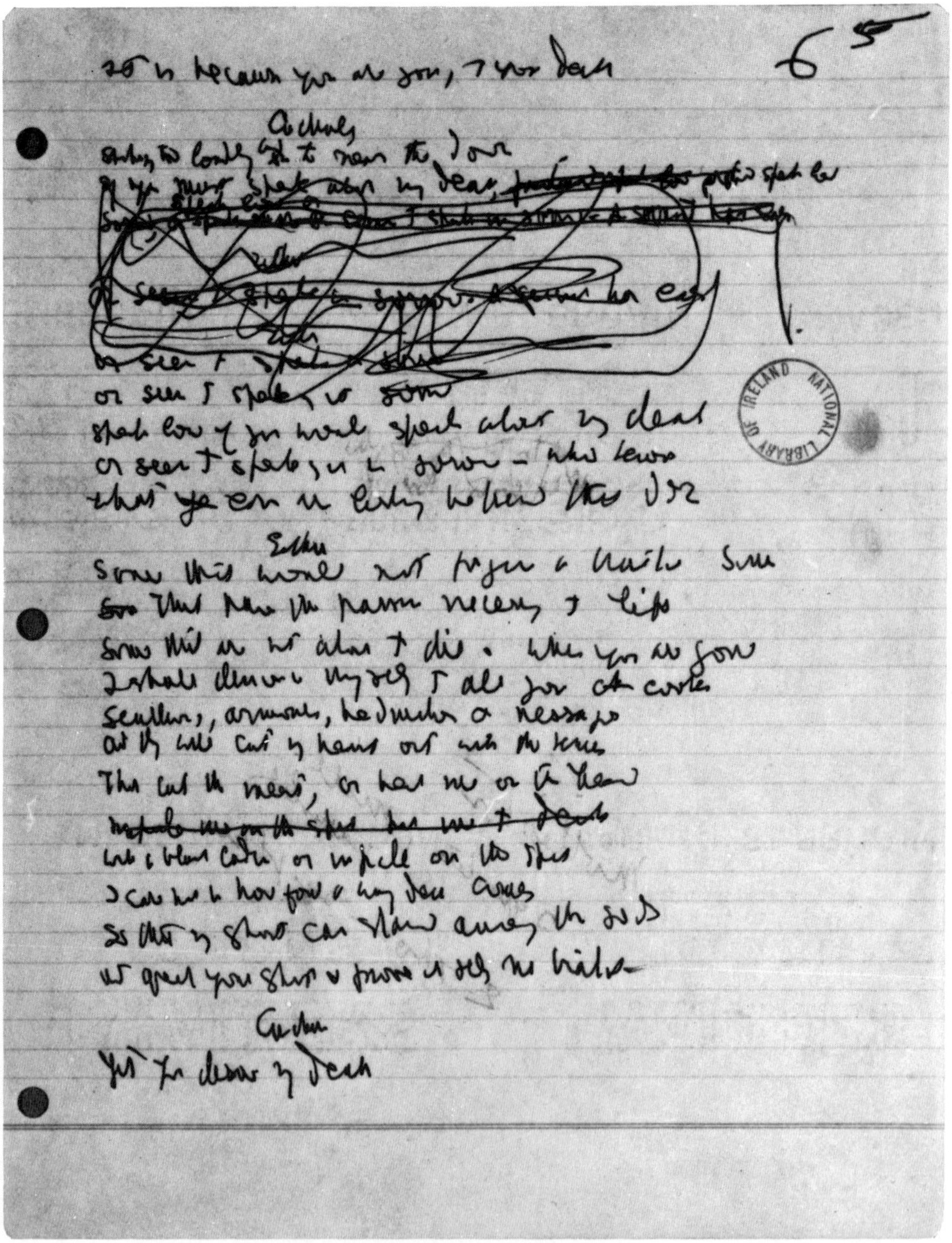

~~5~~
6

It is because you are going to your death
Cuchulain
and
Spoken too loudly or to near the door
If you must speak about my death, ~~pretend speak low pretend~~ speak low
speak low or
~~Sorrow~~, ~~or speak more~~ or seem to speak in sorrow. A servant has ears
Eithne
~~Or seem to speak in sorrow~~. ~~A servant has~~ ears
Eithne
Or seem to speak in sorrow
Or seem to speak of it sorrow
Speak low if you would speak about my death
Or seem to speak of it in sorrow — who knows
What ~~ye~~ ears are listening behind that door
Eithne
Some that would not forgive a traitor Some
~~Som~~ That have the passion necessary to life
Some that are not about to die. When you are gone
I shall denounce myself to all your~~e~~ cooks
Scullions, armorers, bedmakers & messagers
And they will cut my heart out with the knives
That cut the meat, or beat me on the head
~~Impale me on the spit put me to death~~
With a blunt ladle or impale on the spit
I care not in how foul a way death comes
So that my ghost can stand among the gods
And greet your ghost & prove it self no traitor.
Cuchu
Yet you desire my death

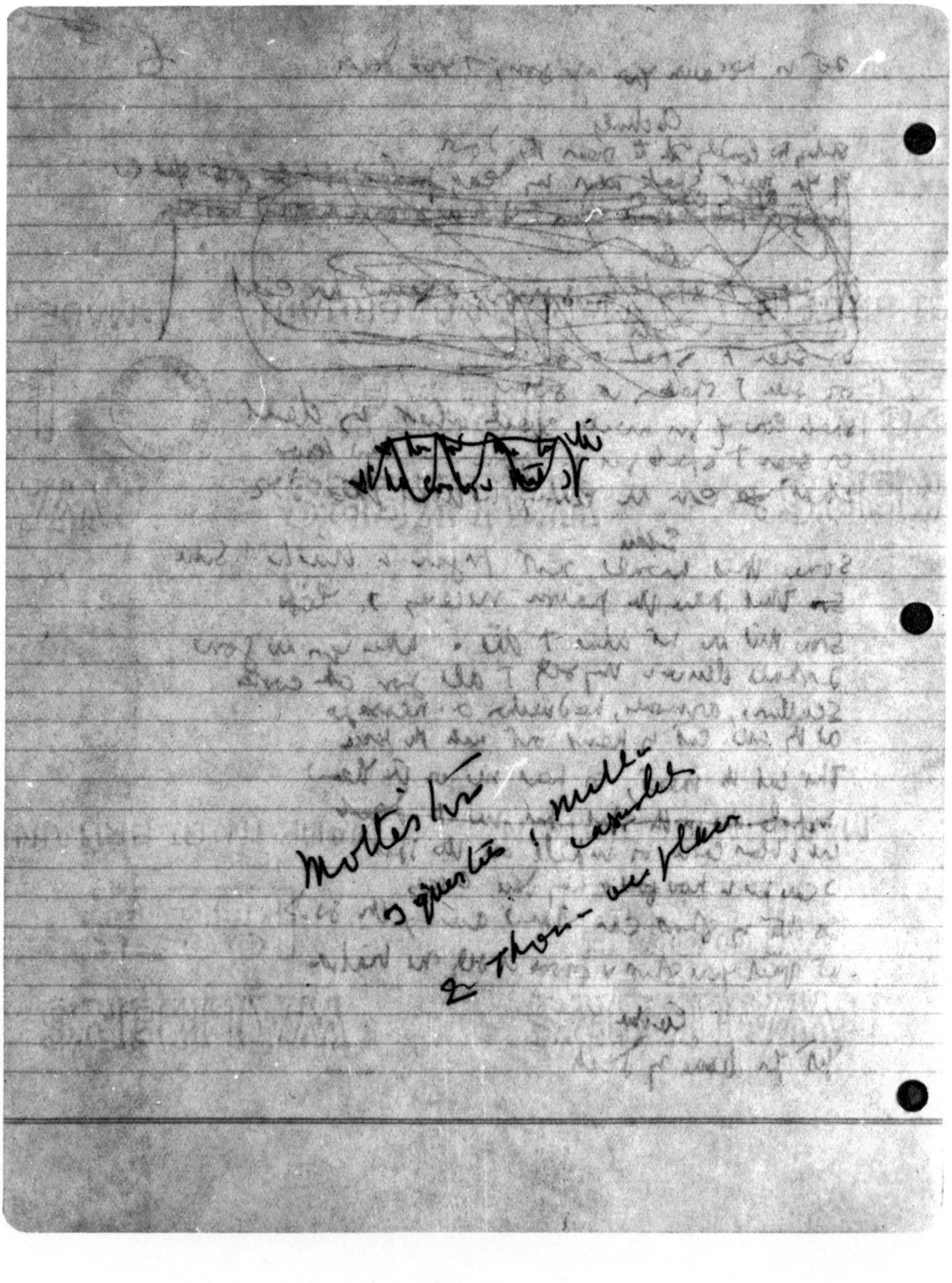

~~& has told me a~~ lie
& has contrived that I

[?]
3 quarters of million
casualies
2 thou — air planes

The first passage is a revision of V7ʳ, ll. 5–6. The lines below do not seem to be part of the play and may have been on the leaf before Yeats used it in the verse draft.

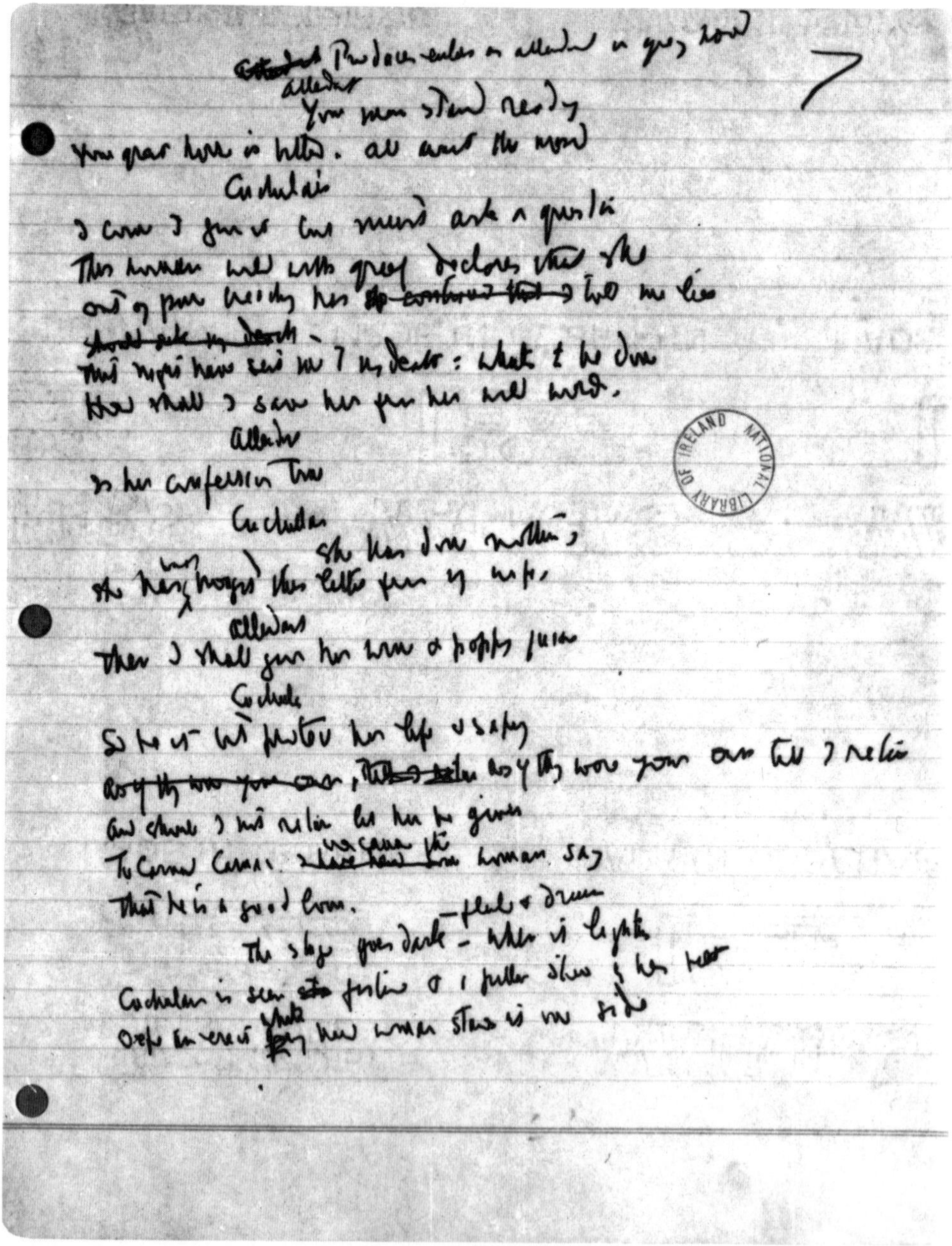
7
NATIONAL LIBRARY OF IRELAND

~~Attendant~~ Producer enters as attendant in grey hood
Attendant 7
Your men stand ready
Your great horse is bitted. All await the word
Cuchulain
I come to give it but must ask a question
This woman wild with grief declares that she
Out of pure treachery has ~~she contrived that~~ I told me lies
~~Should seek my death.~~
That might have sent me to my death: whats to be done
How shall I save her from her wild words.
Attendant
Is her confession true
Cuchullain
She has done nothing
but
She has ^ brought this letter from my wife.
Attendant
Then I shall give her wine & poppy juice
Cuchulain
So be it but protect her life & safety
~~As if they were your own~~. ~~Till I return~~ As if they were your own till I return
And should I not return let her be given
because the
To Carnal Carnac ~~I have heard some~~ woman say
That he is a good lover.
—flute & drum
The stage goes dark – when it lightens
Cuchulain is seen ~~sta~~ fastened to a pillar stone by his belt
white
Oefe an erect ~~grey~~ haired woman stands at one side

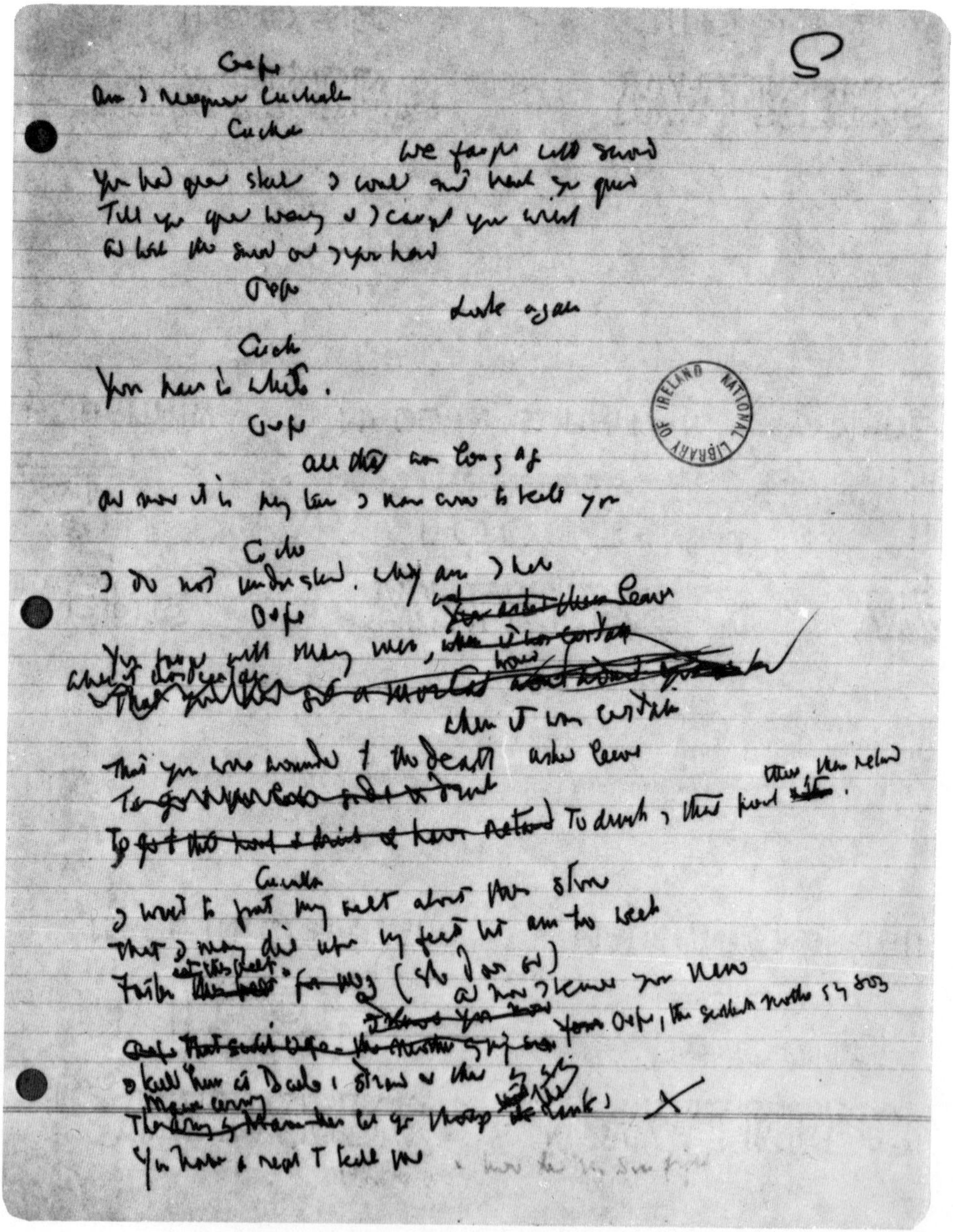

Aoife
Am I recognised Cuchulain
Cuchulain
We fought with sword
You had great skill I could not hold you quiet
Till you grew weary & I caught your wrist
And took the sword out of your hand
Aoife
Look again
Cuchulain
Your hair is white.
Aoife
All that was long ago
And now it is my turn I have come to kill you
Cuchulain
I do not understand. Why am I here
Aoife
You fought with many men, when it was certain
That you were wounded to the death asked leave
To drink, & then found water, then returned.
Cuchulain
I want to put my belt about this stone
That I may die upon my feet but am too weak
Fasten it for me (she does so)
And now I know your name
Aoife, the sedentary mother of my son
I killed him at Baile's Strand
You have a right to kill me

8

Oefe
1 Am I recognised Cuchulain
Cuchu
We fought with sword
2 You had great skill I could not break your guard
3 Till you grew weary & I caught your wrist
4 And took the sword out of your hand
Oefe
Look again
Cuch
5 Your hair is white.
Oefe
All that was long ago
6 And now it is my [?turn/?time] I have come to kill you
Cuchu
7 I do not understand. Wh{y / e} am I here
Oefe ~~and~~
~~You asked their leave~~
8 You fought with many men, ~~when it was certain~~
when it was certain wound
9 ~~That you had got a mortal wound wound you asked~~
10 when it was certain
11 That you were wounded to the death asked leave
12 ~~To go to the lake side & drink~~
there, then returned
13 ~~To go to that pool & drink & have returned~~ To drink of that pool ~~& then~~.
Cucullain
14 I want to put my belt about this stone
15 That I may die upon my feet but am too week
[~~?~~] this belt.
16 Fasten ~~this belt~~ ~~for me~~. (She does so)
And now I know your name
~~I know you now~~
~~Youre~~ Oefe, the Scottish mother of my son
17 ~~Oefe~~ ~~That Scotch Oefe — the mother of my son~~
18 I killed him at Baile s Strand & that is why
Maeve army ~~their~~ the
19 The ~~army of Maeve~~ ~~has~~ let you through ~~its~~ ranks X
20 You have a right to kill me

---

19 The large "X" consists of a line in blue ink crossed by one in black.

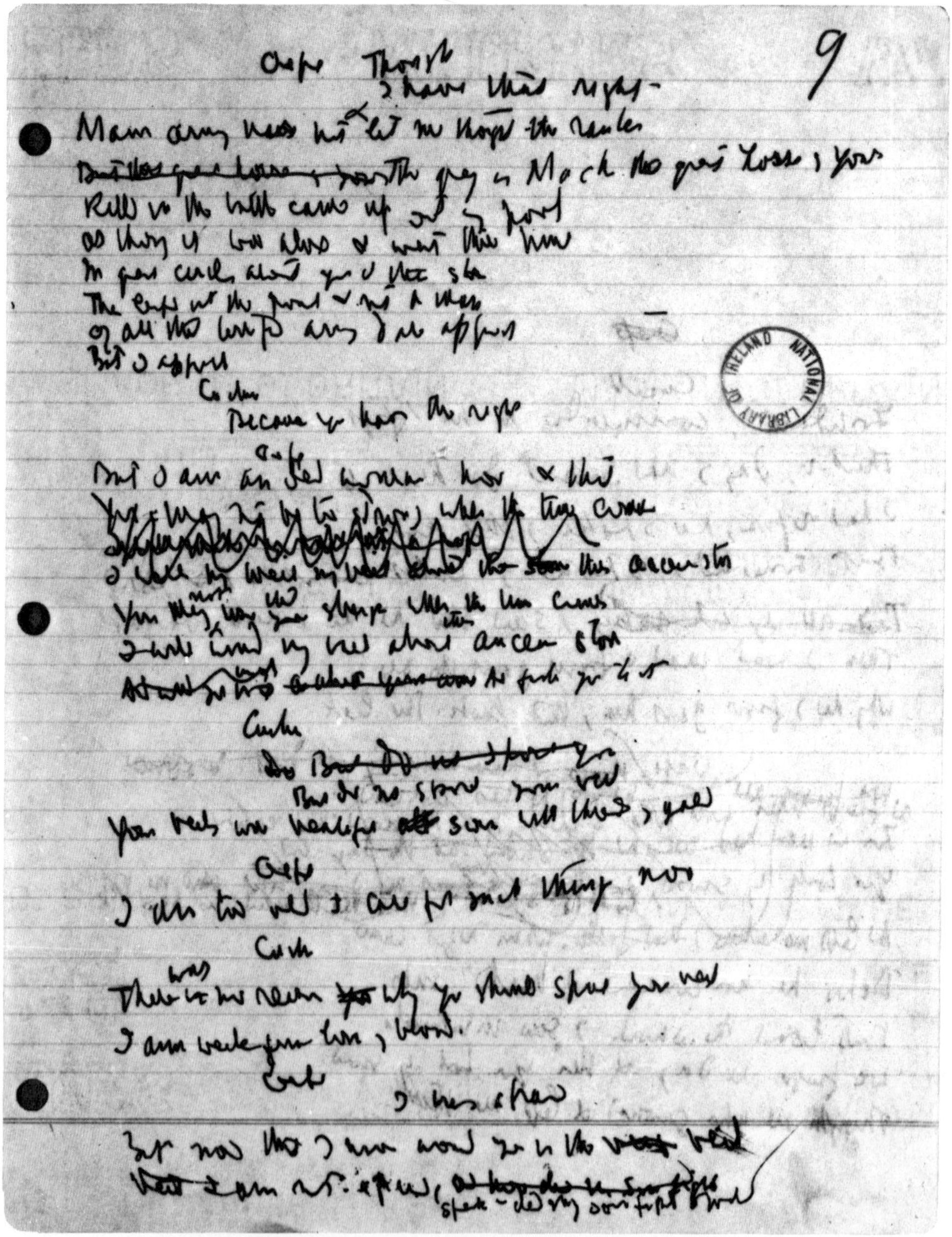

Oefe 9

Though
{s ^I have that right
Maeves army ha{ve not let me through the ranks
{T
~~But that great horse of yours~~ {the grey of Macha that great horse of yours
Killed in the battle came up out of pool
As though it were alive & went three times
In great circles about you & that stone
Then leaped into the pool & not a man
Of all that terrified army dare approach
But I approach
Cuchu
Because you have the right
Oefe
But I am an old woman now & that
[You may not be too strong when the time comes
~~I will make my veil into a rope~~
I will my weil my veil about ~~the stone~~ this ancient stone
not that
You may ^ use ~~your~~ strength when the time comes
this
I will wind my veil about ancent stone
~~in it~~
~~And wind you in it a about your arms~~ And fasten you to it
Cuchu
~~Do But do not spoil your~~
But do not spoil your veil
Your veils were beautiful ~~all~~ some with threds of gold
Oefe
I am too old to care for such things now
Cuch
was
There ~~is~~ no reason ~~you~~ why you should spoil your veil
I am week from loss of blood.
Oefe
I was afraid
But now that I have wound you in the ~~veil~~ veil
~~Veil~~ I am not afraid ~~And how did my son fight~~
(Speak — did my son fight well

---

3 "the" probably omitted after "of."

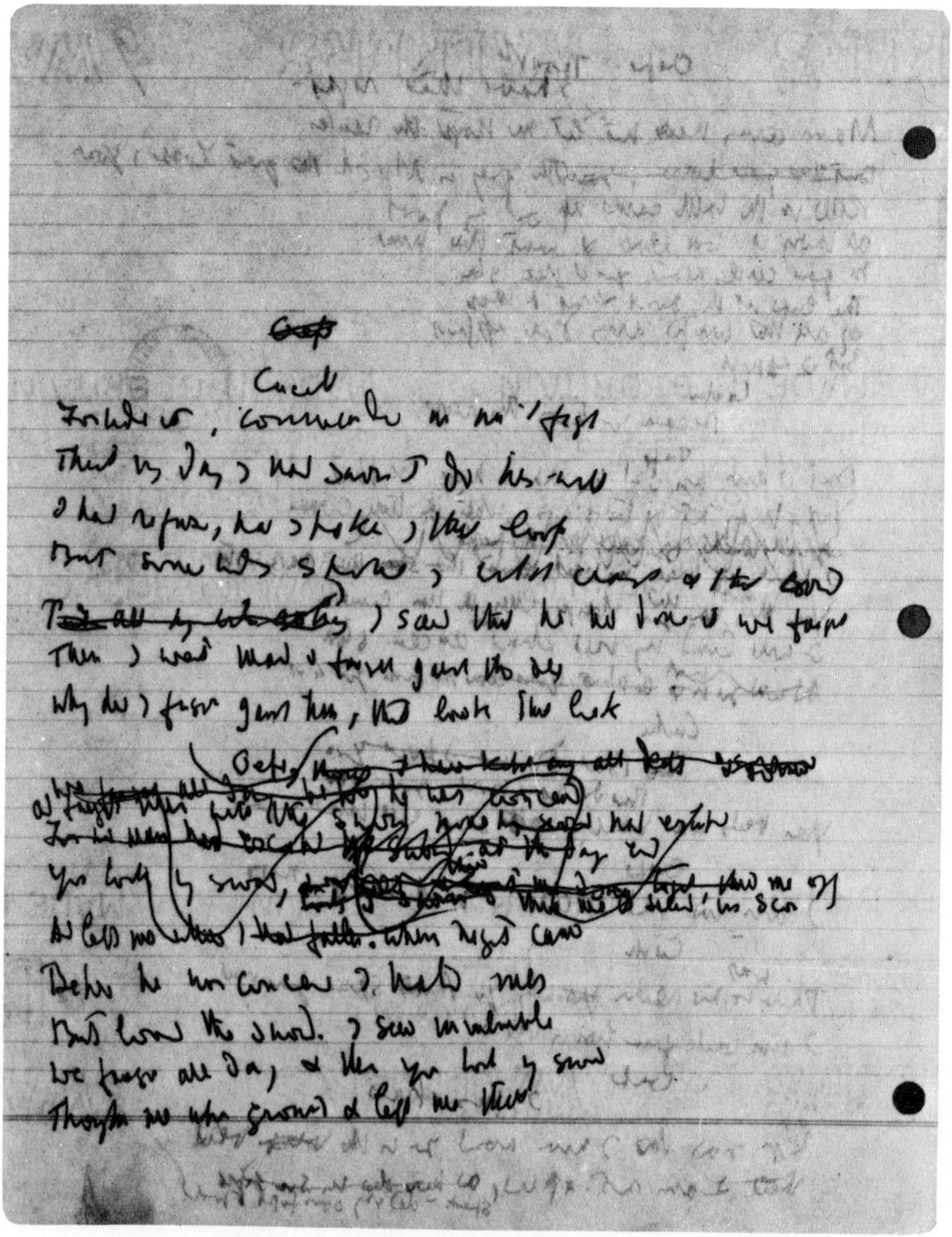

~~Oefe~~

Cucul

Forbade it, commanded me me to fight
That very day I had sworn to do his will
I had refused, had spoken of that look
But some body spoke of witch craft & that word
[?I]
~~Put all my wits astray~~ I said that he had done it we fought
Then I went mad & fought against the sea
Why did I fight against him, that look that look

Oefe

I ~~thought to have kept away all death & sorrow~~
~~We fought all day before he was conceived~~
And fought men with the sword None ~~my sword~~ had escaped
~~For no man had escaped my sword. At the days~~ end
~~threw~~
You took my sword, ~~and &~~ [~~?~~] ~~me down~~ [~~?~~], ~~threw~~ me off
~~took~~ [?~~it scorn~~] threw me it seemed in scorn
And left me where I had fallen. When night came
Before he was conceived I hated men
But loved the sword. I seemed invulnerable
We fought all day & then you took my sword
Through me upon ground & left me there

A revision of V10^{r}, ll. 6–22. The revision was continued on V10^{v}.

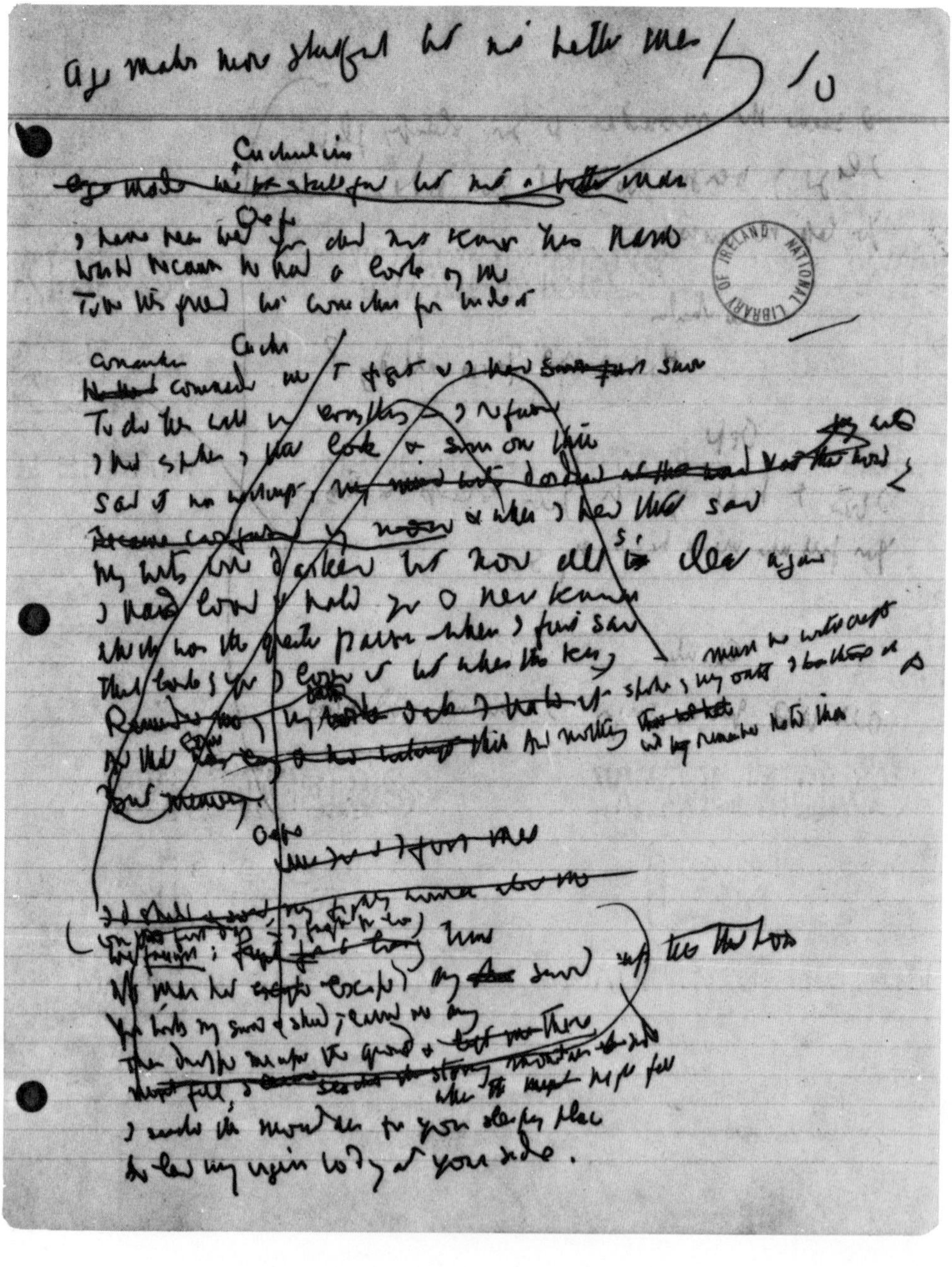

1 Age makes more skilful but not better men

10

Cuchulain
2 ~~Age made~~ [?~~me ?~~] ~~skillful but not a better~~ man
Oefe
3 I have been told you did not know his name
4 Wanted because he had a look of me
5 To be his friend but Concubar for bade it
Cuchu
Concubar
6 ~~He had~~ commanded me to fight & I had ~~sworn just~~ sworn
7 To do his will in everything — I refused
8 I had spoken of that look & some one there
~~my~~ wits
9 Said it was wichcraft, ~~my mind wits darkened at that word & at that~~ word ^
10 ~~Became confused by now~~ & when I heard that said
s
11 My wits were darkened but now all ~~is~~ clear again
d
12 I ha{ve loved & hated you & never known
13 Which was the greater passion when I first saw
14 That look of you I loved it but when the king
~~oath~~
15 ~~Reminded me of my words oath I hated~~ it
~~came~~
16 And that ~~was easy & no witchcraft this~~
17 But ~~memory.~~
Oefe
~~When you & I first met~~
18 ~~I'd shield & sword, my fighting women about me~~
On that first day, I fought for long
19 We ~~fought; fought for a long~~ time
20 No man had ~~escaped~~ escaped my ~~sho~~ sword up till that hour
21 You took my sword & shield; carried me away
22 Then dropped me upon the ground & ~~left me~~ there
23 ~~Night fell; I [?cerched] serched the stormy mountain sh~~ side
when the ~~night~~ night fell
24 I searched the mountain for your sleeping place
25 And laid my virgin body at your side.

---

must be witchcraft
spoke of my oath I ~~ha~~ thought it ^
And nothing ~~that but hate~~
but ~~my~~ remembered hatred this

The passage below the rule is from the right margin (revisions of ll. 15–17).
2 The second illegible word was cancelled first in blue ink, then in black.

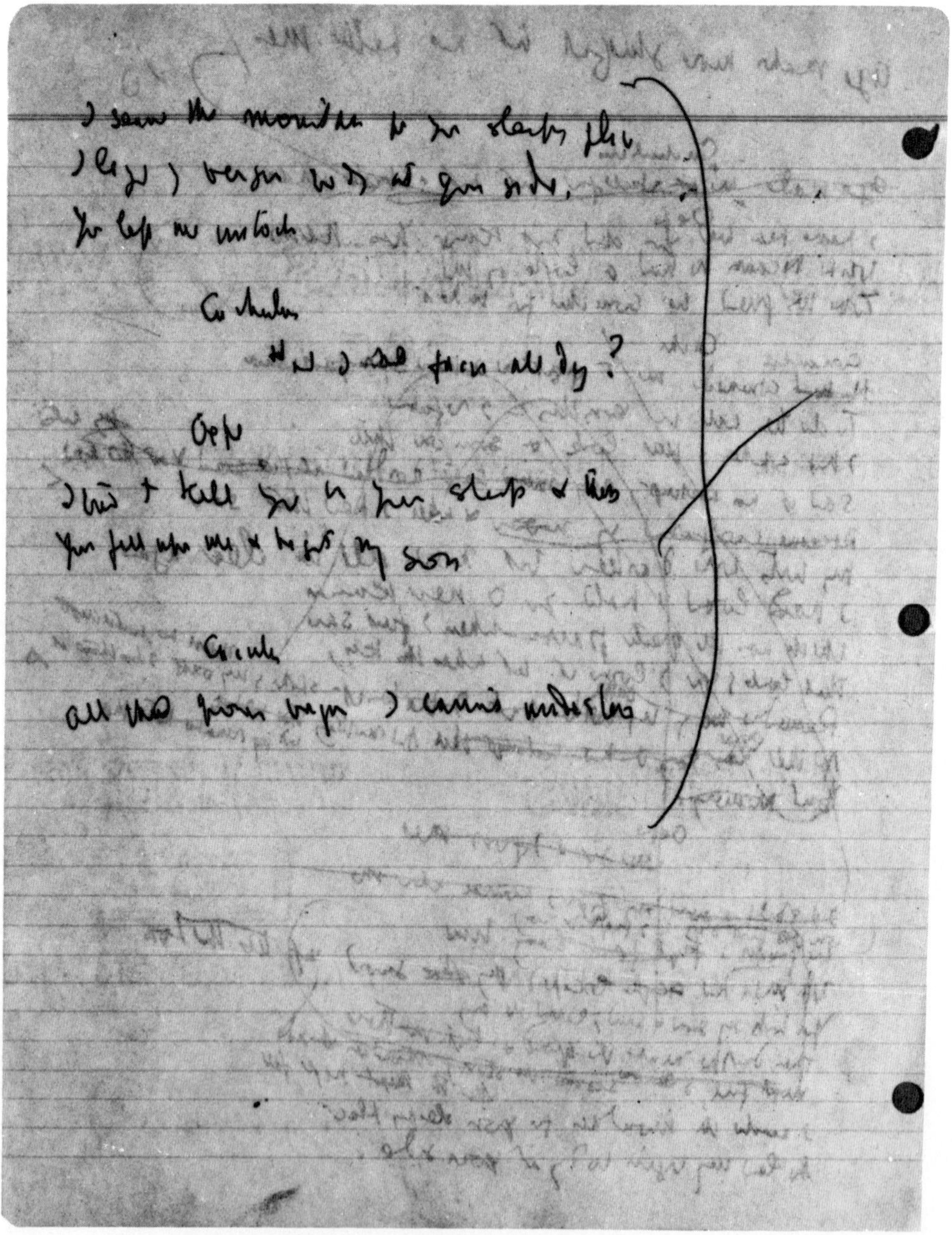

I searched the mountain for your sleeping place
I layed my vergin body at your side,
You left me untouched

Cuchulain

Had I not fought all day?

Oefe

I tried to kill you in your sleep & then
You fell upon me & begot my son

Cuculain

All that grows vague I cannot understand

A revision of V10ʳ, l. 24–V11ʳ, l. 2.

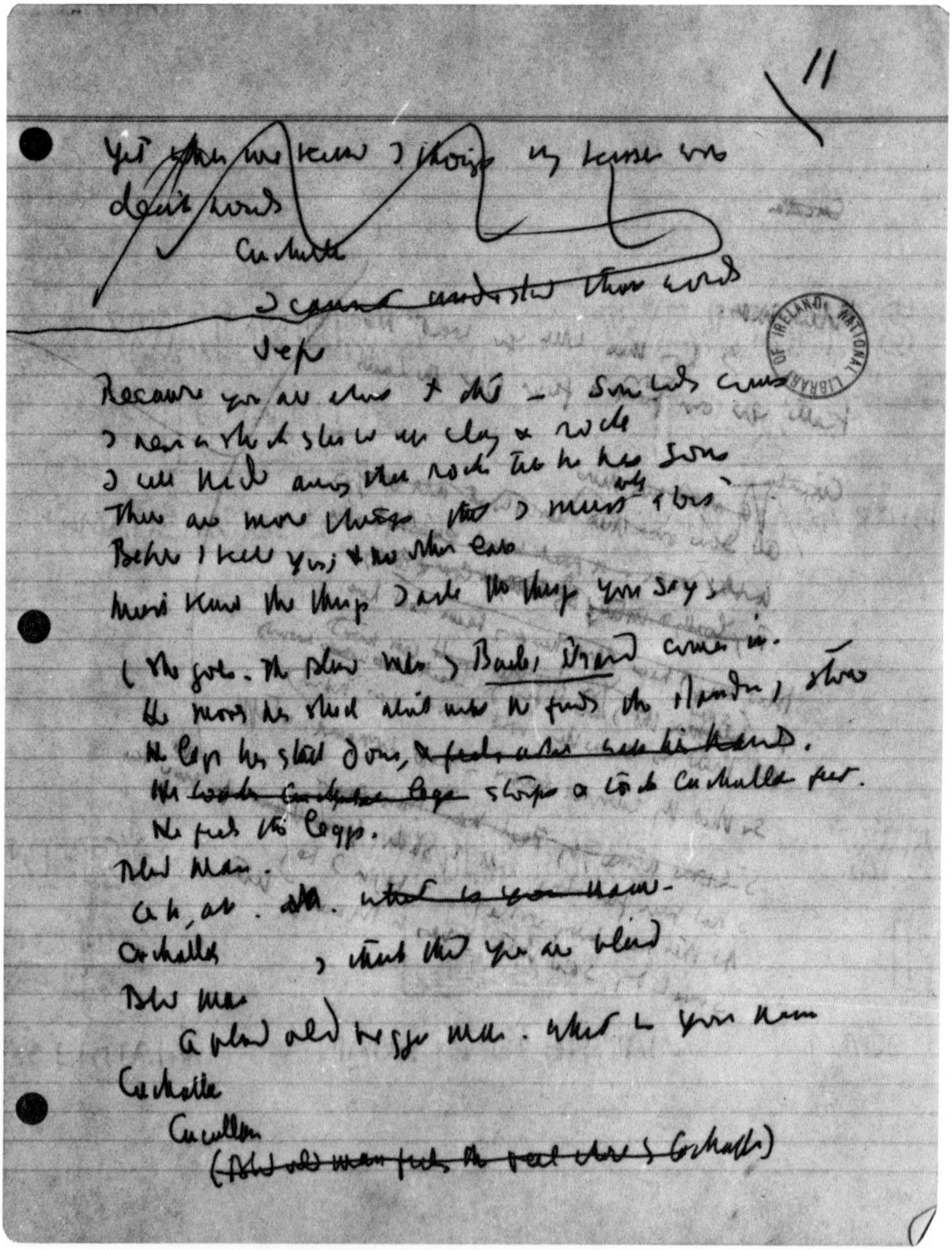

11

Yet when we kissed I thought my kisses were
death wounds
Cuchullain
I cannot understand those words
Oefe
Because you are about to die — Some body comes
I hear a stick strike upon clay & rock
I will hide among these rocks till he has gone
ask
There are more things that I must about
Before I kill you; & no other ears
Must know the things I ask the things you say,

(She goes. The Blind Man of Baile s Strand comes in.
He moves his stick about until he finds the standing stone
He lays his stick down, & ~~feels about with his hands.~~
He ~~touches Cuchulains legs~~ stoops & touches Cuchullains feet.
He feels the leggs.
Blind Man.
Ah, ah. ~~ah.~~ ~~What is your name~~.
Cuchullain
I think that you are blind
Blind Man
A blind old beggar man. What is your name
Cuchullain
Cucullain
(~~Blind old man feels the veil~~ [~~?~~ ?~~by~~/?~~of~~] ~~Cuchullain)~~

8 The punctuation mark may be a period.

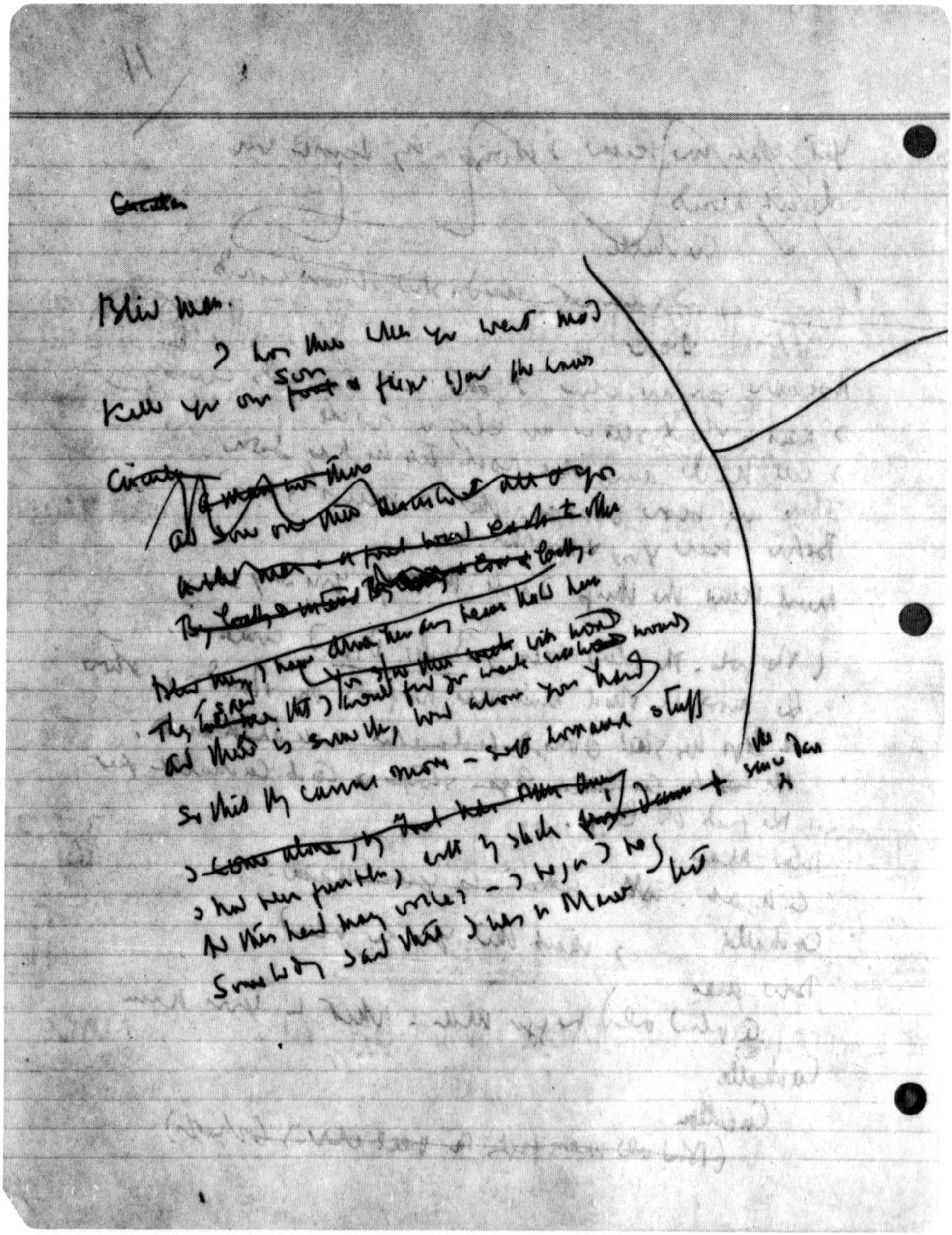

~~Cuculan~~

Blind Man.

1 I was there when you went mad

son

2 Killed your own ~~fool~~ & fought against the waves

~~Cuculain~~

3 [~~A man was there~~

4 [And some one there described it all to you

5 ~~A blind man & a fool bound each to~~ other

6 ~~By loathing & interest~~ ~~By loathing & love &~~ loathing.

7 ~~Blind Man I have driven him away because hated~~ him

said ~~You stood there week~~ with wounds

8 They ~~told me~~ that I would find you week with ~~wounds~~ wounds

9 And there is something bound about your hands

10 So that they cannot move — soft womanish stuff

11 ~~I come alone, my Fool has run away~~

the

12 I had been fumbling with my stick ~~from dawn~~ ~~f~~ since dawn

^

13 And then heard many voices — I began to beg

14 Somebody said that I was in Maeves tent

A revision of V12^r, ll. 4–12.

7 "I" probably omitted after "because."

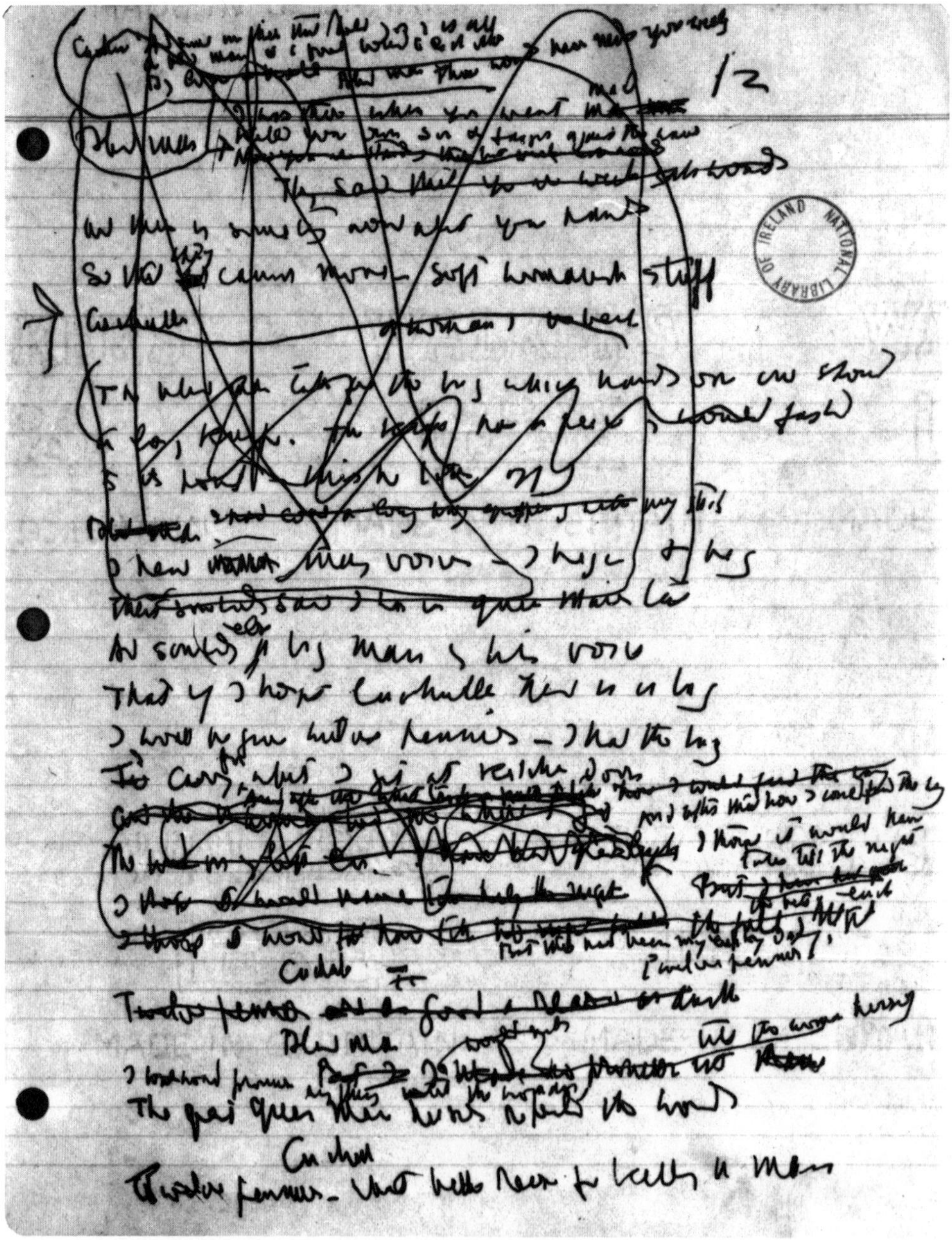

Cuchu 'And some one there that told you of it all
A blind man & a fool bound to each other
By love & hate

Blind Man

Those wounds have made you week
mad 12
I was there when you went ~~ma ma~~
Killed your own son & fought against the waves
Blind Man ~~Now you are standing there but week with wounds~~
~~They said that you are week with wounds~~
And there is something wound about your hands
they
So that ~~you~~ cannot move — soft womanish stuff
~~Cuchullain A woman s v veil.~~

(The blind man takes from the bag which hands on one should
A long knife. The knife has a peice of would fastened
to its point — this he takes off)

I had come a long way gropping with my stick
~~Blind Man~~
I heard ~~voices~~ many voices — I began to beg
Then somebody said I was in Queen Maeves tent
else
And somebody ^ a big man by his voice
That if I brought Cuchullains head in a bag
I would be given twelve pennies — I had the bag
I fo
~~To~~ carry ^ what I get at kitchen doors
And after that what track or path to take
And then the woman told me where to go
The wind in my left ear. I have had great luck
I ~~thought it would have taken half the night~~
I thought it would ~~tak~~ have taken ~~till night fall the fall of night~~

Cuchulain
~~T~~
Twelve pennies
~~Twelve pennies are as good a reason as another~~

Blind Man
~~would make~~ ~~till the woman~~ herself
~~But I~~ I ~~made no promises till Maeve~~
I ~~wo~~ woud promise any thing ~~un~~til the woman,
The great Queen Maeve herself repeated the words

Cuchul
T
A welve pennies. What better reason for killing a man

~~how I could find the way~~
And after that how I could find the way
I thought it would have
taken till the night
~~But I have had great~~
the best of luck
But this has been my lucky day.

The passage below the rule is from the right margin (revisions of ll. 17–20).
In the stage directions, Yeats wrote "hands" for "hangs."
23 "not" probably omitted after "woud."

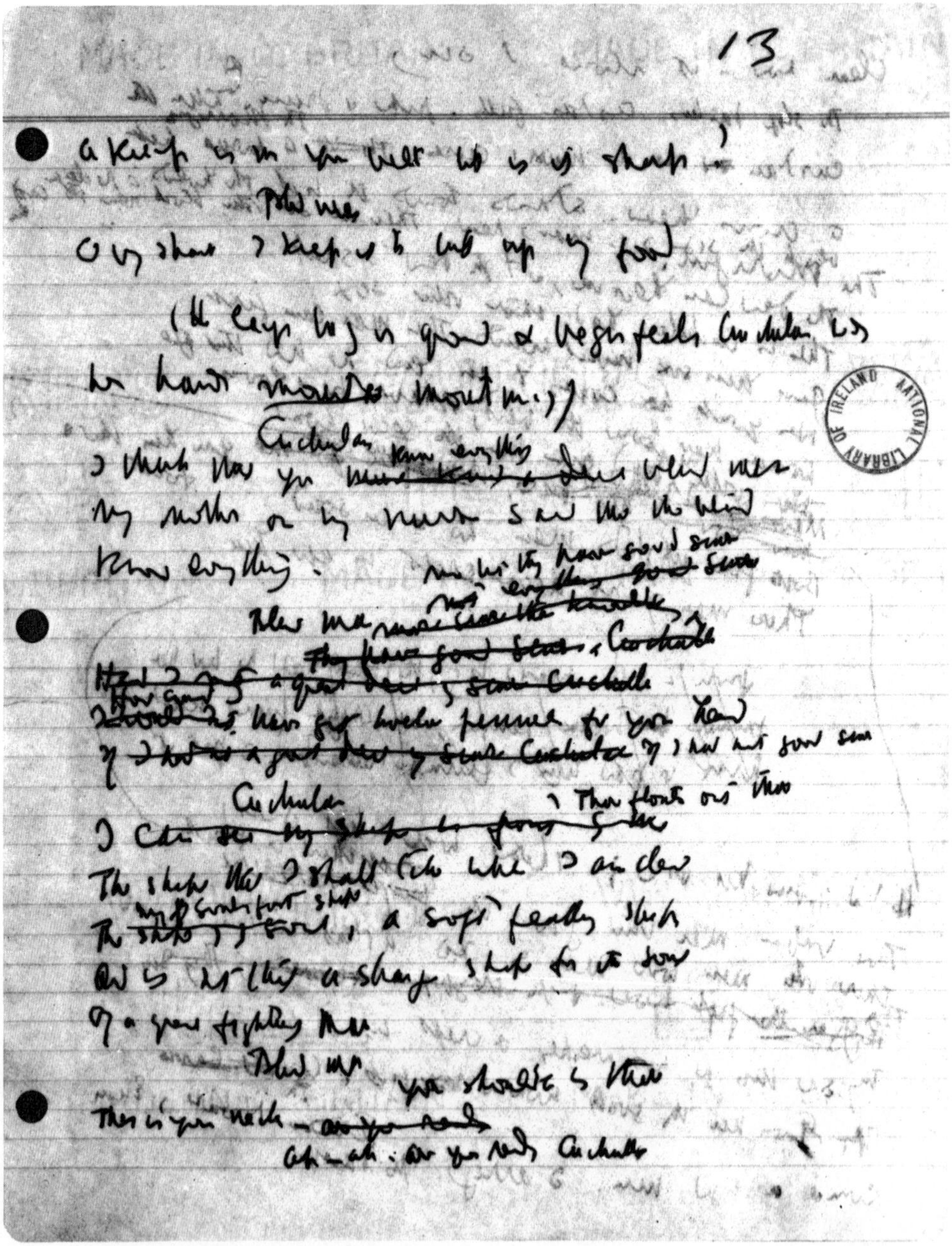
13

a keep [illegible] in your belt [illegible] sharp ?

Blind man

O [illegible] I keep it to cut up my food

(He lays [illegible] Cuchulain [illegible]

his hands ~~moving~~ moving [illegible])

Cuchulain

I think that you ~~[illegible]~~ know everything Blind man

My mother or my nurse said that the blind

know everything.

Blind man

[illegible]

Cuchulain

I can ~~[illegible]~~

The sleep that I shall take when I am [illegible]

~~The [illegible]~~ [illegible], a soft feathery sleep

And is not this a strange sleep for the death

Of a great fighting man

Blind man

This is your neck — ~~are you ready~~ your shoulder is there

Ah — ah: are you ready Cuchulain

13

1 A Knife is in your belt but is it sharp?
Blind Man
2 O very sharp I keep it to cut up my food

(He lays bag on ground & begins feeling Cuchulains body his hands ~~mountai~~ mounting)
Cuchulain
know everything
3 I think that you ~~must know a deal~~ blind man
4 My mother or my nurse said that the blind
5 Know everything.
no but they have good sense
Blind Man ~~not everything good~~ ~~sense~~
~~more sense than knowledge~~ ∧
~~They have good sense~~ ∧ ~~Cuchullain~~
6 ~~Had I not a great deal of sense Cuchullain~~
How could I
7 ~~I would not~~ have got twelve pennies for your head
8 If ~~I hadnt a great deal of sense Cuchulain~~ If I had not good sense
Cuchulain
There floats out there
9 I ~~can see my shape in front of me~~
10 The shape that I shall take when I am dead
my ~~f~~ souls first shape
11 The ~~shape of my soul~~, a soft feathery shape
12 And is not that a strange shape for the soul
13 Of a great fighting man
Blind Man
Your shoulder is there
14 This is your neck — ~~are you ready~~
Ah — ah. Are you ready Cuchullain

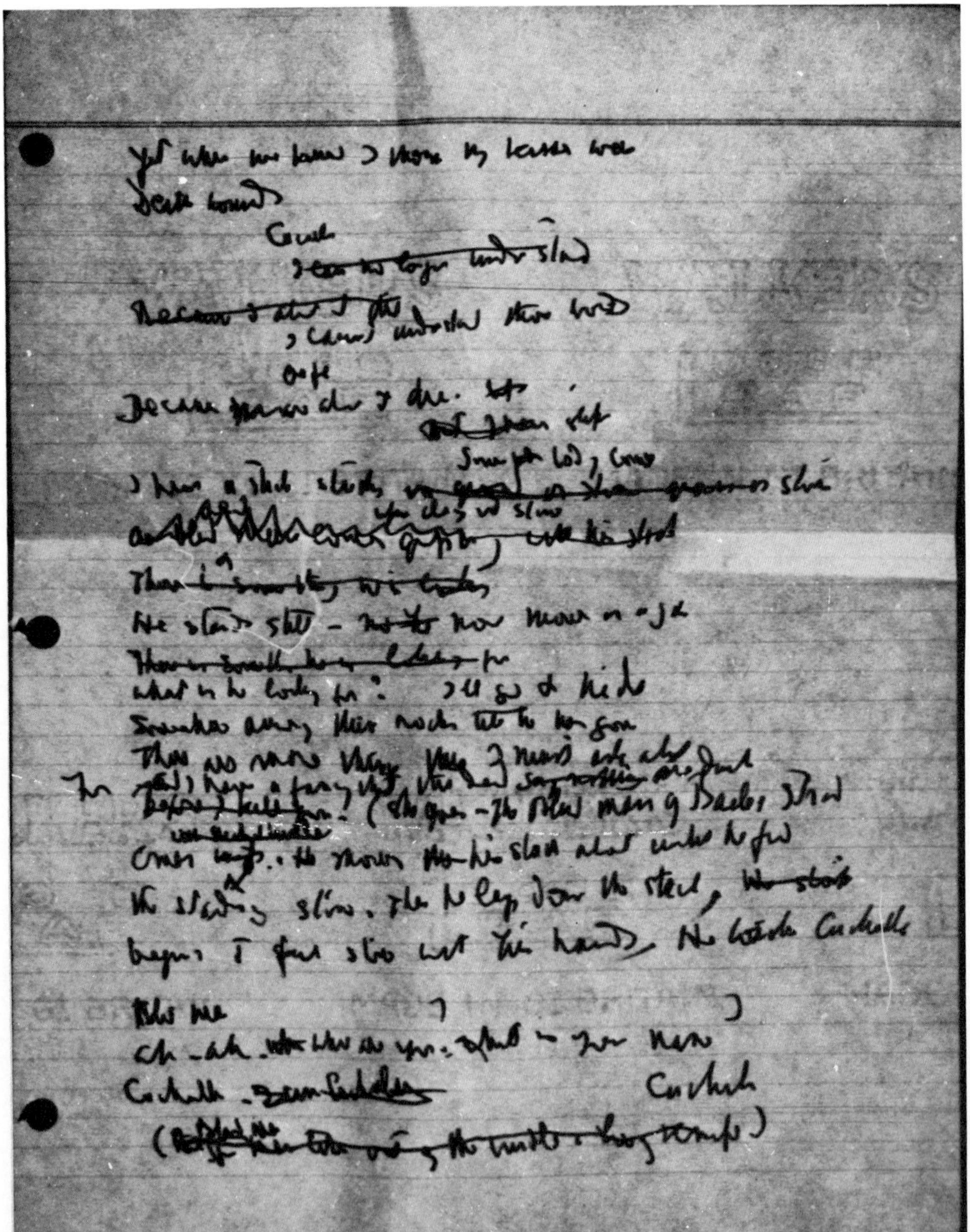

1 Yet when we kissed I thought my kisses were
2 Death wounds
Cucul
3 I ~~can no longer understand~~
4 ~~Because I about to die~~
5 I cannot understand those words

Oefe
6 Because ~~you are~~ about to die. [?~~but~~]
~~But I hear~~ steps.
Some [~~-?-~~] body comes
7 I hear a stick striking ~~on ground or stone grass or~~ stone
upon clay and stone
~~old~~
8 ~~A blind ^ man comes groping with his stick~~
9 ~~There is some thing he is looking~~
10 He stands still — ~~now he~~ now moves on again
11 ~~There is something he is looking~~ for
12 What is he looking for? I ll go & hide
13 Somewhere among these rocks till he has gone
14 There are more things that I must ask about
15 For ~~And~~ I have a fancy that the dead ~~say nothing~~ are dumb
16 ~~Before I kill you.~~ (She goes — The Blind Man of Baile s Strand
~~with stick & bundle~~
17 comes [?~~in~~]. He moves ~~the~~ his stick about until he finds
^
18 the standing stone. Then he lays down the stick. ~~Wi stick~~
19 begins to feel stone with his hands. He touches Cuchullain

Blind Man
20 Ah — ah. ~~Who~~ Who are you? What is your name?
21 Cuchullain. ~~I am Cuchulain~~ Cuchulain
Blind Man
([?~~Ragged] Man takes out of the bundle a long knife~~)

This leaf contains an alternate version of V11^r and was perhaps composed as part of the same rather than an earlier draft.

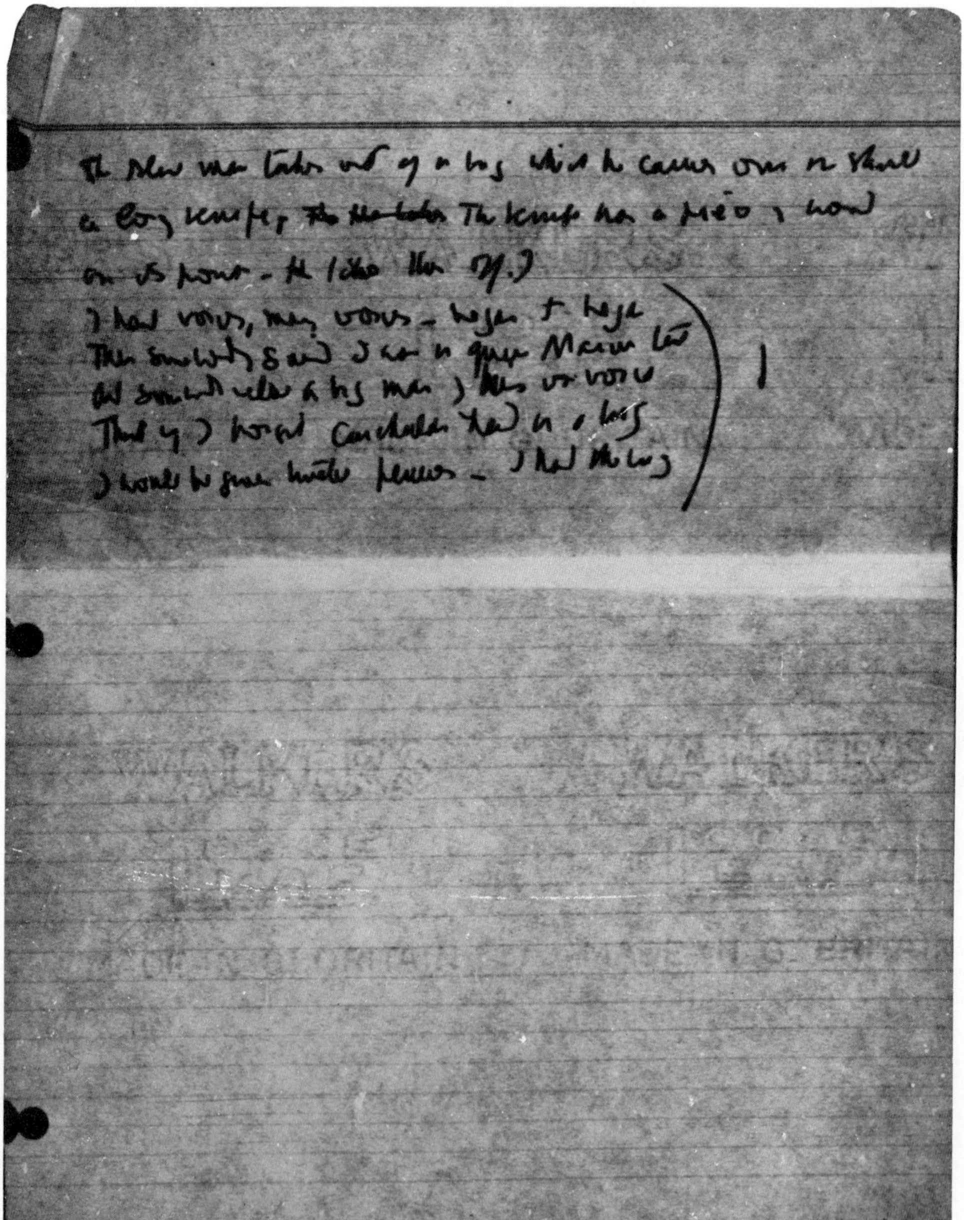

The Blind Man takes out of a bag which he carries over one should a long knife. ~~The He takes~~ The knife has a piece of wood on its point. He takes this off.)

I heard voices, many voices — began to began
Then somebody said I was in queen Maeves tent
And somebody else a big man by his ~~v~~ voice
That if I brought Cuchulains head in a bag
I would be given twelve pennies — I had the bag

A revision of V12^r, stage directions and ll. 10–15. It seems to be earlier than the revision of V12^r on V11^v.

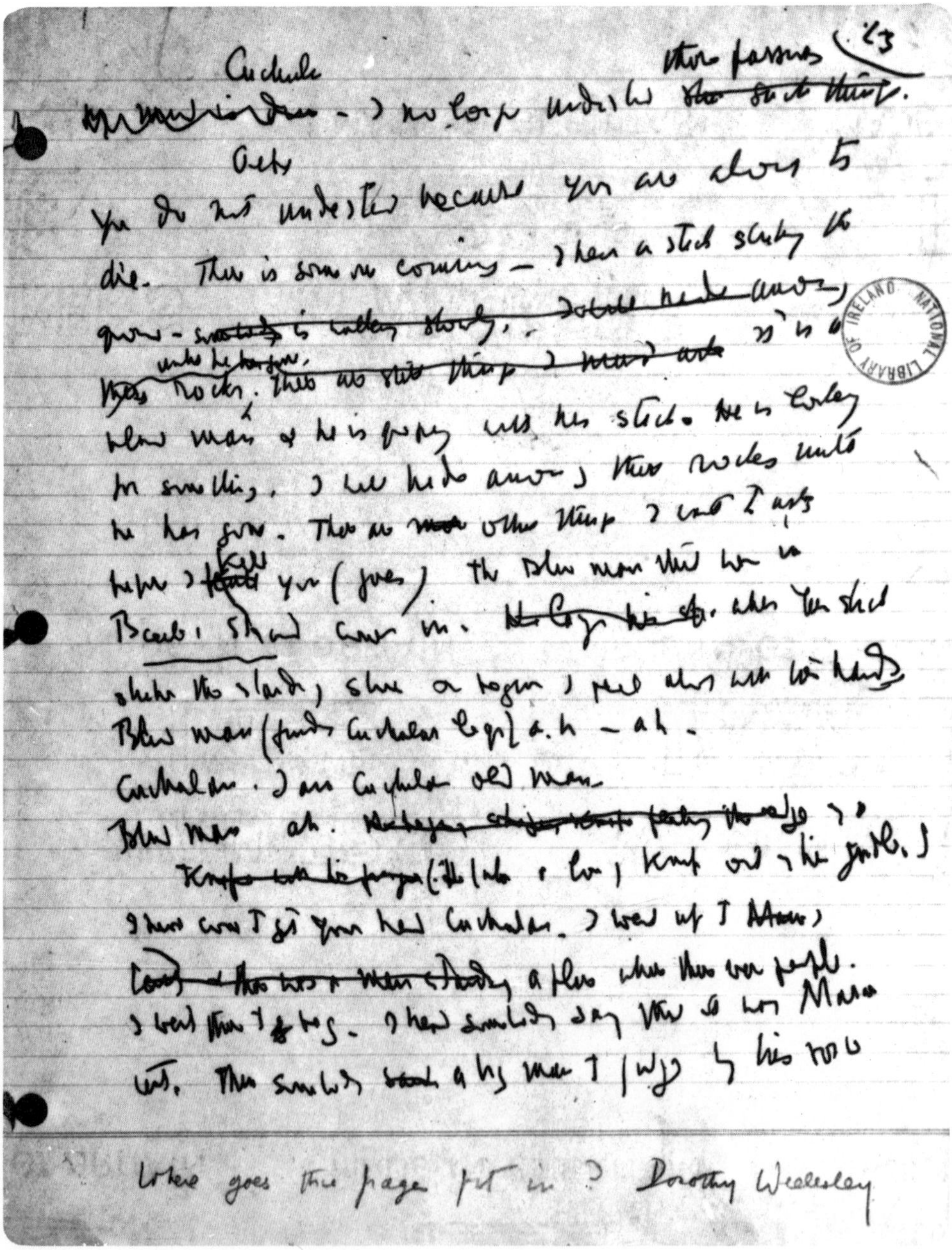

23

Cuchulain — I no longer understand other persons.

Aoife

You do not understand because you are about to die. There is some one coming — I hear a stick striking the ground — somebody is walking slowly [illegible] among these rocks. [illegible] blind man & he is groping with his stick. He is looking for something. I will hide among those rocks until he has gone. There are other things I want to ask before I kill you (goes) The blind man that was in Baile's Strand comes in. [illegible] with the stick shakes the stones or touches [illegible] feels about with his hands.

Blind man (finds Cuchulain legs) ah — ah.

Cuchulain. I am Cuchulain old man.

Blind man ah. [illegible] (He takes a long knife out of his girdle.) I have come to get your head Cuchulain. I was up [illegible] a place where there were people. I went there to beg. I heard somebody say there [illegible] Maeve [illegible]. This somebody [illegible] a big man [illegible] by his [illegible]

Where goes this page if in? Dorothy Wellesley

Cuchulain 13

those passions
~~My mind is dim~~ — I no longer understand ~~sh such things~~.
Oefe
You do not understand because you are about to
die. There is some one coming — I hear a stick striking the
ground — ~~somebody is walking slowly. I will hide~~ among
~~until he has gone.~~
~~these rocks. There are still things I must ask~~ It is a
<
blind man & he is groping with his stick. He is looking
for some thing. I will hide among these rocks until
he has gone. There are ~~more~~ other things I want to ask
kill
{k
before I ~~call~~ you (goes) The Blind Man that was in
<u>Baile s</u> <u>Strand</u> comes in. ~~He lays his sti~~ When his stick
strikes the standing stone and begins to feel about with his hands
Blind Man (finds Cuchulains legs) ah — ah.
Cuchulain. I am Cuchulain old man.
Blind Man ah. ~~He begins sharpening knife feeling the~~ edge of a
~~knife with his finger~~ (. He takes a long knife out of his girdle.)
I have come to get your head Cuchulain. I went up to ~~Maeve~~s
~~tent & there was a man standing~~ a place where there were people.
I went there to [?~~g~~] beg. I heard somebody say that it was Maeves
tent. Then somebody ~~said~~ a big man to judge by his voice

Where goes this page fit in? Dorothy Wellesley

Dorothy Wellesley's note reflects a failure to recognize that this leaf was from the prose draft and so did not go with the verse-draft materials among which she was trying to place it. It corresponds to V11r, l. 2–V12r, l. 13 of the verse draft.

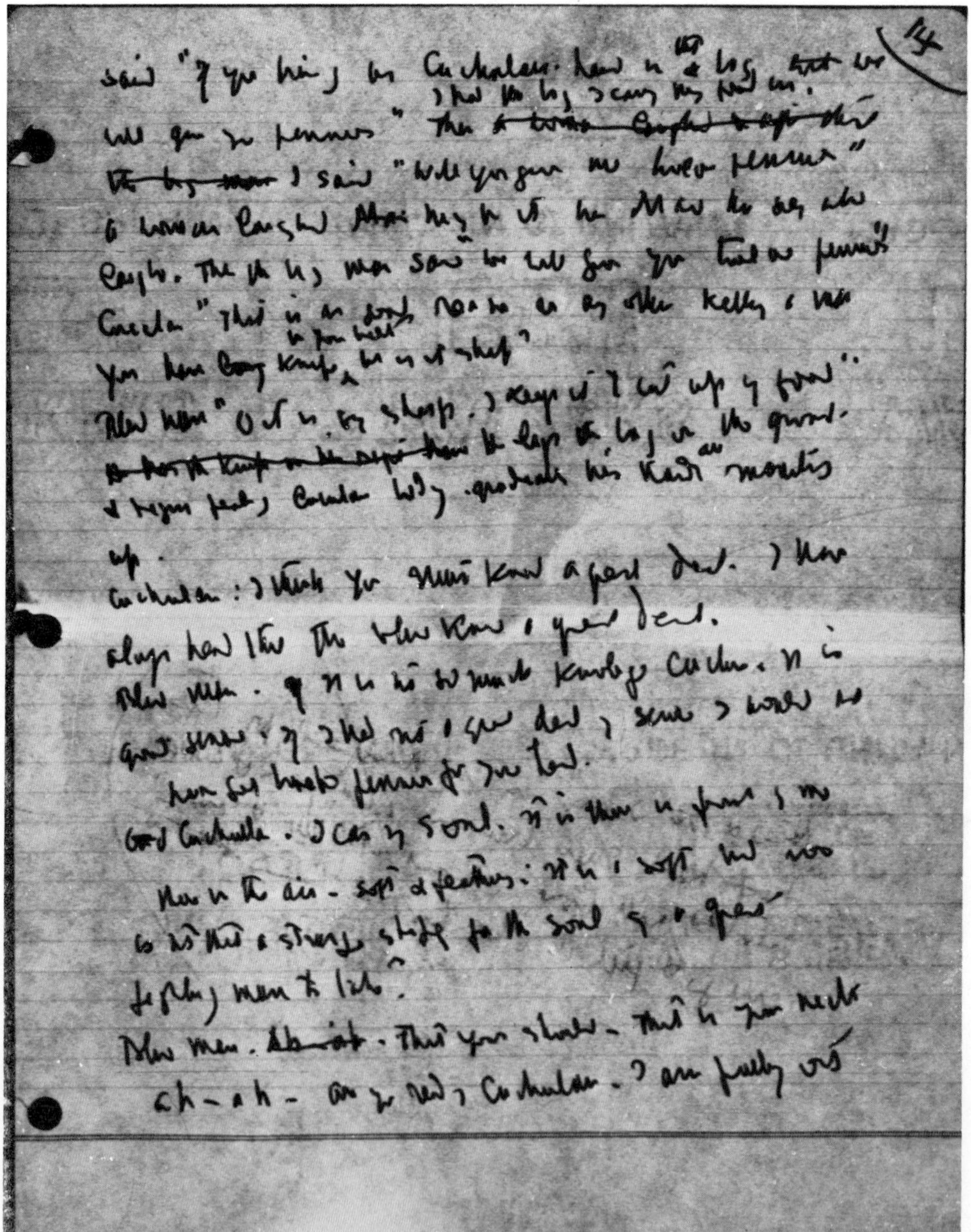
said "If you bring [illegible] Cuchulain [illegible]
will give you pennies" [illegible]
I said "Will you give me [illegible] pennies"
[illegible]
[illegible]
[illegible]
you [illegible]
[illegible] "Out [illegible] shop. [illegible]
[illegible]
[illegible] Cuchulain [illegible]
up.
Cuchulain: I think you must know a great deal. I have
always heard [illegible] know a great deal.
[illegible] knowledge [illegible]
great [illegible]
[illegible] pennies for [illegible]
[illegible] Cuchulain. [illegible] soul. [illegible]
[illegible] air — soft as feathers: [illegible] soft [illegible]
[illegible] strange [illegible] soul [illegible]
[illegible] man to [illegible].
[illegible] — that your [illegible] — [illegible]
oh — oh — [illegible] Cuchulain. I am [illegible]

that 14
said "If you bring us Cuchulains head in ~~a~~ bag ~~wil~~ we
I had the bag I carry my food in.
will give you pennies'' Then ~~a woman laughed & after that~~
~~the big man~~ I said "Will you give me twelve pennies"
A woman laughed ~~Ma~~ high it was Mave her self who
laughed. Then the big man said "we will give you twelve pennies"
Cuculain "That is as good reason as any other killing a man
in your belt
You have ~~long~~ knife ∧ but is it sharp?
Blind Man "O it is very sharp. I keep it to cut up my food"
~~He has the knife in his right han~~ He lays the bag on the ground,
are
& begins feeling Cuculains body, gradually his hands mounting
up.
Cuchulain: I think you must know a great deal. I have
always heard that the blind know a great deal.
Blind Man. [?~~It~~] It is not so much knowledge Cuchu. It is
good sense. If I had not a great deal of sense I would not
have got twelve pennies for your head.
~~Cuch~~ Cuchullain. I can my soul. It is there in front of me
there in the air — soft & feathery. It is a soft bird now
is not that a strange shape for the soul of a great
fighting man to take?
Blind Man. ~~Ah — ah.~~ That your should. That is your neck
ah — ah — are you ready Cuchulain. I am pulling out

Prose draft corresponding to V12^r, l. 14–V13^r, l. 14 of the verse draft.
3 "man" may have been cancelled before the entire phrase was cancelled.
6 "for" probably omitted after "other."
7 "a" probably omitted after "have."
17 "see" probably omitted after "can."

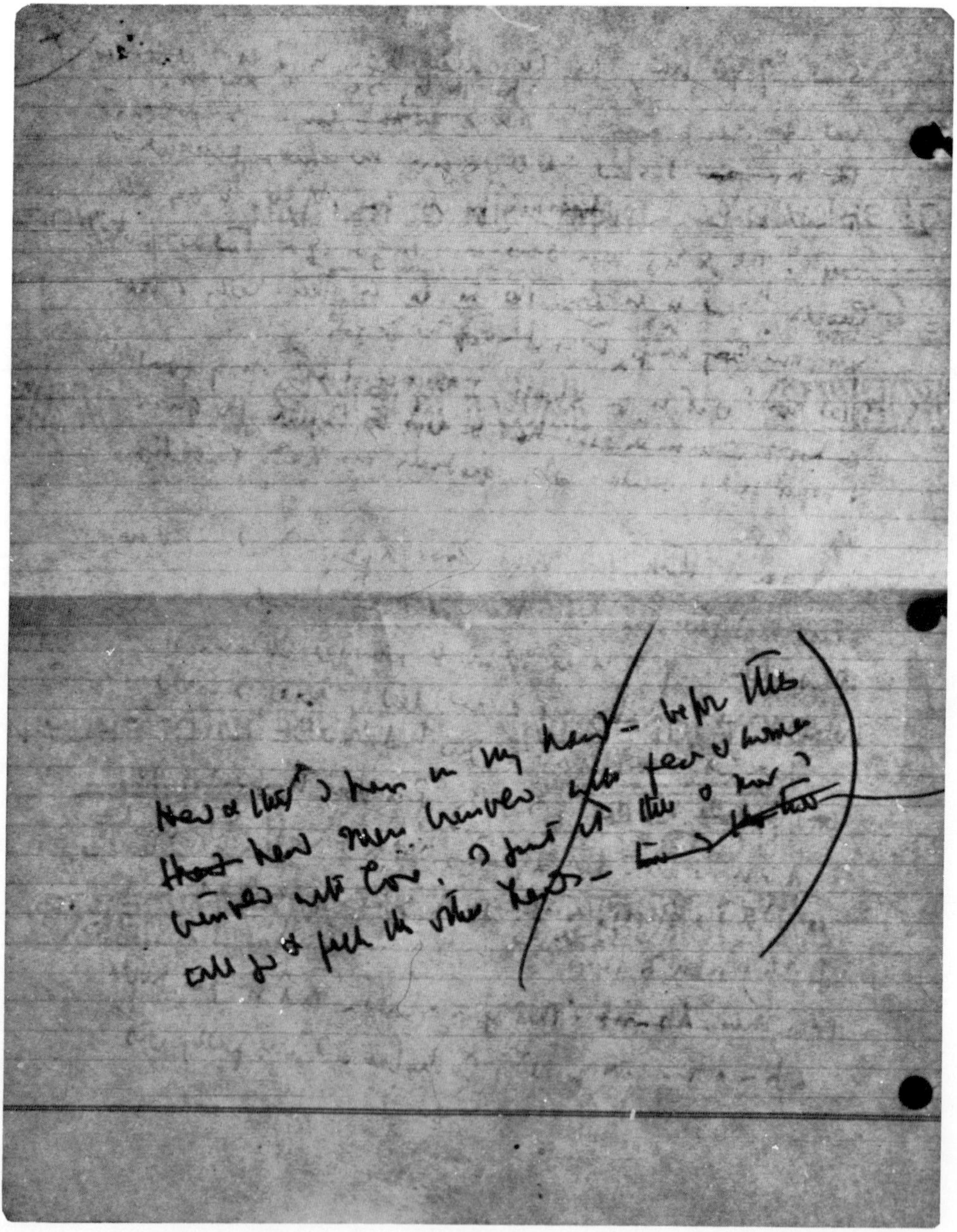

Head & that I have in my hand — before this
~~Head~~ head men trembled with fear & women
trembled with love. I put it there & now I
will go & fetch the other heads — ~~two of the two~~

A revision of P15^{r}, ll. 14ff of the prose draft. It is in a darker blue ink than that used in the bulk of the prose-draft material; it was also used on P15^{v} and for revisions on P15^{r} and PV16^{r}. It seems to represent a stage of revision earlier than the revisions in black ink.

4 The second "the" may have been cancelled before the entire phrase was cancelled.

Manuscripts of the End of the Play

Yeats had a great deal of difficulty writing the end of the play, from the point of Cuchulain's death to the closing lyric. The extant materials for this section show extensive revision and a major change of plan.

The earliest discernible stage is composed of two leaves of prose draft, numbered 15 and 16 (P15, PV16). The Old Man's speech would presumably have been in prose even in the verse draft. It is clear, however, that page 15 is prose draft, for it continues the sentence broken at the bottom of page 14 of the prose draft, and on the verso of 14 is a revision of a passage on page 15. That page 16 is also prose draft is indicated by the fact that it continues the Old Man's speech from the point to which it had been brought by page 15 and that on both 15 and 16 the Old Man is referred to as "Attendant." In addition, on the verso of 15 is a revision keyed by a line to a passage on page 16.

Yeats was clearly dissatisfied with this version. He cancelled that portion of the Attendant's speech on page 15 and wrote a new version, numbering the new leaf 14 (V14). (Cancelled revisions of two passages appear on V13^{v}.) After cancelling page 15 and writing page 14, Yeats was still trying to salvage page 16, as it has corrections in black ink, and as in place of one cancelled passage he wrote in black ink and then cancelled several lines on the verso of page 14.

Still dissatisfied, he cancelled pages 14 and 16 in their entirety, turned to the verso of page 13 of the verse draft, and wrote a new version in which he abandoned the idea of having the Old Man reappear at this point in the play and gave the role of "choreographer" of Emer's dance to the Morrigu.

The stage direction following the Morrigu's speech that describes Emer's dance and introduces the closing lyric is not found in the holograph materials, though a passage which may be a revision of part of it has survived. That passage seems also to be connected with the evolution of the lyric itself, and is reproduced in the next section, p. 120.

The materials are transcribed in the following order:

a. P15^{r}	d. V14^{r}
b. P15^{v}	e. V14^{v}
c. PV16^{r}	f. V13^{v}

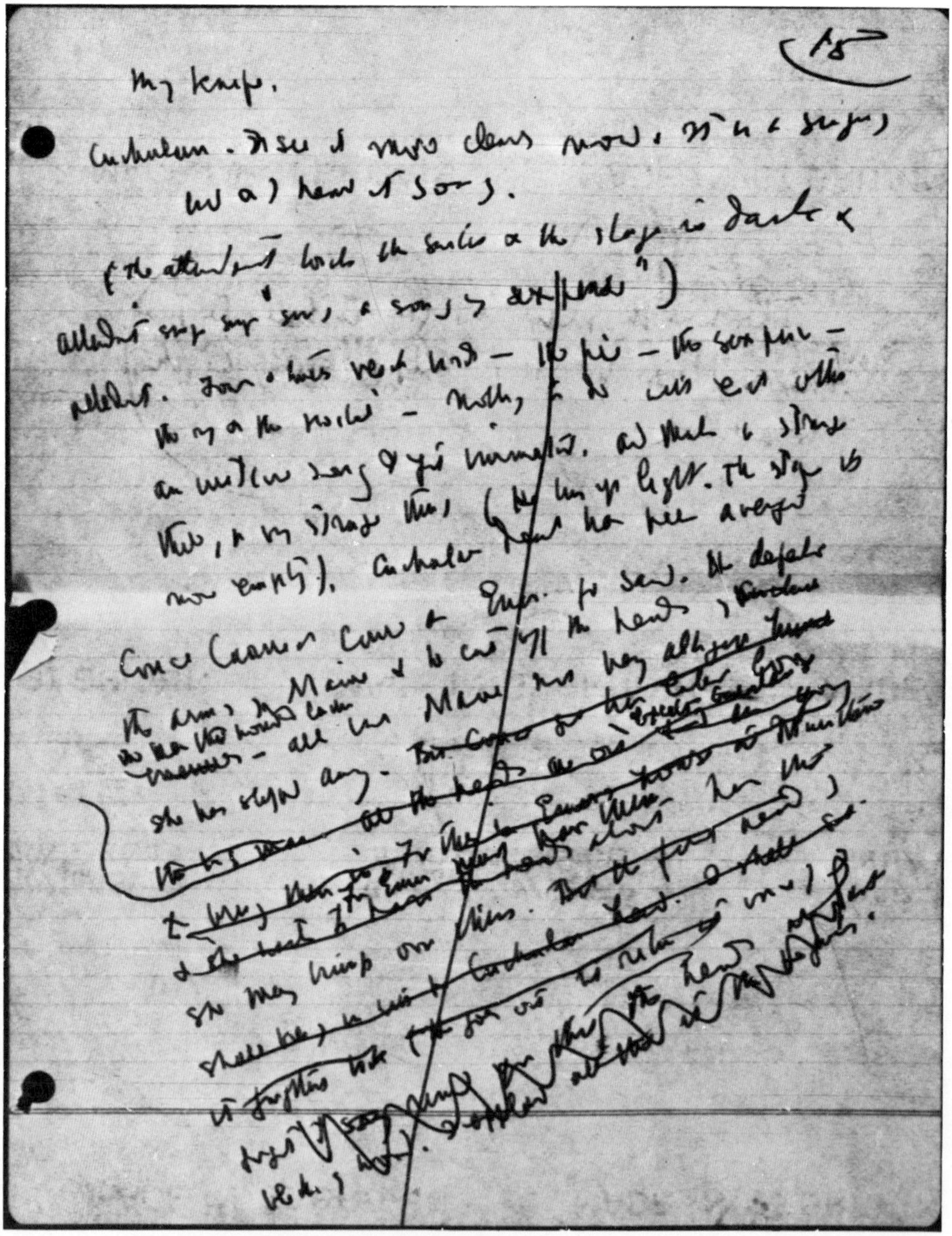

15

My knife.
Cuchulain. I see it more clearly now. It is a singing
bird & I hear it song.

(The attendant touches the switch & the stage is dark &
Attendant sings sings "sing a song of six pense")

Attendant. Four & twenty black birds — the pie — the six pence —
the ry & the pocket — nothing to do with each other
an untrue song & yet immortal. And thats a strange
[?thing], a very strange thing (He turns up light. The stage is
now empty). Cuchulains death has been avenged
Conal Carnach came as Emer for saw. He defeated
the army of Maive & he cut off the heads of ~~Cuchulains~~
the men that wounded Cuch
~~enemies~~ — all but Mave not being altogether human
she has slipped away. ~~But Conal got her latest lover~~
~~except Cuculain s~~
~~the big man~~. ~~All the heads are out~~ & ~~I am going~~
to ~~bring them in. For this is Emer s house at Muirthemne~~
For Emer must have them
~~& she wants to have the heads~~ about her that
she may triumph over them. ~~But the first head~~ I
~~shall bring in will be Cuchulains head. I shall~~ [?~~get~~/?~~set~~]
it ~~frightens~~ [?~~her~~] (~~He goes out but returns at~~ once) I
forgot to ~~say~~ remind you that the heads are but
blocks of wood. I explained ~~all that~~ at the beginning.

There are several revisions in the darker blue ink, including the vertical cancellation line, the cancellation line in l. 14; all cancellation lines except that through "the big man" and the words "except Cuchulain s" in l. 15; the cancellation line and the words "For Emer must have them" in l. 17; the cancellation lines in ll. 18, 19, 20; and the wavy cancellation line in ll. 21–22.

19–20 This sentence could be "I shall get it [it] frightens her" or conceivably "I shall bet it frightens her."

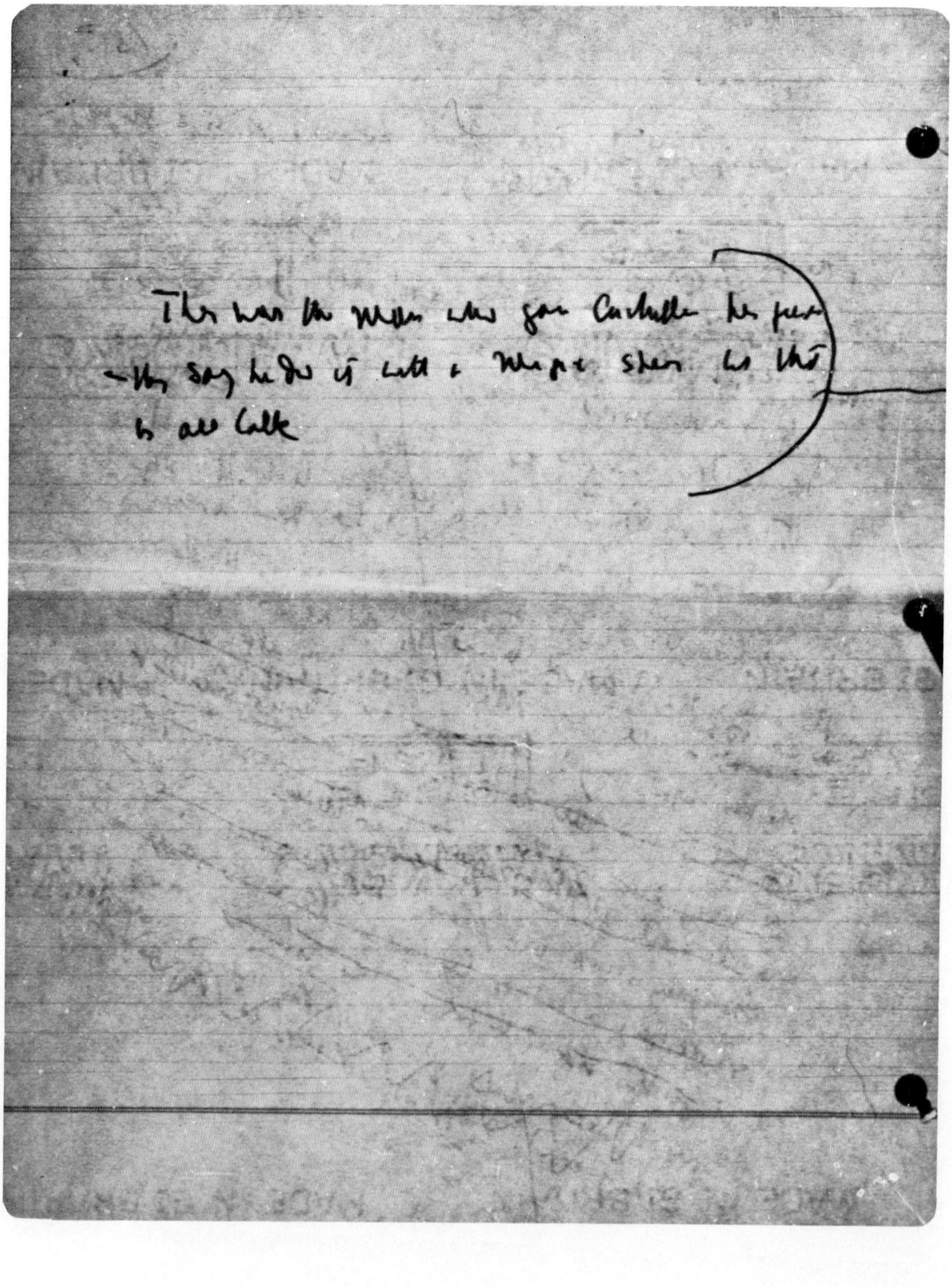
This was the person who gave Cuchulain his [illegible]
—they say he did it with a whisper. [illegible] [illegible] [illegible]
is all talk

This was the man who gave Cuchullain his first
— they say he did it with a magic spear but that
is all talk

A revision, in the darker blue ink, of PV16^{r}, l. 6.

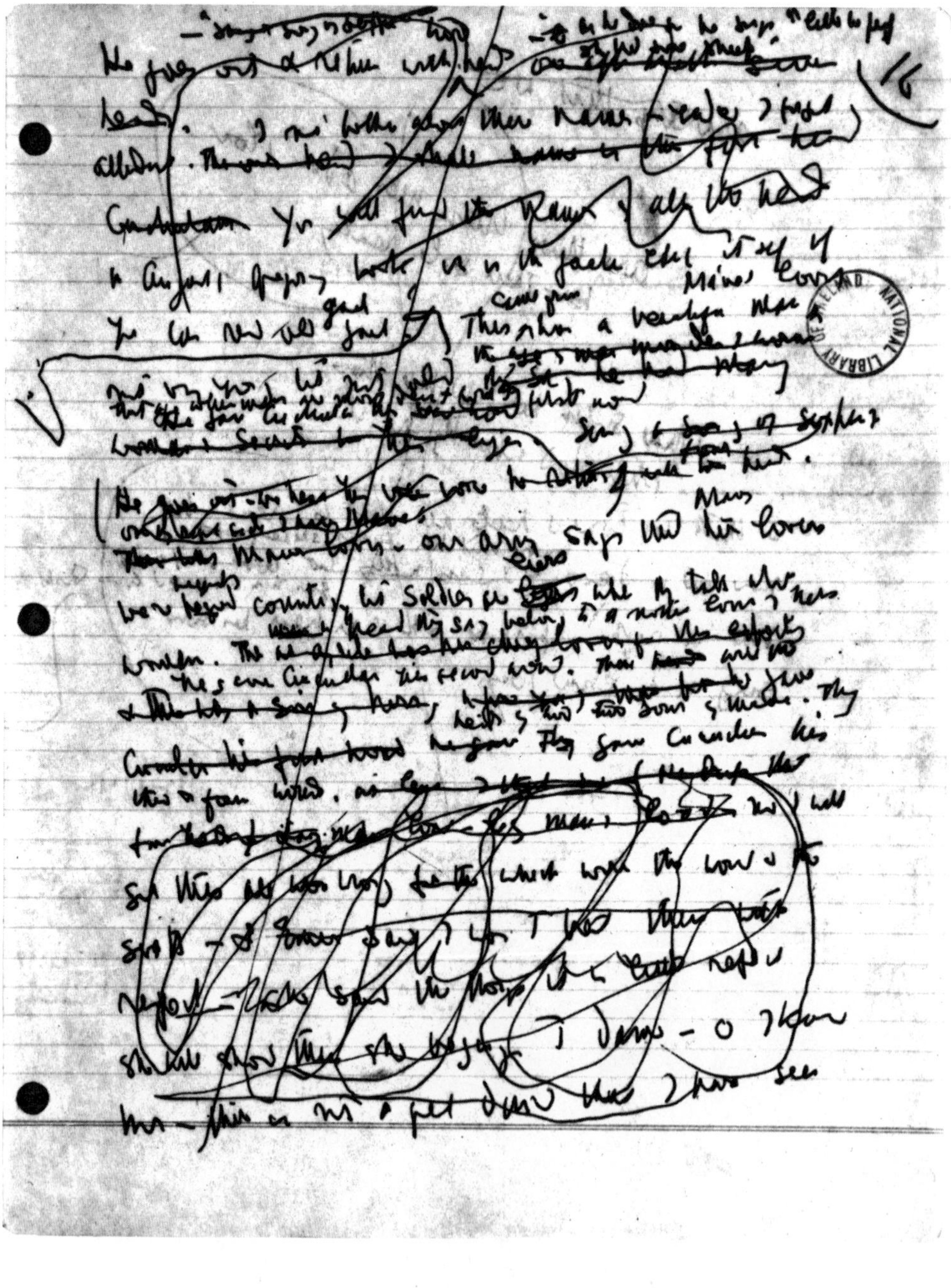

— ~~"sing a song of sixpence~~
— ~~C~~ as he does so he sings "little bo peep
two she had some sheep —
He goes out & returns with ∧ heads ~~one after another seven~~ 16
~~heads.~~
I not bother about their names — indeed I forget
Attendant. ~~The only head I shall name is the first head~~
~~Cuchulains.~~ You will find the names of all the heads
in Augusta Gregorys book, or in the Gaelic epic it self if
Gael came from Maive s lover
you can read old gael. This ∧ was a beautiful man ∧
~~the age of man most dear to woman~~
not very young but not old ~~they say he had many~~
That age when men are most dear to woman
He gave Cuchulain his ~~second wound~~ first wound
~~woman s secrets in his eyes.~~ Sing ~~a song of sixpense~~
~~four~~
~~(He goes out — we hear his vice voice he returns with two heads.~~
~~on my right side I have Mave's~~ Maves
~~This was~~ Maves lover — our army says that her lovers
beyond liers
were ~~beyond~~ counting but soldiers are ~~lyers~~ when they talk about
~~man s~~ head they say belong to a nother lover of hers
women. The ~~at any rate was her chief lover for this expedition~~
he gave Cucullain his second wound. These ~~heads~~ were the
~~& this was a son of hers,~~ a ~~fine young man but he~~ gave
heads of two two sons of Mave. They
~~Cuculain his first wound~~ ~~he gave~~ ~~They~~ gave Cucullain his
third & fourth wounds. At least I think so —(He drops the
four heads) Lazy man load — lazy man s load Now I will
get this all ~~wron~~ wrong ~~for the~~ which were the [?wound] and the
[?sons/?suitors] — & ~~Emer said I was to treat them with~~
respect — ~~she said that though it is little~~ respect
she will show them she begins to dance — O I know
her — this is not a quiet dance that I have seen

Prose draft adapted for use in the verse draft. There are several revisions in the darker blue ink, including all the revisions except "two" in l. 1; the cancellation line and the revisions in l. 3; the cancellation line through "they say he had many" and the words "the age of man most dear to woman" (but not the cancellation line) in l. 7; the cancellation line through "woman s secrets in his eyes" and the words "He gave Cuchulain his second wound" (but not the cancellation line) in l. 8; the cancellation line through "two," the word "four," and possibly the period, in l. 9; the cancellation line through "This was" and the words "on my right side I have Mave's" (but not the cancellation line) in l. 10; the cancellation lines through "beyond" and "lyers" and the words "beyond" and "liers" in l. 11; the cancellation line through "fine young man but he" in l. 13. Starting with "he gave" in l. 14, the remainder of the page, except the cancellation line through "They" in l. 14 and the lines cancelling the entire passage, is in the darker blue.

3 "shall" probably omitted after the first "I" in the revisions.
19 The first "respect" was possibly cancelled.
20 "when" probably omitted after "them."

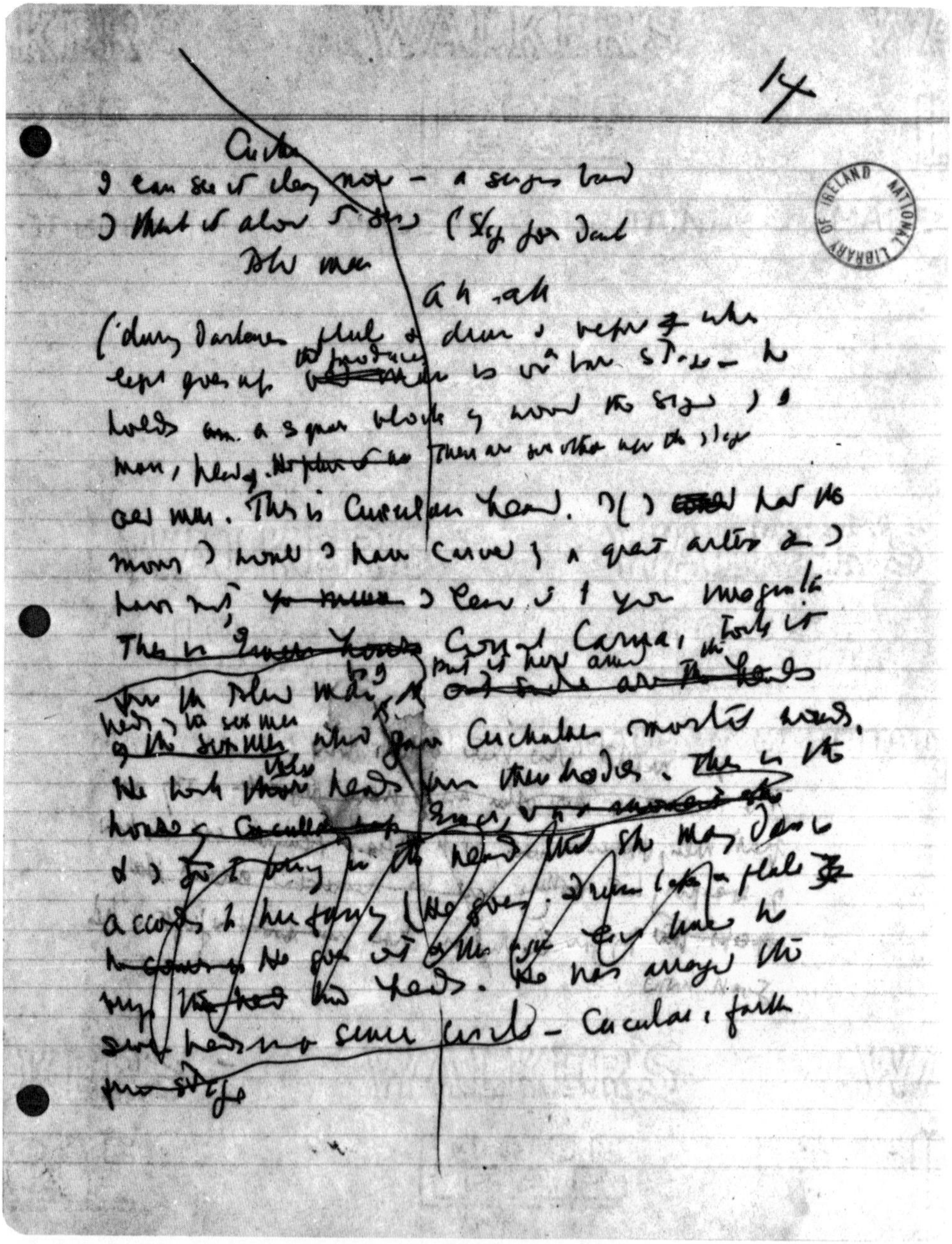
NATIONAL LIBRARY OF IRELAND

14

Cuchu
I can see it clearly now — a singing bird
I think it about to sing (Stage goes dark
Blind Man
Ah, ah
(during darkness flute & drum as before~~)~~ when
the producer a
light goes up ~~Old Man~~ is on bare stage — he
holds ~~an~~ a square block of wood the size of a
man s head.) ~~He places it on~~ There are six others upon the stage
Old Man. This is Cuchulains head. If I ~~could~~ had the
money I would [?I] have carved by a great artist as I
have not, ~~you must~~ I leave it to your imagination
~~This is Emers house~~ Conal Carnac took it
bag put it here amid the
from the Blind Man^^. ~~Out side are the heads~~
heads of the six men
~~of the six men~~ who gave Cuchulain mortal wounds.
their
He took ~~those~~ heads from their bodies. This is the
house of Cucullains wife Emer, in a moment she
& I go to bring in the heads that she may dance
according to her fancy (He goes. Drum taps & flute~~)~~
~~he comes in~~ He goes out & then again each time he
brings ~~two heads~~ two heads. He has arranged the
seven heads in a semi circle — Cuculain s farthest
from stage

A revision of P15r.
2 "is" probably omitted after "it."
4 "had it" probably omitted after "have."

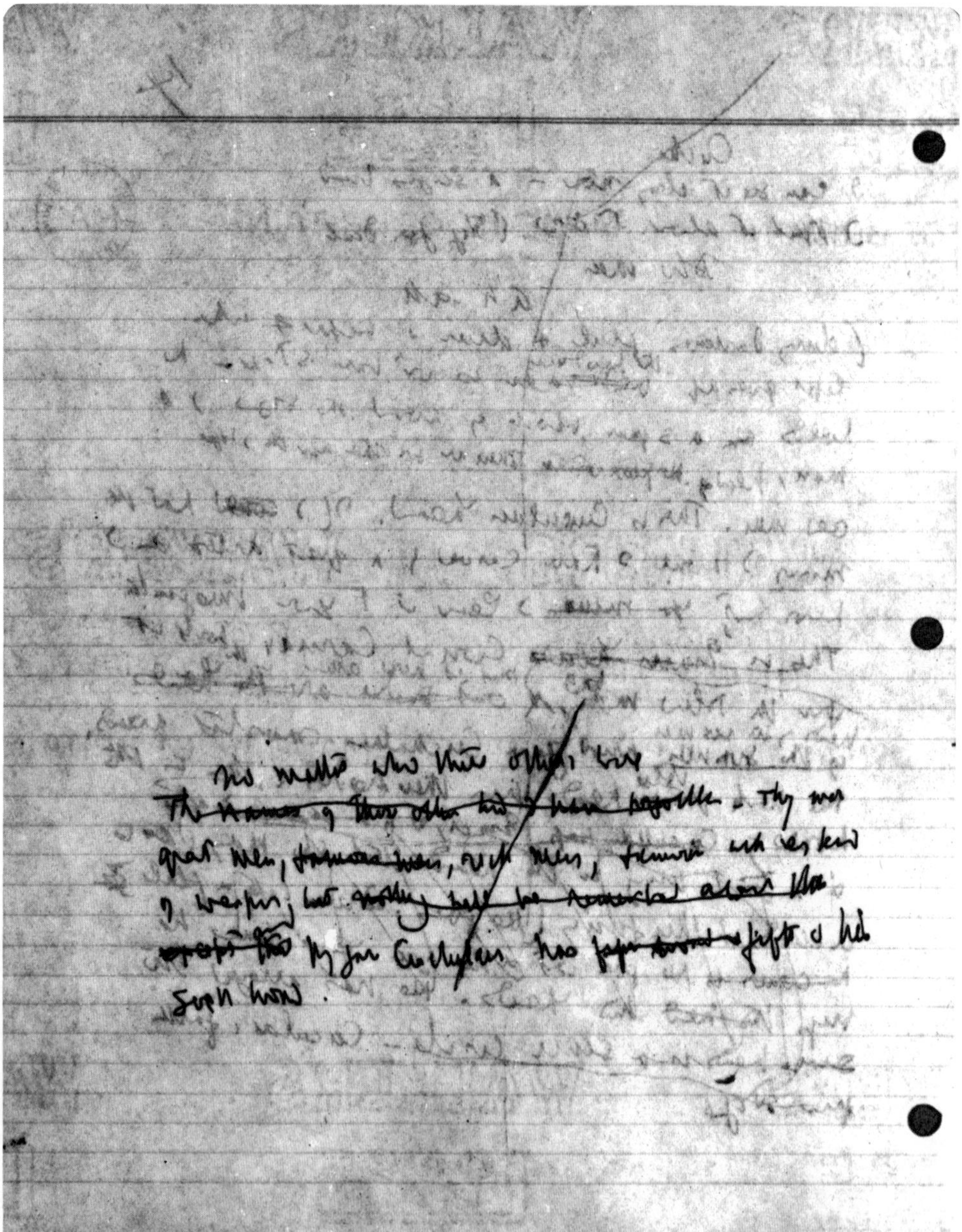

no matter who these others were
~~The names of these other two I have forgotten~~. They were
great men, ~~famous men,~~ rich men, famous with every kind
of weapon, but ~~nothing will be remembered about them~~
and
~~except that~~ they gave Cuchulain his ~~fifth wound &~~ fifth & his
sixth wound.

A revision of PV16r, ll. 16ff.

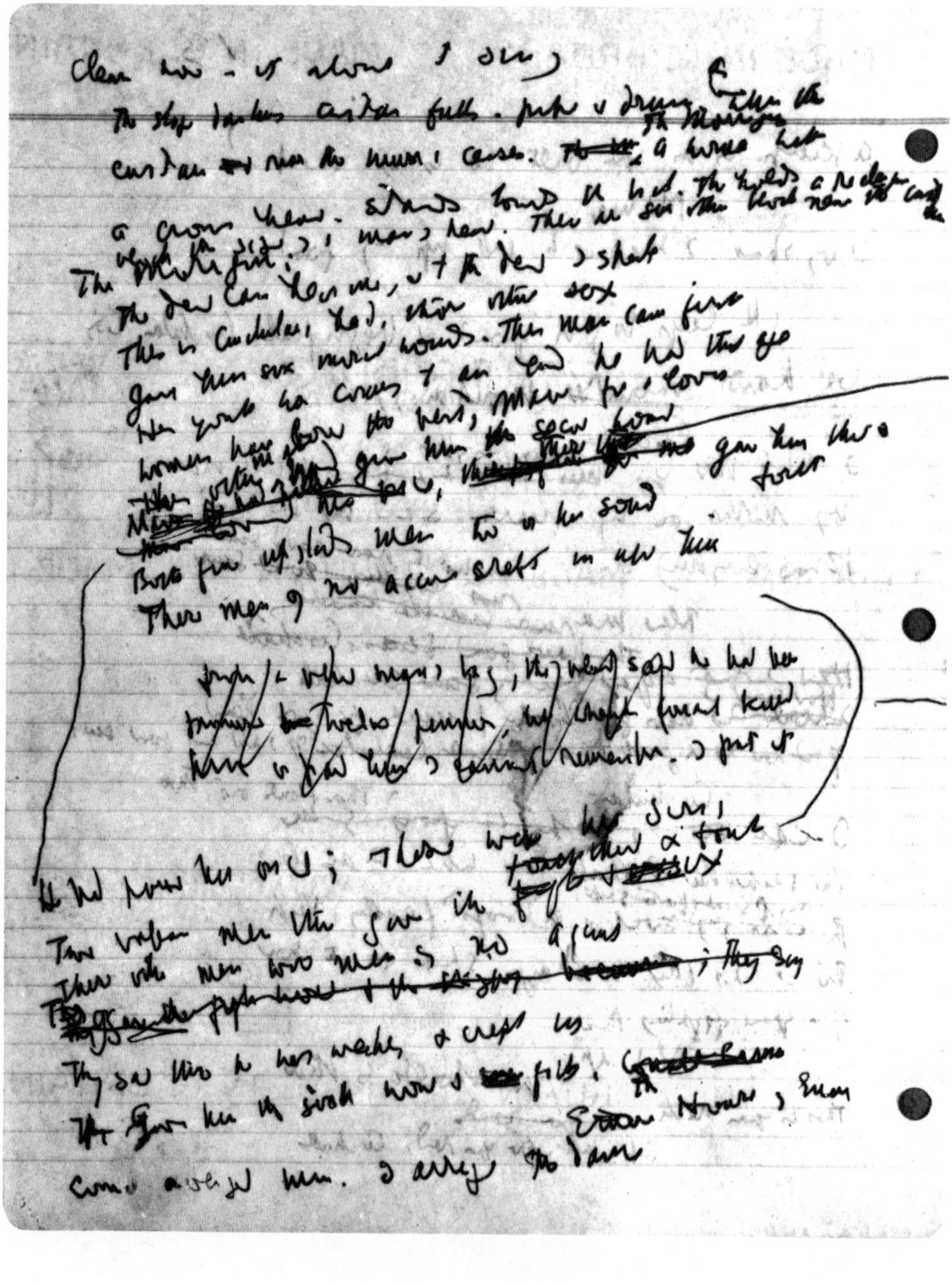

1 Clear now — it about to sing

The stage darkens curtain falls. Pipe & drum. When the
Th Morrigue
curtain [~~?~~] rises the music ceases. ~~The M~~ a woman with
<
a crows head stands towards the back. She holds a rectangular
block the size of a man s head. There are six other blocks near the curtain

The Morigue:

2 The dead can hear me, & to the dead I speak
3 This is Cuchulain s head, those other six
4 Gave him six mortal wounds. This man came first
5 His youth was coming to an end he had that age
6 Women have loved the best, Mave for a lover
man
7 This other ^ had given him the second wound
~~Mave He had possessed~~ these [?~~two~~]
8 ~~Mave loved his voice, these~~ [?~~two~~] ~~fine young men~~ gave him third & fourth
9 Both fine upstanding men two of her sons
10 These men of no account crept in upon him

11 from a blind man s bag, the blind said he had been
12 promised ~~tw~~ twelve pennies, but whether Conal killed
13 him or paid him I cannot remember. I put it

14 He had possessed her once; these were her sons
~~forth~~ third & forth
15 Two valient men that gave the ~~fifth & cix six~~
16 These other men were men of no account
~~They~~
17 ~~They gave the fifth wound & the~~ [?~~the~~]~~sixth because; They say~~
18 They saw that he was weakening & crept in
19 ~~They~~ Gave him the sixth wound & ~~six~~ fifth. ~~Conall Carna~~
The
~~Emers~~ House of Emer
20 Conal avenged him. I arrange the dance

Lines 11–13 and "The / ~~Emers~~ House of Emer" between lines 19 and 20 are revisions of specific passages on V14^r, and predate the remainder of the page, which was written after V14^r had been cancelled in its entirety.

In the stage directions, there may be a comma after the first "head."

1 "is" probably omitted after "it."

11 "man" probably omitted after the second "blind."

19 The "G" may have been cancelled or written over a lowercase "g."

Manuscripts of the Lyric

In Yeats's original conception of the play there were to have been two lyrics (corresponding to lines 196–211 and 212–227 of the final version), one before the action and one at the very end. Two drafts (L1^{v}, L2^{v}) of the "first" lyric appear on versos of leaves used in the composition of "The Man and the Echo" and "John Kinsella's Lament. . . ," respectively. They are both in the darker blue ink. A cancelled version of the first eight lines appears as part of the earliest extant draft of the prologue (PV1^{v}). An unnumbered leaf of manuscript (L3^{r}) contains a version of the remaining lines of the "first" lyric. Here and in the first eight lines Yeats again used the darker blue ink. A revised version of the entire first lyric is found on page V2A^{r}, in the lighter blue ink used for the original composition of the verse draft. This version is quite close to the version of these lines found in the earliest extant typescript.

One early draft of the second part of the lyric appears on the verso of L3. The use of ink of the same color used on L3^{r} may indicate contemporaneity. Another unnumbered leaf (L4^{r}) contains a draft of lines 222–227; it is also in the darker blue ink. It may have been a continuation of L3^{v}, or part of a separate draft the rest of which has apparently not survived.

In black ink, on the verso of page 16, Yeats wrote and then cancelled a prose passage that was possibly connected with now-missing stage directions for Emer's dance but which deals with a question that Yeats developed in the lyric.

The next draft of the second part of the lyric, in black ink, is on the recto of a leaf that Yeats numbered "20." At some point in the process of composition this leaf must have come in Yeats's loose-leaf binder immediately after page 16, for on the verso of that page, above the prose passage, he worked on some troublesome lines in the first stanza of the "second" lyric. Finally he wrote out a clean version of the first stanza below the second stanza. This version of the second lyric was then virtually identical with that in the earliest extant typescript. (See page 163 for evidence that the separation into two lyrics persisted through at least one typescript stage.)

The materials are transcribed in the following order:

a. L1^{v} (196–211)
b. L2^{v} (196–211)
c. PV1^{v} (196–203)
d. L3^{r} (204–211)
e. V2A^{r} (196–211)
f. L3^{v} (212–227)
g. L4^{r} (222–227)
h. PV16^{v} (212–227)
i. V20^{r} (212–227)

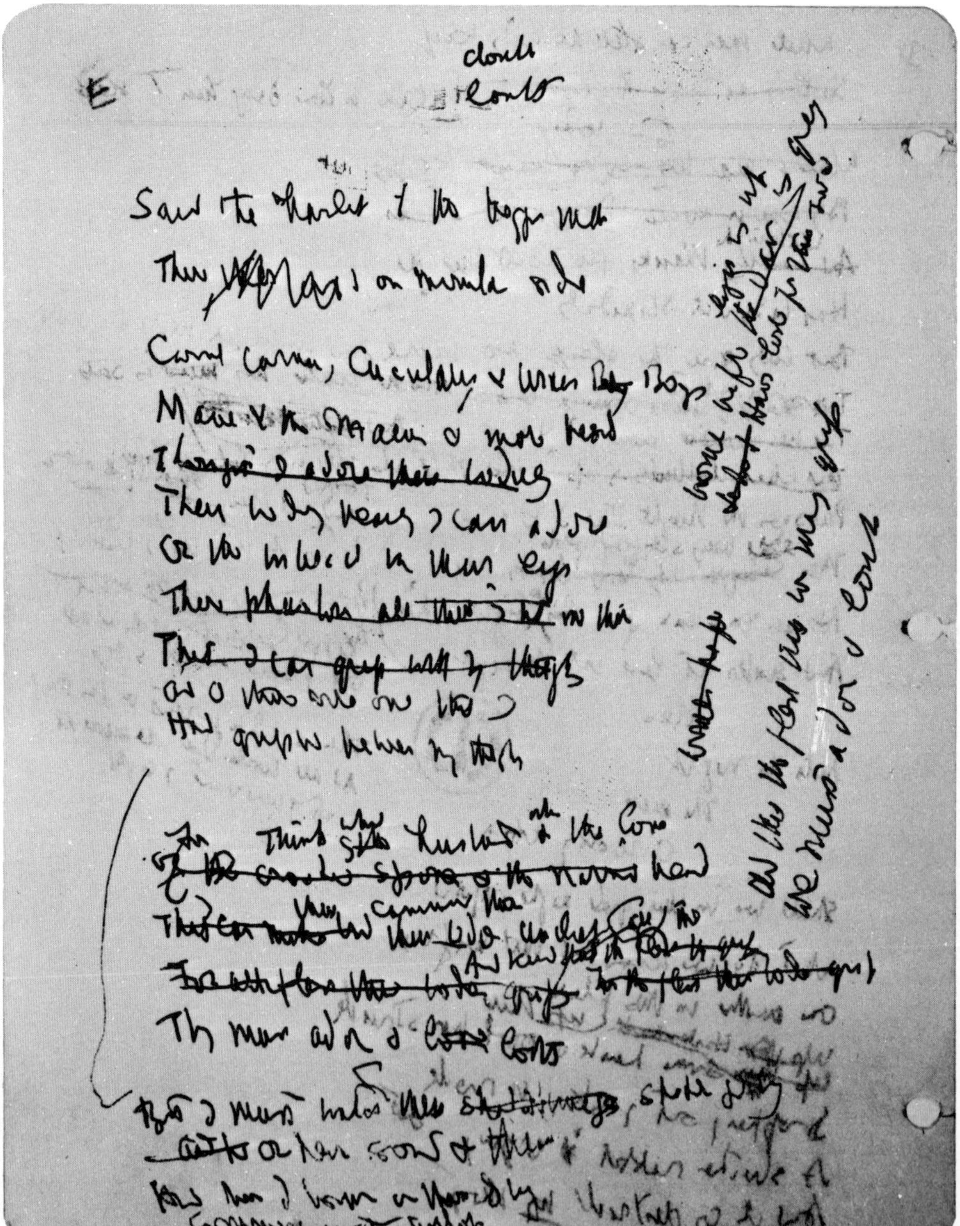

cloath
loath

Said the harlot to the beggar man
There ~~ther~~ up [?t] on mountain side
Conal Carna, Cuculain, & Usnas ~~Boy~~ Boys
Mave & the Maeve & more beside
~~Though I adore their bodily~~
Their body beauty I can adore
Or the intellect in their eyes
~~There phantoms all there's not~~ one there
~~That I can grip with my thighs~~
And O there were one that I
Had gripped between my thighs

[?what] [?wh]
For Think of ~~the~~ husband & the lover
~~Of the crooked~~ [?~~spine~~] ~~& the narrow~~ [?head]
[?I] [?these] command that
~~That can make two~~ their bodies uncloath
~~all~~ the
And [?knew] ~~that the flesh they grip~~
~~For all flesh their bodies grip~~ ~~For the flesh their bodies grip~~
They must adore & ~~love~~ loath

But I must watch their ~~shades~~ ~~images~~ shapes go by
~~And he~~ Or hear sound & then
How those [?] boys or these [?] boys
Command me to uncloth

---

light is up
[?women] before ~~the dawn is~~ grey
[~~? ?~~] Have listened for their sound

~~women ha~~ [~~?~~]

And that the flesh that we may grip
We must adore & loath

The recto of this leaf contains a partial draft of "The Man and the Echo," not reproduced in this edition. The passages below the rule are from the right margin.

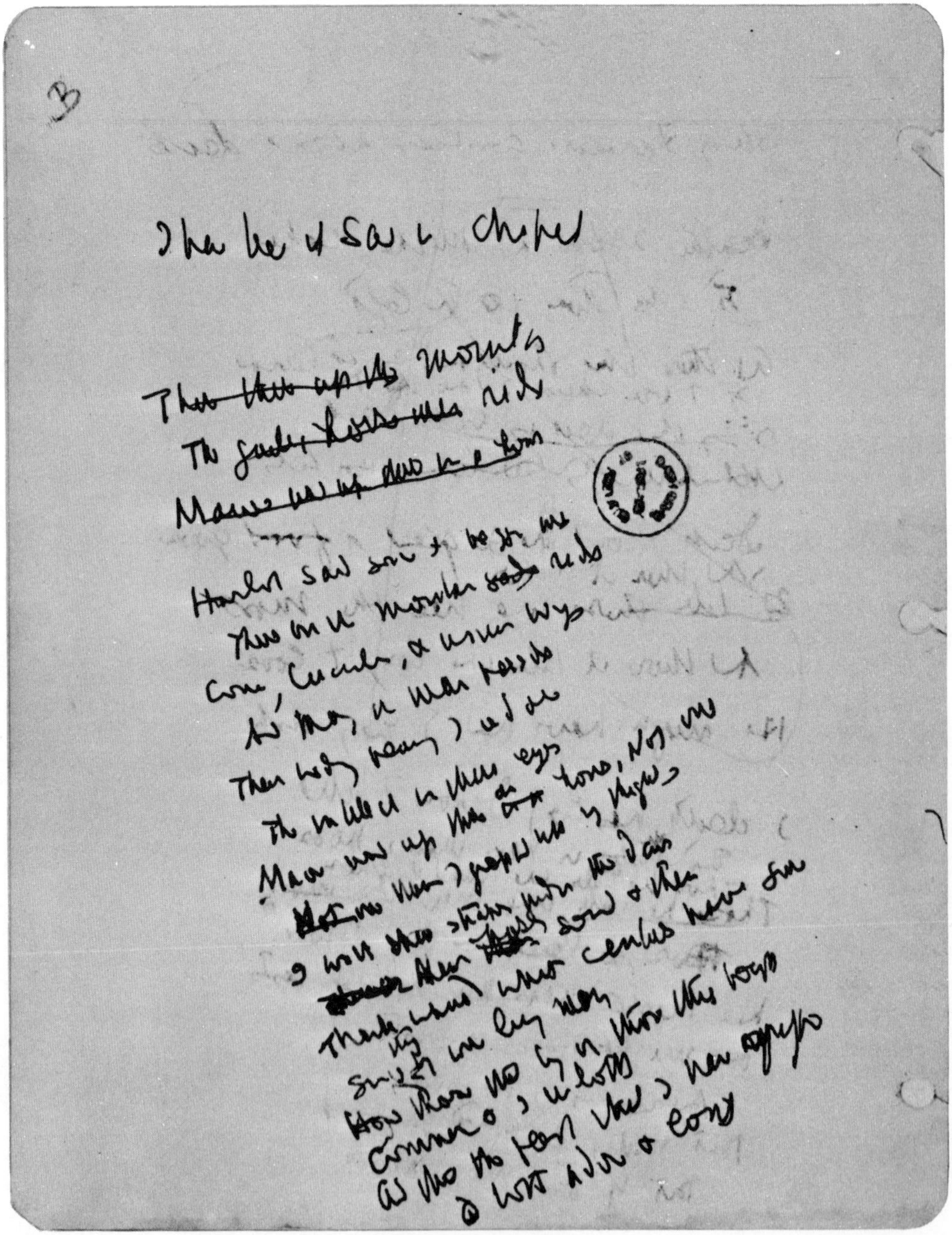

I have heard it said in chapel

~~There there up the~~ mountain
The ~~Gaelic horse men~~ ride
~~Maeve used up two in a hour~~

Harlot said sang to beggar man
There on the mountain [?~~gods~~/?~~side~~] ride
Conal, Cuculain, & Usnas boys
And many a man beside
Their body beauty I adore
The intellect in their eyes
an
Mave used up three ~~in an~~ hour, Not one
~~Not~~ one have I gripped with my thighs,
I watch their shapes under the dawn
{H horses
~~Their~~ {hear ~~their~~ sound & then
Think about what centuries have gone
they
Since ~~boy~~ were living men
How those two boys or those three boys
Command & I uncloth
And that the flesh that I have gripped
I both adore & loath

The recto of this leaf contains a partial draft of "John Kinsella's Lament for Mrs. Mary Moore," not reproduced in this edition. The line "I have heard it said in chapel" is also from the draft of that poem.

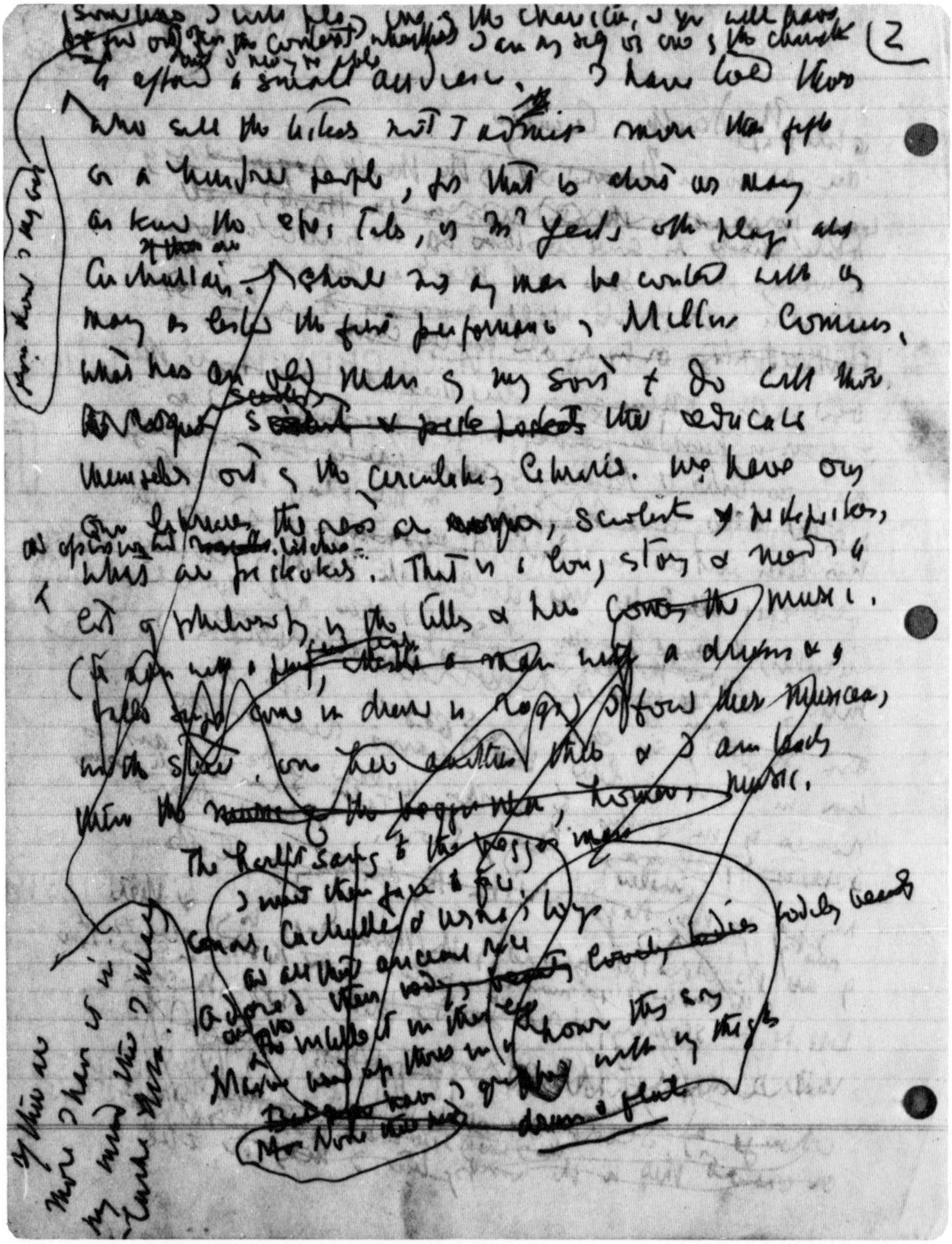

1 The harlot sang to the beggar man
2 I meet them face to face
3 Conal, Cuchullain & Usna's boys
4 And all that ancient race
5 Adored their ~~body's beauty~~ ~~lovely bodies~~ bodily beauty
And the
6 ∧ ~~The~~ intellect in their eye
7 Maeve used up three in an hour they say
8 ~~But none have~~ I gripped with my thighs
[?~~Mo~~] None there have
drum & flute

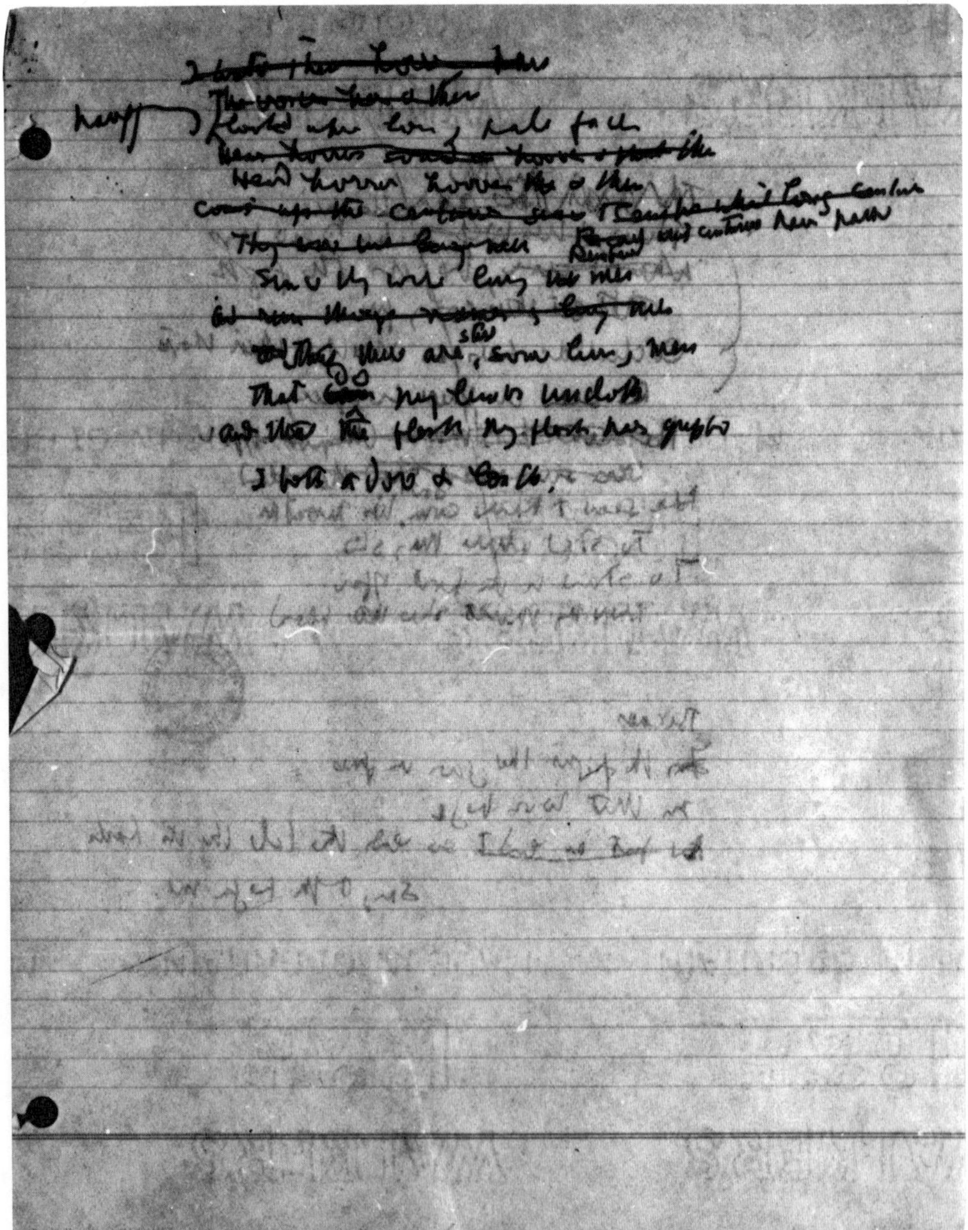

1 ~~I watch their horses pass~~
2 ~~The voices hear & then~~
3 have ⊢ I ∧ looked upon long pale faces
4 ~~Hear horses sound & hooves & that then~~
Heard horses hooves ~~the~~ & then
5 Count ~~up the centuries since Remember what long centuries~~
~~Recall~~ what centuries have passed
Remembered
6 ~~They were but living men~~
7 Since they were living ~~m~~ men
8 ~~And run through names of living men~~
{T still
9 ~~And~~ {that there are ∧ some living men
do
10 That ~~can~~ my limbs uncloth
11 And that the flesh my flesh has gripped
12 I both adore & loath.

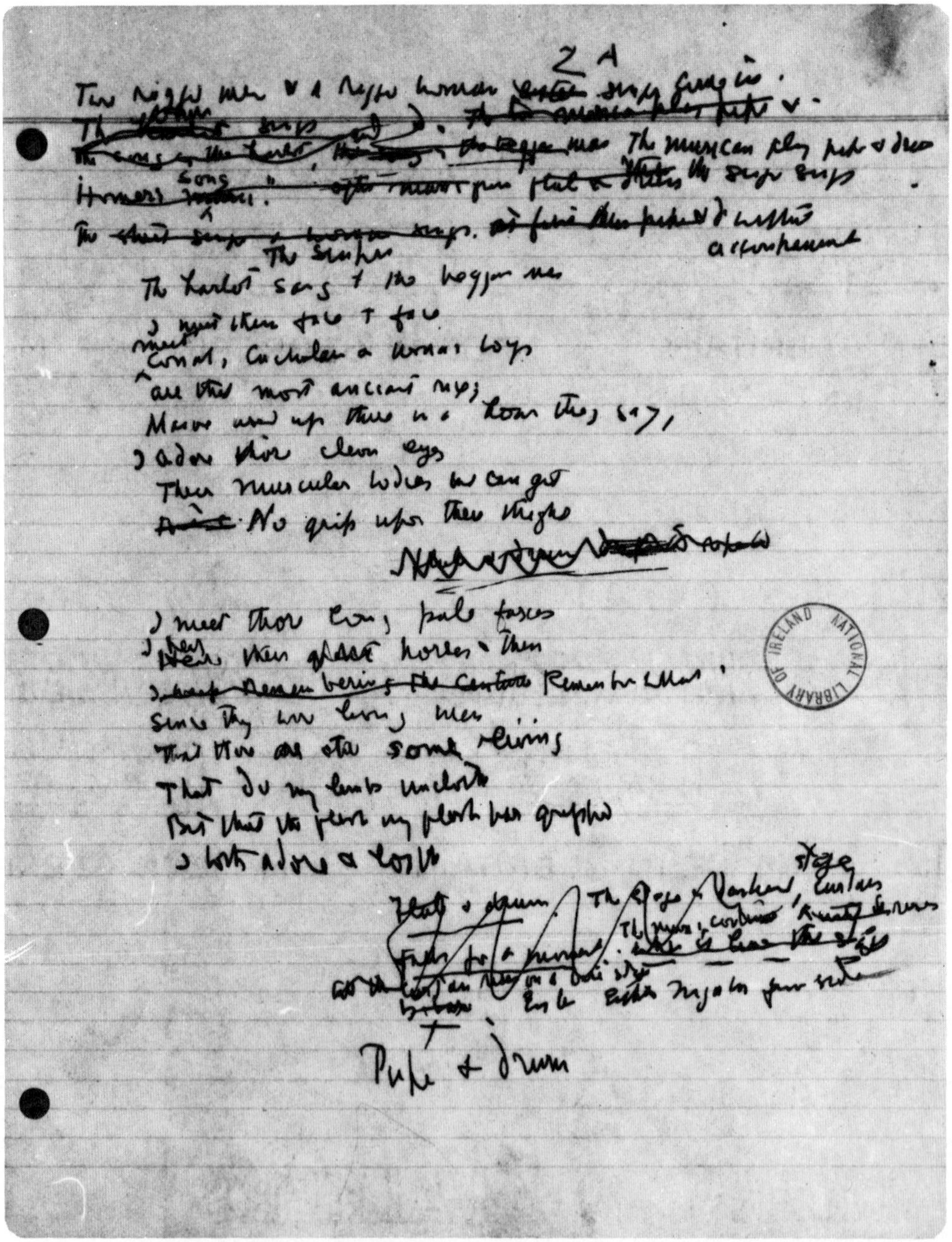
2 A

The harlot sang to the beggar man

I meet them face to face
Conal, Cuchulain & Usna's boys
All that most ancient race;
Maeve ... up there in a ... they say,
I adore those clean eyes
Their muscular bodies we can get
No grip upon their thighs

I meet those long pale faces
I hear their great horses & then
... Remember what
Since they were living men
That there are other some living
That do my limbs unclothe
But that the first my flesh has gripped
I both adore & loathe

Pipe & drum

The singer
The harlot sang to the beggar man
I meet them face to face
Meet
^ Conal, Cuchulain & Usna s boys
All that most ancient race;
Maeve used up three in a hour they say,
I Adore those clever eyes
Their muscular bodies but can get
~~But c~~ No grip upon their thighs

~~flute & drum defeated repeated~~

I meet those long pale fasces
I hear
Hear their ~~great~~ horses & then
~~I weep remembering the centuries~~ Remember what
Since they were living men
That there are still some living
That do my limbs uncloth
But that the flesh my flesh has gripped
I both adore & loath

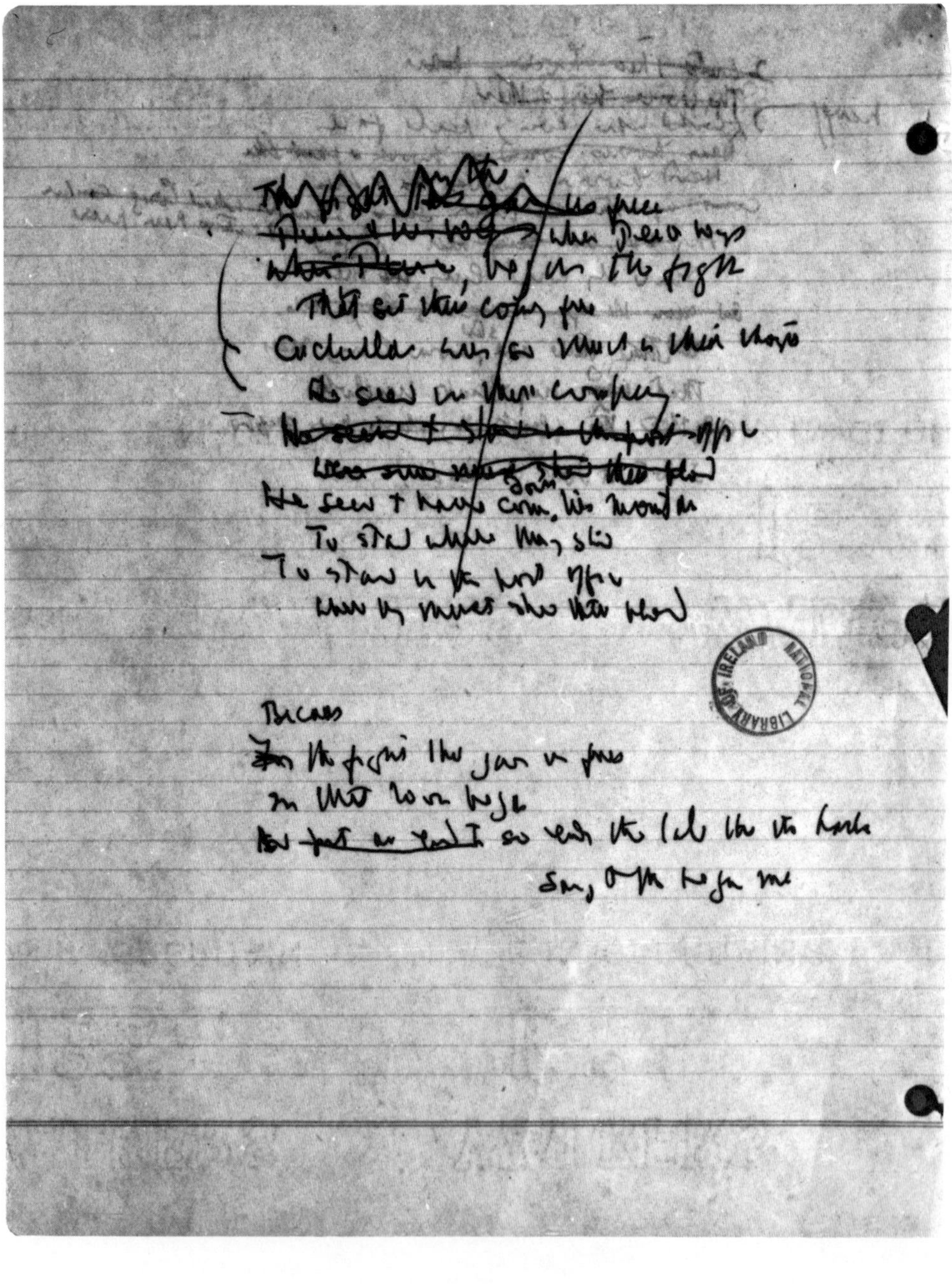

~~in the~~
~~The fight~~ ~~that gave us~~ freed
~~Pearse & his boys~~ When Perces boys
~~When Pearce~~ began the fight
That set their country free
Cuchullain was so much in their thought
He seemed in their company
~~He seemed to stand in the post~~ office
~~Were some must shed their blood~~
down
He seemed to have come ^ his mountain
To stand where they stood
To stand in the post office
Where they must shed their blood

Because
~~For~~ the fight that gave us freedom
In that hour began
And ~~put an end to~~ so ends the tale that the harlot
sang to the begar man

---

3 There may be a comma after "Pearce."

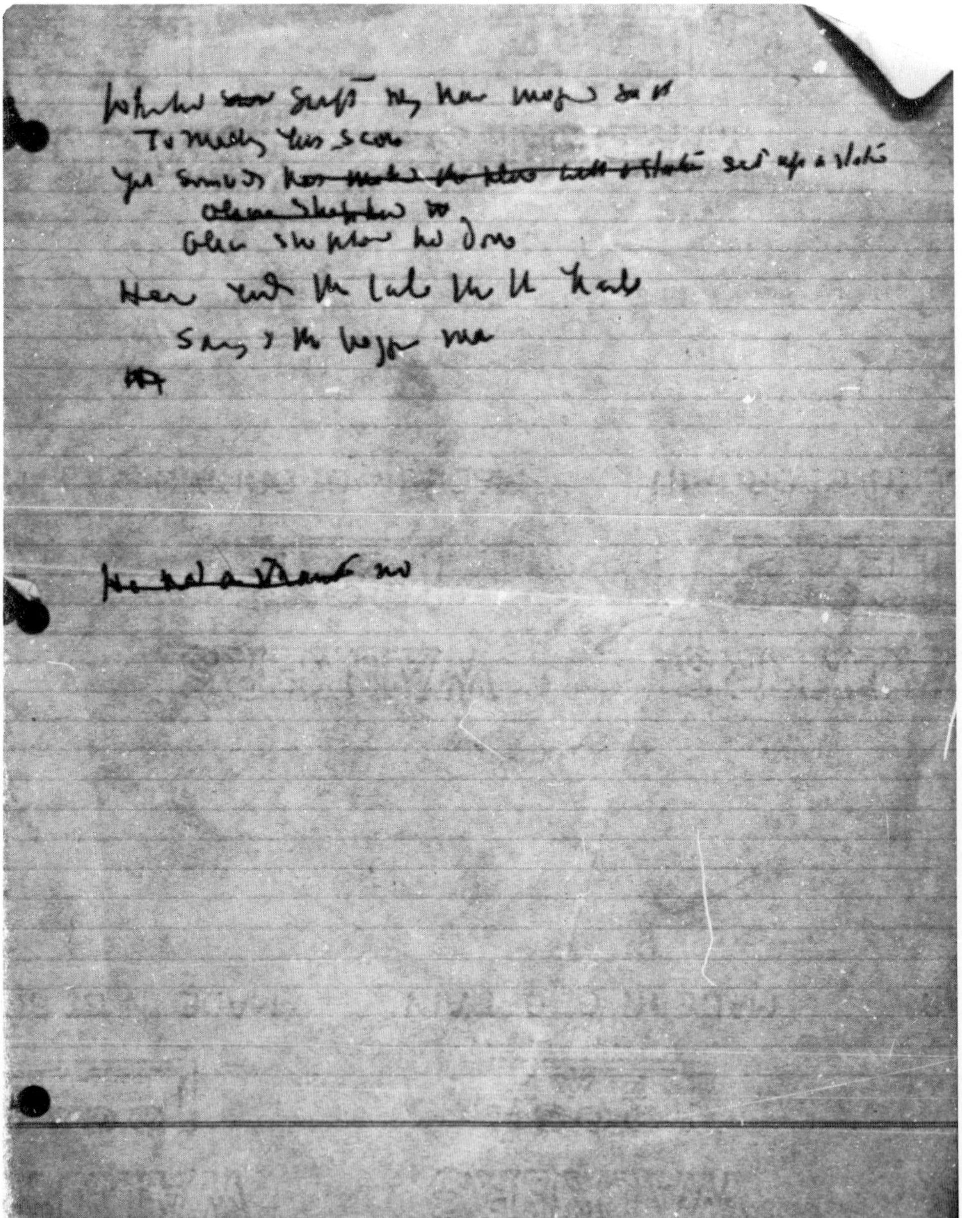

[?In?hatred] ~~sw~~ Swift may have imagined such
        To mollify his scorn
Yet somebody ~~has marked the place with a statue~~ set up a statue
        ~~Oliver Shepherd~~ ~~m~~
      Oliver Shepherd had done
Here ends the tale that the harlot
      Sang to the beggar man
~~He~~

~~He had a stran~~[?] no

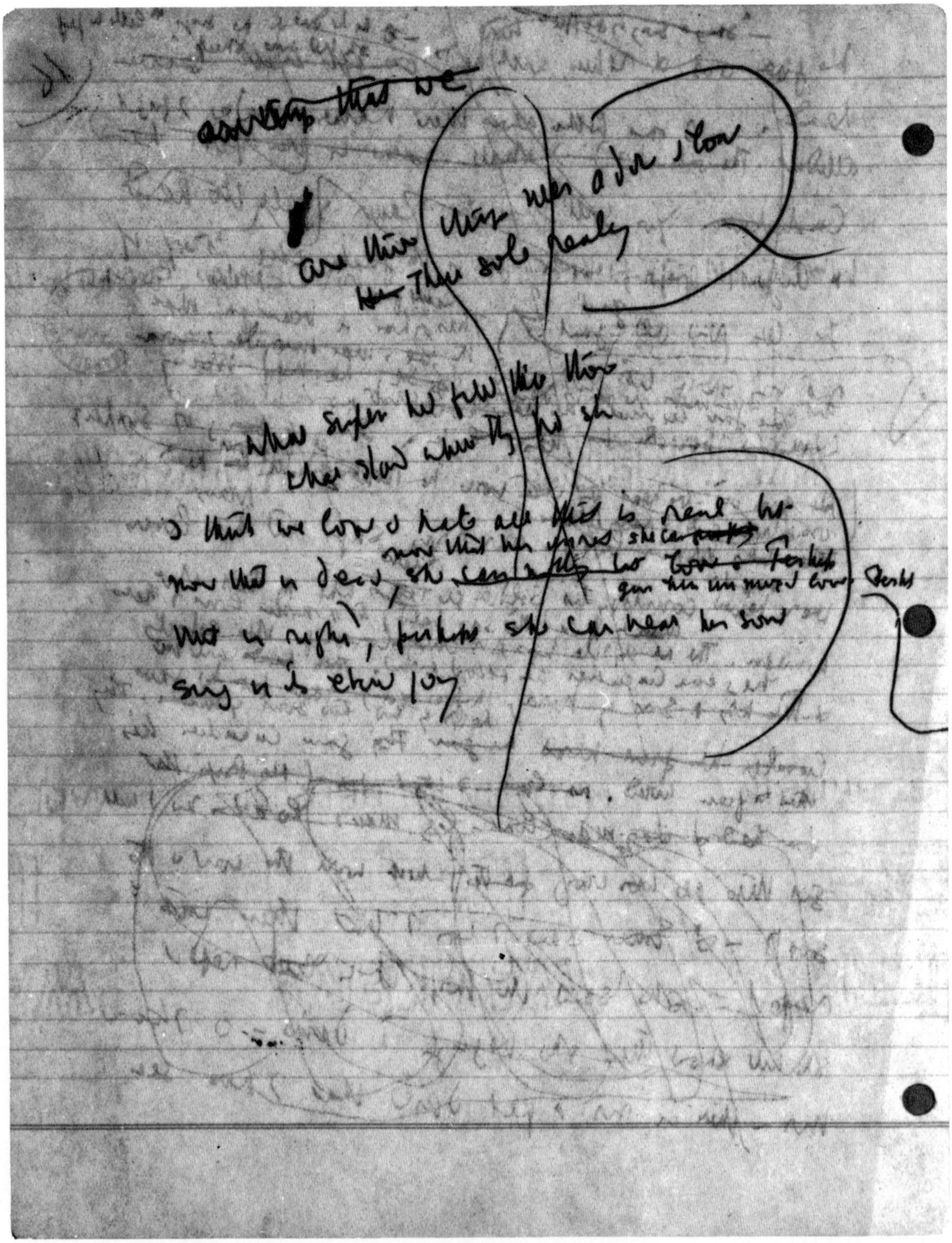

1 ~~Are things that we~~

2 Are those things men adore & loath
3 ~~His~~ Their sole reality

4 What singer had filled their thought
5 What stood where they had stood

6 I think we love & hate all that is real but
now that hes unreal she can ~~give him~~
7 now that is dead, she ~~can nothing but~~ ~~love. Perhaps~~
give him un mixed love. Perhaps
8 that is right, perhaps she can hear his soul
9 Sing in its eternal joy

Lines 1–5 are revisions of V20^{r}, and may have been added later than ll. 6–9. Those lines were perhaps related to the stage directions for Emer's dance which must have been present in the verse draft but have not survived (the line keying ll. 6–9 to a facing recto does not seem to connect to V20^{r}); but their subject matter allies them with the lyric.

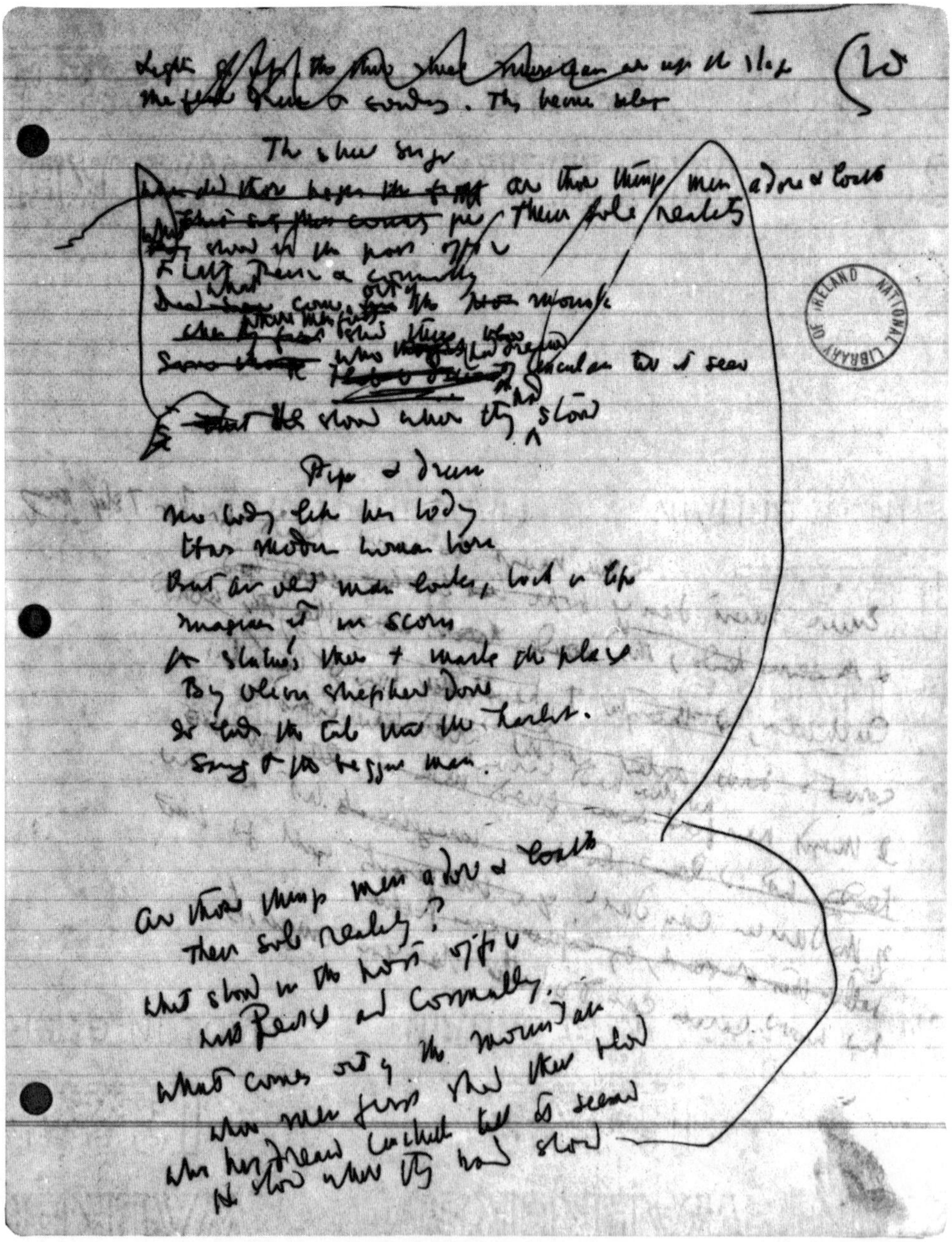
The Three Songs
Pipe & drum
No body like her body
That modern woman bore
But an old man looks,
Imagines it in scorn
A statue's there & marks the place
By Oliver Sheppard done
So tell the tale that the harlot
Sang to the beggar man.
Are those things men adore & loathe
Their sole reality?
What stood in the Post Office
With Pearse and Connolly?
What comes out of the mountain
Where men first shed their blood
Who thought Cuchulain till it seemed
He stood where they had stood

Lights go up. The three street musiceans are upon the stage 20
The flute drum & [?sounding]. They become silent

The street singer
~~When did those begin the fight~~ Are those things men adore & loath
~~That set their country~~ free Their sole reality
What
~~They~~ stood in the post office
^
With Pearce & Connolly
What out of
~~Did some~~ come ^ ~~from~~ the ~~mou~~ mountain
where men first
~~Whe they first~~ shed their blood
~~Some thought~~ Who ~~thought~~ had dreamed
~~Flute & drum~~ of Cuculain till it seemed
{H had
~~That~~ {he stood where they ^ stood

Pipe & drum
No body like his body
Has modern woman borne
But an old man looking back on life
Imagines it in scorn
A statue's there to mark the place
By Oliver Shepherd done
So ends the tale that the harlot
Sang to the beggar man.

Are those things men adore & loath
Their sole reality?
What stood in the post office
{P
With {pearce and Connolly.
What comes out of the mountain
Where men first shed their blood
Who has dreamed Cuchullain till it seemed
He stood where they had stood

The stage directions show that when Yeats wrote this page he still intended to have *two* lyrics. The directions were eventually cancelled, but the plan seems to have survived into the typescript stage.

The Death of Cuchulain

TYPESCRIPTS

The typescript versions of *The Death of Cuchulain* are on white wove paper measuring 25.4 cm × 20.4 cm and watermarked SWIFT BROOK / BOND. The typeface differs from that in typescripts of several of the *Last Poems* but is the same as that in the typescript of "The Black Tower."

The most important typescript, National Library of Ireland MS 8772#6, with Yeats's holograph corrections and revisions in blue-black ink, is transcribed below. Following the transcription is a collation of TS6 with the other extant nonposthumous typescript (NLI MS 8772#7) and the major published texts.

Typescript leaves are identified by "TS" followed by the National Library of Ireland folder number and a page number, for example, TS6, 2. Page numbers coincide with Yeats's own. He made no use of versos in the typescripts, so all references are to rectos.

TS6: Transcriptions and Photographic Reproductions

Yeats's major post-manuscript work on *The Death of Cuchulain* was done on a typescript now identified as NLI MS 8772#6. After he had revised this typescript, Mrs. Yeats wrote out on another copy of it (now NLI MS 8772#7) the changes he had made, presumably to increase their legibility. There are in fact variants between the two corrected typescripts, the significance of which is discussed in the introductory note to the collation of TS6 with TS7 and the printed texts (pp. 167–168).

When TSS 6 and 7 were being typed, the typist (Mrs. Yeats?) made an error in numbering the pages, skipping from 7 to 9. (Also, TS6 changes from ribbon to carbon at this point, TS7 the reverse.[1]) When Mrs. Yeats, in the process of preparing the corrected TS7, came to the end of page 7, she inserted a page 8 from what was apparently an earlier, now-lost typescript, and altered *it* in accordance with Yeats's revisions of page 9, which he had renumbered "8." (When she came to page 9 of TS7, which contained essentially the same material as page 8 of the lost typescript, she was forced simply to cancel nearly all of it.)

A second indication that there was an earlier typescript stage is provided by the insertion into TSS 6 and 7 of ribbon and carbon copies of a page (TS6, 17) containing the first half of the lyric. This page was originally numbered "3" and was renumbered "17" in TSS 6 and 7. The change would presumably reflect Yeats's decision to remove that portion of the lyric from the beginning of the play to the conclusion.

A comparison of page 8 with the corresponding portions of the manuscript and of TS6 gives some direct indication of the relationship of that intermediate stage to those preceding and following it.

The speech by Eithne with which page 8 begins:

> The Morrague's my friend.
> What matter! Cuchullain is about to die.

is neither in the manuscript nor in TS6, though in Yeats's revision of the latter he added some lines that correspond to it—"I might have peace that know / The Morrigue, the woman like

[1]There are a number of corrections in *pencil* in the typescript, all made on ribbon-copy pages, which means that they were put in before the mixing of ribbon and carbon versions. Yeats's revisions are partly on ribbon, partly on carbon, dividing between pages 7 and 9; thus it is possible that while revising he came to the point at which the ribbon copy skips from 7 to 9 and, in consulting the carbon to see if the "missing" page was there, inadvertently switched the parts of the two copies.

a crow, / Stands to my defence & cannot lie / But that Cuchulain is about to die." The most plausible explanation of its absence is that the typist not only skipped a page in numbering but also omitted a few lines of the text of the ur-typescript. (The stage directions for Aoife's entrance were also missing from TS6.) When Yeats noticed the error he wrote in the missing material. The surviving page 8 is a carbon, and in the original the lines in question may already have been changed to the version found in TS6; otherwise, Yeats made the revision when he noticed the omission and restored the passage. With this exception, the manuscript version and the two typescript stages are virtually identical, the differences of slight significance: for example, "You fought . . ." for "We fought . . . ," "To die . . ." for "That I may die . . . ," insertion of a second "Look again!"

Comparison between the verse draft as a whole and TSS 6 and 7 reveals that whatever intervening version or versions there may have been produced only minor alterations in the text. (This generalization cannot be applied to the prologue, as the extant manuscripts of it do not bring the text to as late a point of development as do those for the body of the verse draft.)

Yeats's revisions of TS6 *were* both extensive and significant. In one instance, he even resorted to a separate, unnumbered leaf (TS6, 6B) to work out a new draft of a particularly troublesome passage. He then wrote an expanded version of that passage (TS6, 6C) and incorporated it into the typescript. (The paper used for both holograph leaves is the same as that used for the other holograph manuscripts.)

THE DEATH OF CUCHULLAIN

~~(A bare stage of any period. A very old man looking like something out of mythology)~~

Old Man I have been asked to produce a play called "The Death of Cuchullain". It is the last of a series of plays which has for theme ~~the~~ his life and death. ~~of a legendary Irish figure.~~ I have been selected because I am out of fashion and out of date like the antiquated romantic stuff the thing is made of. I am so old that I have forgotten the name of my father and mother, unless indeed I am, as I affirm, the son of Talma, and he was so old that ~~men~~ his friends & acquaintances still read Virgil and Homer. When they told me that I could have my own way I wrote certain guiding principles on a bit of newspaper. I wanted an audience of fifty or a hundred, and if there are more I beg them not to shuffle their feet or talk when the actors are speaking. I am sure that as I am producing a play for people I like it is not ~~likely~~ probable in this vile age that they will be more in number ~~numerous~~ than those who listened to the first [illegible] performance of Milton's Comus. On the present occasion they must know the old epics and Mr Yeats' plays about them; such people however poor have libraries of their own. [illegible] If there are more than a hundred I wont be able to escape people who

THE DEATH OF CUCHULLAIN

(A bare stage of any period. A very old man looking like
something out of mythology)

Old Man **I have been asked to produce a play called "The**
Death of Cuchullain". It is the last of a series
his
of plays which has for theme ^ ~~the~~ life and death. ~~of~~
~~that~~
~~a~~ ^ ~~legendary Irish figure.~~ I have been selected
because I am out of fashion and out of date like
the antiquated romantic stuff the thing~~s~~ is made of.
I am so old that I have forgotten the name of my
father and mother, unless indeed I am, as I affirm,
his friends & acquaintances
the son of Talma, and he was so old that ~~men~~ still
^
read Virgil and Homer. When they told me that
I could have my own way I wrote certain guiding
principles on a bit of newspaper. I wanted an
audience of fifty or a hundred, and if there are
more I beg them not to shuffle their feet or talk
when the actors are speaking. I am sure that as
I am producing a play for people I like it is not
probable
~~likely~~ ^ in this vile age that they will be more in number
~~numerous~~ than those who listened to the first per-
on the present occasion they must
formance of Milton's "Comus"; ^ ~~they know the old~~
~~know the old~~
no matter what the because
epics and Mr. Yeats' plays and though they are poor
~~they must~~
men ^ have their own libraries. If there are more
than a hundred I wont be able to escape people who

---

performance of Milton s Comus
On the present occasion they
must know the old epics and
M[r] Yeats' plays about them.
Such people however poor
have libraries of their own

~~must~~
~~even though poor~~
~~men,~~

The passages below the rule are from the left margin (revisions of ll. 19–21).

3 The period after "death" was added in ink.

2

Old Man are educating themselves out ~~of the circulating libraries~~, sciolists all, pickpockets and opiniated bitches. Why pickpockets? I will explain that, I will make it all quite clear.

(drum and pipe behind the scene, then silence)

That's from the musicians; I asked them to do that if I was getting excited. If you were as old you would find it ~~is~~ easy to get excited. Before the night ends you will meet the music. There is a singer, a piper and a drummer. I have picked them up here and there about the streets, and I will teach them, if I ~~can~~ live, the music of the beggarman, Homer's music, ~~then~~ I promise a dance. I wanted a dance because where there are no words there is less to spoil. Emer must dance, there must be severed heads for her to dance ~~among~~ before. ~~I am old, I belong to mythology~~. I had thought to have had those heads carved, but no, if the dancer can dance properly no woodcarver can ~~do~~ look as well as a parallelogram of painted wood. But I was at my wit's end to find a good dancer; I could have got sucha dancer once, but she has gone; the tragi-comedian dancer, the tragic dancer, upon the same neck love and loathing, life and death. I spit three times. I spit upon the dancers painted by Degas. I spit

2

book societies, book clubs
Old Man **are educating themselves out ~~of the circulating~~**
and the like
~~libraries,~~ sciolists all, pickpockets and opiniated
bitches. Why pickpockets? I will explain
that, I will make it all quite clear.
(drum and pipe behind the scene, then silence)
That's from the musicians; I asked them to do
that if I was getting excited. If you were as
old you would find it ~~as~~ easy to get excited. Before
the night ends you will meet the music. There is
a singer, a piper and a drummer. I have picked
them up here and there about the streets, and I will
live,
teach them, if I ~~can~~ the music of the beggarman,
[?&] ~~I am old & belong to mythology and~~
Homer's music. ~~and~~ I promise a dance. I wanted a
^
dance because where there are no words there is less
to spoil. Emer must dance, there must be severed
before
heads for her to dance ~~among@.~~ ~~I am old, I~~
^
~~belong to mythology~~. I had thought to have had
those heads carved, but no, if the dancer can dance
look
properly no woodcarver can ~~do~~ as well as a parallel-
^
ogram of painted wood. But I was at my wit's end
to find a good dancer; I could have got sucha
dancer once, but she has gone; the tragi-comedian
dancer, the tragic dancer, upon the same neck|love
and loathing, life and death. I spit three times.
I spit upon the dancers painted by Degas. I spit

— I am old, I belong
to mythology — severed heads

The passage below the rule is from the left margin; it is marked for insertion in l. 15, after "heads."
7 In "before," "or" was typed, then written over in ink; "e" was added in ink.
11 The comma after "them" was added in ink.
12 The period after "music" was added in ink over a typed comma.

The night has could timeless
Remembers the great, but not

3

Old Man upon their short bodices, their stiff stays, their toes whereon they spin like peg-tops, above all upon that chambermaid face. The chambermaid, that old maid history. I spit! I spit! I spit!

(The stage is darkened, the curtain falls. The pipe and drum continue until the curtain rises on the stage lights up a minute or half a minute later. Ethne Inguba enters.)

Ethne Cuchullain! Cuchullain!

(Cuchullain enters from back)

Ethne I am Emer's messenger,
I am your wife's messenger, she has bid me say
You must not linger here in sloth for Maeve
With all those Connacht ruffians at her back
Burns barns and houses up at Emain Macha:
Your house at Muirthemne already burns.
No matter what's the odds, no matter though
Your death may come of it, ride out and fight.
The scene is set and you must out and fight.

Cuchullain You have told me nothing. I am already armed
I have sent a messenger to gather men,
And wait for his return. What have you there?

3

1 **Old Man** **upon their short bodices, their stiff stays, their**
2 **toes whereon they spin like peg-tops, above all**
the
3 **upon that chambermaid face. ~~That~~ chambermaid,** lc/
4 **that old maid history**! **I spit! I spit! I spit!**
(The stage is darkened, the curtain falls. ~~The~~ [?~~on a~~]
begin and ~~again~~
pipe anddrum continue until the curtain rises ~~and~~
~~A bare stage~~
~~the stage lights up a minute or~~ half a minute later,
Eithne Inguba enters.~~at one side~~.)
5 **Ethne** **Cuchullain! Cuchullain!** again on a
(Cuchullain enters from back) bare stage
I am Emer's messenger,
6 **I am your wife's messenger, she has bid me say**
7 **You must not linger here in sloth for Maeve**
8 **With all those Connacht ruffians at her back**
9 **Burns barns and houses up at Emain Macha:**
10 **Your house at Muirthemne already burns.**
11 **No matter what's the odds, no matter though**
12 **Your death may come of it, ride out and fight.**
13 **The scene is set and you must out and fight.**
14 **Cuchullain** **You have told me nothing. I am already armed**
15 **I have sent a messenger to gather men~~n~~,**
16 **And wait for his return. What have you there?**

They might have looked timeless
Rameses the Great, but not

The passage below the rule is from the top margin; it is marked for insertion in l. 3, after "face."

3 Yeats originally intended to change the "T" in "That" to a lowercase letter, then cancelled the entire word and substituted "the."

4 The exclamation point after "history" was added in ink over a typed period.

4

Eithne I have nothing

Cuchullain There is something in your hand.

Eithne No.

Cuchullain Have you not a letter in your hand?

Eithne I do not know how it got into my hand.
I am straight from Emer. We were in some place.
She spoke. She saw.

Cuchullain This letter is from Emer.
It tells a different story. I am not to move
Until tomorrow morning, for, if now,
I must face odds no man can face and live.
Tomorrow morning Cohal Caernach comes
With a great host.

Eithne I do not understand.
Who can have put that letter in my hand?

Cuchullain And there is something more to make it certain
stir
I shall not [illegible] till morning; you are sent
To be my bedfellow, but have no fear
All that is written but I much prefer
Your own unwritten words. I am for the fight
I and my handful are set upon the fight

4

1 **Eithne** I have nothing
Cuchullain There is something in your hand.
2 **EEithne** No.
~~No.~~
Cuchullain Have you not a letter in your hand?
3 **EEithne** I do not know how it got into my hand.
4 I am straight from Emer. We were in some place.
5 She spoke. She saw.
Cuchullain This letter is from Emer.
6 It tells a different story. I am not to move
7 Until tomorrow morning, for, if now,
8 I must face odds no man can face and live.
9 Tomorrow morning Conal Caernach comes
10 With a great host.
Eithne I do not understand.
11 Who can have put that letter in my hand?
12 **Cuchullain** And there is something more to make it certain
stir
13 I shall not @@@@ till morning; you are sent
14 To be my bedfellow, but have no fear
15 All that is written but I much prefer
16 Your own unwritten words. I am for the fight
17 I and my handful are set upon the fight

---

2 "No." was cancelled in pencil.
13 The cancelled word was "move."

5

Cuchullain	We have faced great odds before, a straw decided.
	(The Morrigu enters & stands between them)
Eithne	I know that somebody or something is there
	Yet nobody that I can see.
Cuchullain	There is nobody.
Eithne	Who among the gods, ~~among those that watch,~~ of the air & the upper air
	~~Has a crow's body?~~
	Has a bird's head
Cuchullain	Morrague ~~has a crow's body.~~ or head like a crow
Eithne (Dazed)	Morrague, war goddess, stands between.
	~~Her black wing touched me upon the shoulder, and now~~
	The Morrigu goes out
	~~All is clear again. [illegible] foul witch~~
	~~[illegible] has an eye in the middle of her forehead,~~
	~~That witch had put her words into my mouth.~~
	woman that has an eye in the middle of her forehead
Cuchullain	~~Fine stories!~~ A ~~woman with an eye in~~ her forehead
	A woman that has a head like a crow
	~~A woman with a body like a crow,~~
	But she that put those words into your mouth
	Had nothing monstrous; you put them there yourself.
	You need a younger man, a friendlier man,
	But fearing what my violence might do
	Thought out those words to send me to my death,
	And were in such excitement you forgot
	The letter in your hand. ~~O Eithne, Eithne~~

5

1 **Cuchullain We have faced great odds before, a straw decided.**
(The Morrague enters & stands between them)
2 **E ithne I know that somebody or something is there**
3 **Yet nobody that I can see.**
Cuchullain There is nobody.
of the air & the upper air
4 **E ithne Who among the gods~~, among those that watch~~,**
~~**Is headed like a crow**~~
5 ~~**Has a crow's body?**~~
Has a bird's head Has a birds head is headed like a crow
Cuchullain Morrague ~~has a crow's~~ body.
6 **E ithne** (Dazed) **Morrague, war goddess, stands between.**
7 **Her black wing touched me upon the shoulder, and now**
The Morrague goes out ~~put me to sleep into a t~~
8 **All's clear again. Queen Maeve ~~sent her foul witch~~**
She used to be as pretty as a bird put me into a trance
9 ~~**That has an eye in the middle of her forehead**~~**,**
10 **That witch had put her words into my mouth.**
woman that ~~for~~
~~witch has~~ ~~that~~ has an an eye in the middle of [?her]
^
11 **Cuchullain ~~Fine stories!~~ A ~~woman with an eye in~~ her forehead**
~~A The war goddess~~ A woman that is headed like a crow
12 ~~stet~~ ~~**A woman with a body like a crow**~~**,**
^
13 **But she that put those words into your mouth**
14 **Had nothing monstrous; you put them there yourself.**
15 **You need a younger man, a friendlier man,**
16 **But fearing what my violence might do**
17 **Thought out those words to send me to my death,**
18 **And were in such excitement you forgot**
19 **The letter in your hand. ~~O Eithne, Eithne~~**

~~Though when Cuchulain~~
~~slept with her as a boy~~
All is is intelligable. Mave put me into a trance
Though when Cuchulain slept
with her as a ~~yo~~ boy
~~But~~
She seemed as pretty as a bird
she has changed
She has an eye in the middle
of her for head
~~Or is it some~~[?~~thing~~] [?~~else~~]
[~~? ? ? ?~~]

The passage below the rule is from the left margin (revisions of ll. 8–10).

4 Yeats struck out the comma with his cancellation line.

5 The "has a bird's head" in the margin is in the hand of Mrs. Yeats and was apparently inserted to clarify the same phrase in Yeats's own hand.

6–13 See Notes on Textual Problems, p. 181.

12 Yeats cancelled the "stet" marks.

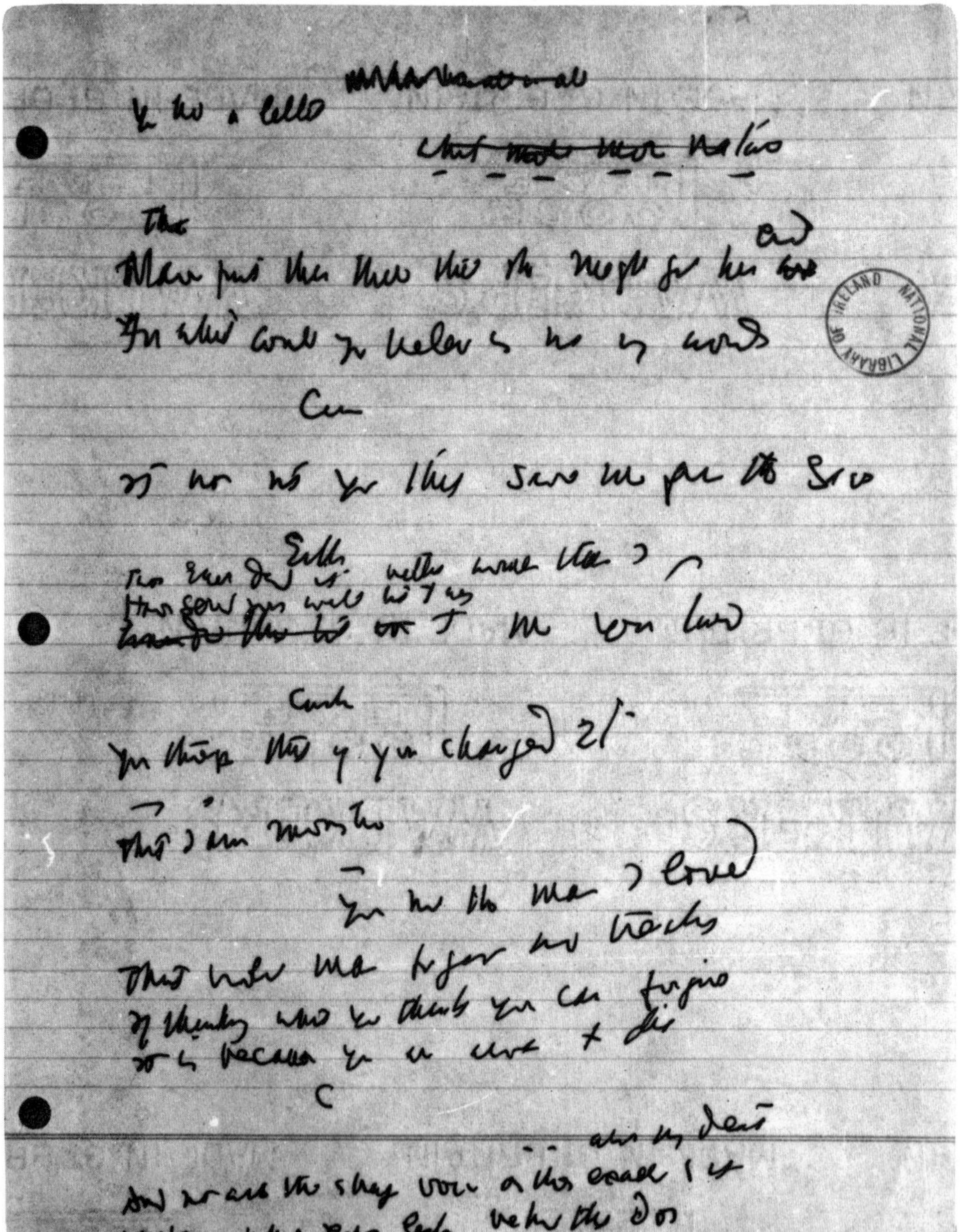
NATIONAL LIBRARY OF IRELAND

~~we have been all in all~~
You ha a letter
~~what more more natural~~
~~Tha~~
{M end
{Tave put them there that she might get her[?~~way~~]
For what could you beleve if not my words
Cu
It was not you that saved me from the sea
Eithne
Twas Emer did it better women than I
Have served you well but t was
~~Emer did that but~~ ~~was~~ to me you turned
Cuch
You thought that if you changed [?etc]
—— –
That I am monstrous
—
You not the man I loved
That violent man forgave no treachery
If thinking what you think you can forgive
it is because you are about to die
C
— — about my death
And not with that strange voice as though exalted by it
Who knows what ears listen behind the dor

This leaf is primarily a revision of TS6, 6A.

6 For a holograph revision of this line, see V2D[v].

8 The symbol at the end of the line was perhaps intended to indicate that the revision was to incorporate the two following lines as they appear in the typescript passage being corrected: "When everything subliminal must change / And if I have not changed that goes to prove" (TS6, 6A, ll. 2–3).

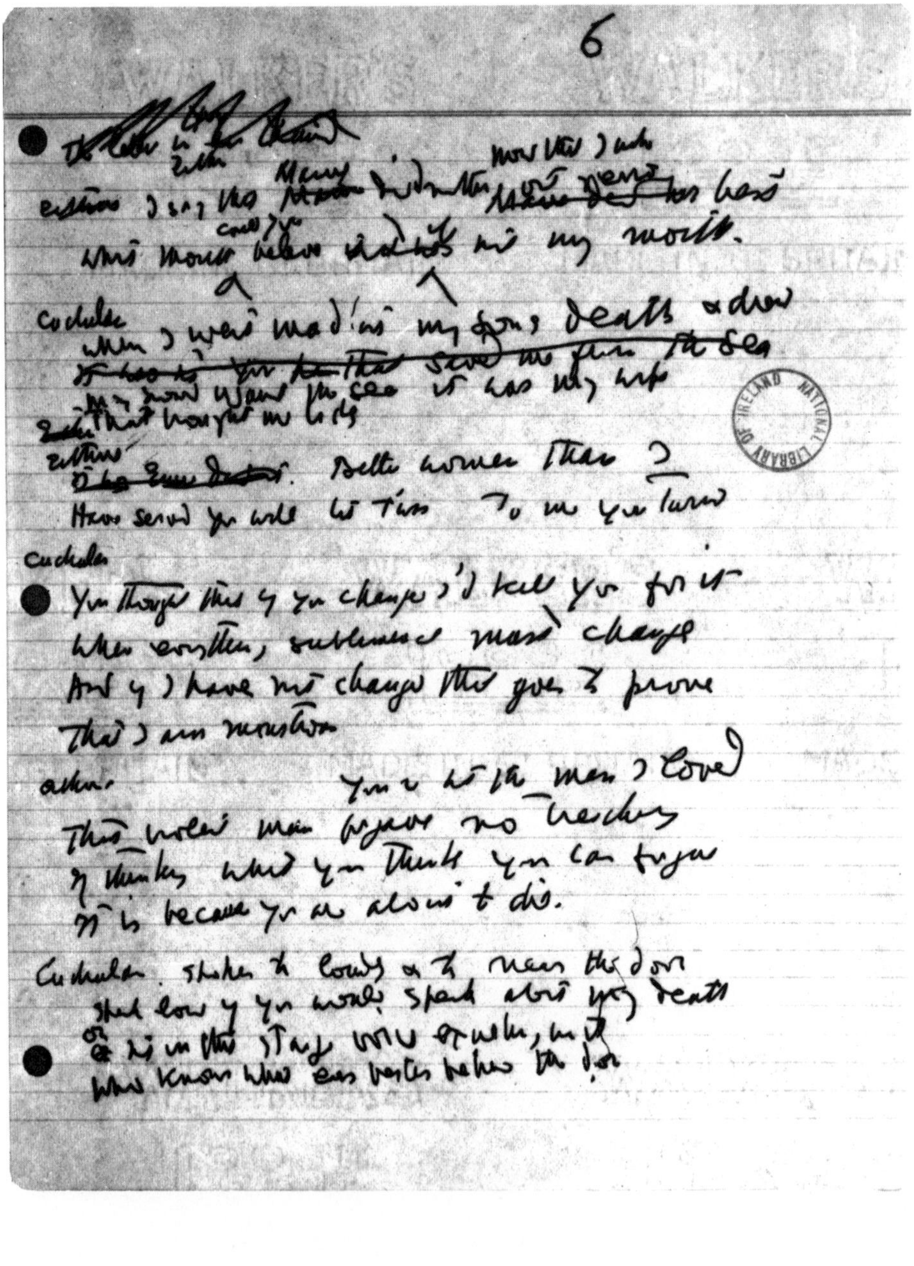
6

~~The Leeds in the Chamber~~ Enter Eithne

Eithne I say the Morrigan ~~Maeve~~ & not that I who must ~~Maeve~~ has bent
What mouth could you believe that it is not my mouth.

Cuchulain When I went mad at my sons death & drew
~~It was to you that~~ saved me from the sea
My sword against the sea it was my wife
Emer that brought me back

Eithne ~~I be Emer~~. Better women than I
Have served you well but 'twas to me you turned

Cuchulain
You thought that if you changed I'd kill you for it
When everything sublunary must change
And if I have not changed that goes to prove
That I am monstrous

Eithne You're not the man I loved
That violent man forgave no treachery
If thinking what you think you can forgive
It is because you are about to die.

Cuchulain Spoken too loudly & too near the door
Speak low if you would speak about my death
Or not in that strange voice exulting in it
Who knows what ears listen behind the door

6

your
[The letter in her hand
Eithne Now that I wake
Maeve
~~Eithne~~ I say that ~~Maeve~~ did nothing out of error
~~Mave did her~~ best
could you if
What mouth ^ beleve ~~if it was~~ not my mouth.
^
Cuchulain
When I went mad at my son s death & drew
~~It was not you ha that saved me from the sea~~
My sword against the sea it was my wife
That brought me back
~~Eithne~~
Eithne
~~It was Emer did it~~. Better women than I
Have served you well but t'was to me you turned
Cuchulain
You thought that if you changed I'd kill you for it
When everything subliminal must change
And if I have not changed that goes to prove
That I am monstrous
Eithne You re not the man I loved
That violent man forgave no treachery
If thinking what you think you can forgive
It is because you are about to die.
Cuchulain Spoken too loudly & too near the door
Speak low if you would speak about my death
Or
[?~~O~~] not in that strange voice exulting in it
Who knows what ears listen behind the dor

This leaf is an expanded and revised version of the revision on TS6, 6B.

6a

Cuchullain You thought that if you changed I'd kill you for it
When everything subliminal must change
And if I have not changed that goes to prove
That I am monstrous.

EEithne I am not indeed
You, not I, have changed.
You are not the violent man that I have loved;
That man forggve no treachery. If you forgive
It is because you are going to your death.

Cuchullain Spoken too loudly and too near the door.
Speak low if you would speak about my death,
Or seem to speak of it in sorrow, who knows
What ears are listening behind that door.

EEithne Some that would not forgive a traitor, some
That have the passion necessary to life,
Some not about to die. When you are gone
I shall denounce myself to all your cooks,
until they cut with knives, batter with ladles
Scullions, armourers, bed-makers and messengers,
And they will cut my heart out with their knives,
until they cut with knives, hammer with ladles
Or hammer me upon the head with ladles,
until they hammer me with a ladle, cut me with a knife
Impale me upon a spit, put me to death
By what foul way best please their fancy,
So that my shade can stand among the shades
And greet your shade and prove it is no traitor.

Cuchullain Women have spoken so plotting men's deaths

a
6

1 **Cuchullain You thought that if you changed I'd kill you for it**
2 **When everything subliminal must change**
3 **And if I have not changed that goes to prove**
4 **That I am monstrous.**
I am awake indeed
EEithne ~~**You, not I, have changed.**~~
5 **You are not the violent man that I have loved;**
6 **That man forgave no treachery. If you forgive**
7 **It is because you are going to your death.**
8 **Cuchullain Spoken too loudly and too near the door.**
9 **Speak low if you would speak about my death,**
10 ~~**Or seem to speak of it in sorrow; who knows**~~
11 **What ears are listening behind that door.**
12 **EEithne Some that would not forgive a traitor, some**
13 **That have the passion necessary to life,**
14 **Some not about to die. When you are gone**
15 **I shall denounce myself to all your cooks,**
~~until they cut with knives, hammer with ladles~~
16 Stet ~~**Scullions, armourers, bed-makers and messengers,**~~
17 ~~**And they will cut my heart out with their knives,**~~
~~cut~~
~~Until they cut with knives, hammer with ladles~~
18 ~~**Or hammer me upon the head with ladles,**~~
~~until they cut me with a knife or hamer hammer~~ with a ladle
19 **Impale me upon a spit, put me to death**
20 **By what foul way best please their fancy,**
21 **So that my shade can stand among the shades**
22 **And greet your shade and prove it is no traitor.**
23 Cuchulain Women have spoken so ~~& plotted~~ plotting man's death

---

until they hammer me
with a ladle, cut me with
a knife

After producing the holograph leaf numbered "6" (TS6, 6C), Yeats renumbered the typed page 6 as "6a." The passage below the rule is from the left margin (revisions of ll. 17–18).

20 The comma after "fancy" was added in ink.

7

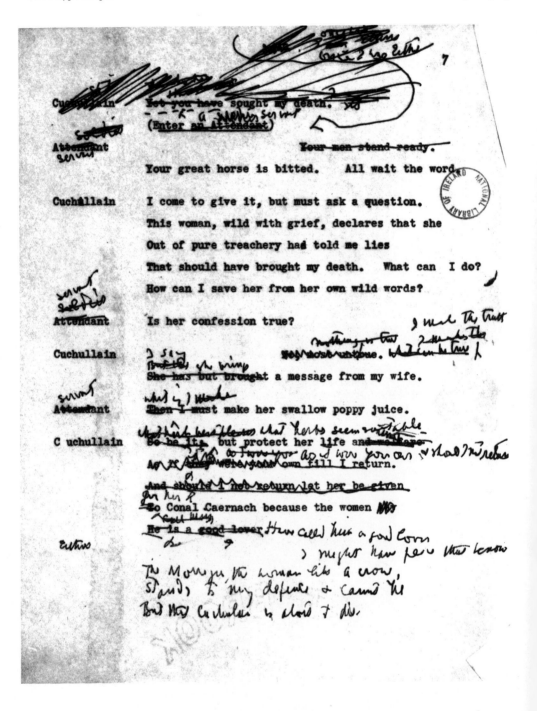

Cuchullain ~~Not you have~~ sought my death.

(~~Enter an Attendant~~) [a servant]

~~Attendant~~ [servant] ~~Your men stand ready.~~

Your great horse is bitted. All wait the word.

Cuchullain I come to give it, but must ask a question.

This woman, wild with grief, declares that she

Out of pure treachery had told me lies

That should have brought my death. What can I do?

How can I save her from her own wild words?

~~Attendant~~ [servant] Is her confession true?

Cuchullain [I say] ~~Not most untrue.~~ [nothing is true] [I make the truth]

~~She has but brought~~ a message from my wife.

~~Attendant~~ [servant] ~~Then I must~~ make her swallow poppy juice.

C uchullain ~~Be be it,~~ but protect her life ~~and welfare~~

As ~~if they were your own~~ till I return. [as if it were your own if should I not return]

~~And should I not return let her be given~~

~~To~~ Conal Caernach because the women

~~He is a good lover~~ [Have called him a good lover]

[Eithne] [I might have peace that know

The Morrigu, the woman like a crow,

Stands to my defence & cannot lie

But that Cuchulain is about to die.]

once was
Eithne I ~~am~~ Eithne
once I was Eithne
7

Then who has
stet Has she not
1 **Cuchullain** ~~**Yet you have**~~ **sought my death**? [?stet]
^ a ~~soldier~~ servant
(Enter ~~**an Attendant**~~**)**
~~Soldier~~
~~**Attendant**~~ ~~**Your men stand ready.**~~
Servant
2 **Your great horse is bitted. All wait the word.**
3 **Cuchullain I come to give it, but must ask a question.**
4 **This woman, wild with grief, declares that she**
5 **Out of pure treachery has told me lies**
6 **That should have brought my death. What can I do?**
7 **How can I save her from her own wild words?**
Servant
~~Soldier~~
8 ~~**Attendant**~~ **Is her confession true?**
I make the truth
~~nothing is true~~ ~~I make the~~
Cuchullain ~~**No, most untrue.**~~ ~~What can be true~~ ^
I say
~~But that~~ she brings
9 ~~**She has but brought**~~ **a message from my wife.**
Servant What if I make
10 ~~**Attendant**~~ ~~**Then**~~ ^ ~~**I must**~~ **make her swallow poppy juice.**
~~What herb best pleases~~ what herbs seem suitable
[?]
11 **Cuchullain** ~~**So be it;**~~ ^ **but protect her life** ~~**and welfare**~~
it [?] ~~as t were your~~ As it were your own & should I not return
12 ~~**As if they were your own till I return.**~~
^
13 ~~**And should I not return let her be given**~~
Give her [?~~to~~]
14 ~~**To**~~ **Conal Caernach because the women** ~~**say**~~
^ ~~call him~~
15 ~~**He is a good lover.**~~ Have called him a good lover
^
Eithne [?~~I~~] I might have peace that know
16 The Morrigue, the woman like a crow,
17 Stands to my defence & cannot lie
18 But that Cuchulain is about to die.

1 The question mark after "death" was added in ink over a typed period.

Aoife Am I recognised, Cuchullain?

Cuchullain You fought with sword,
~~You had great skill, I could not break~~ your guard
~~Till you grew weary and I caught your wrist~~
~~And took the sword out of your hand.~~

Aoife look again! ~~Look again!~~

Cuchullain Your hair is white.

Aoife ~~All that~~ was long ago
And now it is my time, I have come to kill you.

Cuchullain ~~I do not understand. Why am I here?~~

Aoife ~~You fought with many men when it was certain~~
~~That you were wounded to the death, asked leave~~
To drink of this pool. ~~there and then returned~~

Cuchullain ~~I want to put my belt about this stone~~
To die upon my feet, but am too weak.
Fasten this belt.
(she helps him to do so)
And now I know your name,
~~Aoife, the Scottish mother of my son,~~
I killed him at Baile's Strand, ~~and~~ that is why
~~The army of Maeve has let you through its ranks~~

Pipe & Drum. The stage is dark for a moment { 8
when it lights up again ~~the st~~ it is empty. Cuchulain { **9**
enters wounded. He tries to fasten himself to the stage with his belt. ~~Aiofe~~ Aoife enters

1 **Aoife** **Am I recognised, Cuchullain?**

a

Cuchullain **You fought with sword,**

It seemed that we should kill each other; then

2 ~~**You had great skill, I could not break your guard**~~

3 ~~**Ti*ll* you grew weary and I caught your wrist**~~

Your body wearied & I took your sword.

4 ~~**And took the sword out of your hand.**~~

{ l

5 **Aoife** But look again, Cuchulain { **Look again!** ~~**Look again!**~~

6 **Cuchullain** **Your hair is white.**

That time

Aiofe ~~**All that**~~ **was long ago**

7 **And now it is my time, I have come to kill you.**

Where am I? Why am I here?

8 **Cuchullain** ~~**I do not understand. Why am I here?**~~

their leave

You asked ~~when certain~~

9 **Aoife** ~~**You fought with many men when it was certain**~~

certain When that you had six mortal wounds ~~permission~~

10 ~~**That you were wounded to the death, asked leave**~~

out the

11 **To drink** ^ **of** ~~**that**~~ **pool.** ~~**there and then returned**~~

^

I have put my belt

12 **Cuchullain** ~~**I want to put my belt about this stone**~~

about this stone & want to fasten it

13 and ~~**To**~~ **die upon my feet, but am too weak.**

14 **Fasten this belt.**

(she helps him to do so)

And now I know your name,

15 Aoife the mother of my son, we met

{ A

~~We met~~ { at the Hawks Well under the withered trees

16 ~~**Aoife, the Scottish mother of my son**~~,

~~I met you at the Great Hawks withered well~~

17 upon **I killed him** ~~**at**~~ **Baile's Strand,** ~~**and**~~ **that is why**

18 ~~**The army of Maeve has let you through its ranks**~~

~~Maeve's army parted ranks to let you through~~

Maeve parted ranks that she might let you through.

Confused by the omission of a typed page 8, Yeats renumbered this leaf, leaving no page 9.

1 The arrow was added in pencil.

3 The typed "Tii" was corrected in pencil to "Till."

5 The capital "L" was changed to lowercase in ink.

11 The period after "pool" was added in ink.

16 The comma after "son" was added in pencil.

10

Cuchullain You have a right to kill me.

Aoife Though I have
and no part of it let me
Her army ~~has not let me~~ through. ~~the ranks~~
The grey of Macha that great horse of yours
Killed in the battle, came out of the pool
As though it were alive, and went three times
In a great circle round you and that stone
Then leaped into the pool and not a man
Of all that terrified army dare approach
But I approach.

Cuchullain , Because you have the right.

Aoife But I am an old woman now and that
Your strength wanes and so if
~~You may not use that strength~~ when the time comes
I ~~will~~ wind my veil about ~~round~~ this ancient stone
And fasten Down your hands ~~you to it~~.

Cuchullain But do not spoil your veil
Your veils are beautiful, some with threads of gold

Aiofe I am too old to care for such things now.
(she has wound the veil about him)

10

1 **Cuchullain** **You have a right to kill me.**
Aoife **Though I have**
did not part to let me
2 **Her army ~~has not~~ ^ ~~let me~~ through.** ~~**the ranks**~~
3 **The grey of Macha that great horse of yours**
4 **Killed in the battle, came out of the pool**
5 **As though it were alive, and went three times**
6 **In a great circle round you and that stone**
7 **Then leaped into the pool and not a man**
8 **Of all that terrified army dare approach**
9 **But I approach.**
Cuchullain , **Because you have the right.**
10 **Aoife** **But I am an old woman now and that**
Your strength may not sart up
11 ~~**You may not use that strength**~~ **when the time comes**
about
12 **I ~~will~~ wind my veil ~~round~~ this ancient stone**
down your hands.
13 **And fasten ^ ~~you to it~~.**
Cuchullain **But do not spoil your veil**
14 **Your veils are beautiful, some with threads of gold**
15 **Aiofe** **I am too old to care for such things now.**
(she has wound the veil about him)

---

2 The period after "through" was added in ink.
11 In the revision Yeats may have begun to write "might" and then changed the word to "may."
12 "round" was cancelled and "abou " added in pencil.

II

Cuchullain — There was no reason so to spoil your veil
I am weak from loss of blood.

Aoife — I was afraid,
But now that I have wound you in the veil
Our son – how did he fight.
I am not afraid. ~~But how did my son fight?~~

Cuchullain — Age makes more skilful but not better men.

Aoife — I have been told you did not know his name,
And wanted, because he had a look of me,
To be his friend, but Concubar forbade it.

Cuchullain — Forbade it and commanded me to fight;
That very day I had sworn to do his will,
Yet, him and about a
~~I had~~ refused, ~~had~~ spoken ~~of that~~ look,
? said
But somebody spoke of withhcraft and ~~at that word~~
witchcraft had made the look & fought & killed him
~~I said that he had done it, and we fought,~~
Then I went mad, ~~and~~ fought ~~against the sea.~~
~~Why did I fight against him, that look, that look!~~
with the rich vague sea.

Aoife — ~~Before he was conceived, I hated men~~
~~But I loved the sword, I seemed invincible;~~
invulnerable
~~We fought all day but then~~ you took my sword
You
Threw me upon the ground and left me there.
I searched the mountain for your sleeping place
And laid my virgin body at your side,
And yet because you had left me hated you
~~You left me untouched.~~

11

1 **Cuchullain** **There was no reason so to spoil your veil**
2 **I am weak from loss of blood.**
Aoife **I was afraid**,
3 **But now that I have wound you in the veil**
Our son — how did he fight.
4 **I am not afraid.** ~~**But how did my son fight?**~~
5 **Cuchullain** **Age makes more skilful but not better men.**
6 **Aoife** **I have been told you did not know his name,**
7 **And wanted, because he had a look of me,**
8 **To be his friend, but Concubar forbade it.**
9 **Cuchullain** **Forbade it and commanded me to fight;**
10 **That very day I had sworn to do his will,**
Yet I him and about ~~at~~ a
11 ~~**I had**~~ **refused,**∧ ~~**had**~~ **spoke**n ~~**of that**~~ **look,**
∧
I said
12 **But somebody spoke of witchcraft and** ~~**at that word**~~
Witchcraft had made the look & fought & killed him
13 ~~**I said that he had done it, and we fought,**~~
I ~~I knew not what~~.
14 **Then I went mad,** ~~**and**~~ **fought** ~~**against the sea.**~~
~~with the vague cold sea~~
15 ~~**Why did I fight against him, that look, that look!**~~
with the rich vague sea.
~~Our fight over by the~~
16 **Aoife** ~~**Before he was conceived I hated men**~~
17 ~~**But loved the sword, I seemed invincible;**~~
I seemed invulnerable;
18 ~~**We fought all day but then**~~ **you took my sword**
You
19 ∧**Threw me** ~~**up**~~**on the ground and left me there.**
20 **I searched the mountain for your sleeping place**
21 **And laid my virgin body at your side,**
And yet because you had left me hated you
22 ~~**You left me untouched.**~~

---

2 The comma after "afraid" was added in pencil.
10 The "w" in "will" was added in ink.
11 Yeats seems to have intended the carat to cancel the comma after "refused."
14 The comma after "mad" was added in ink.

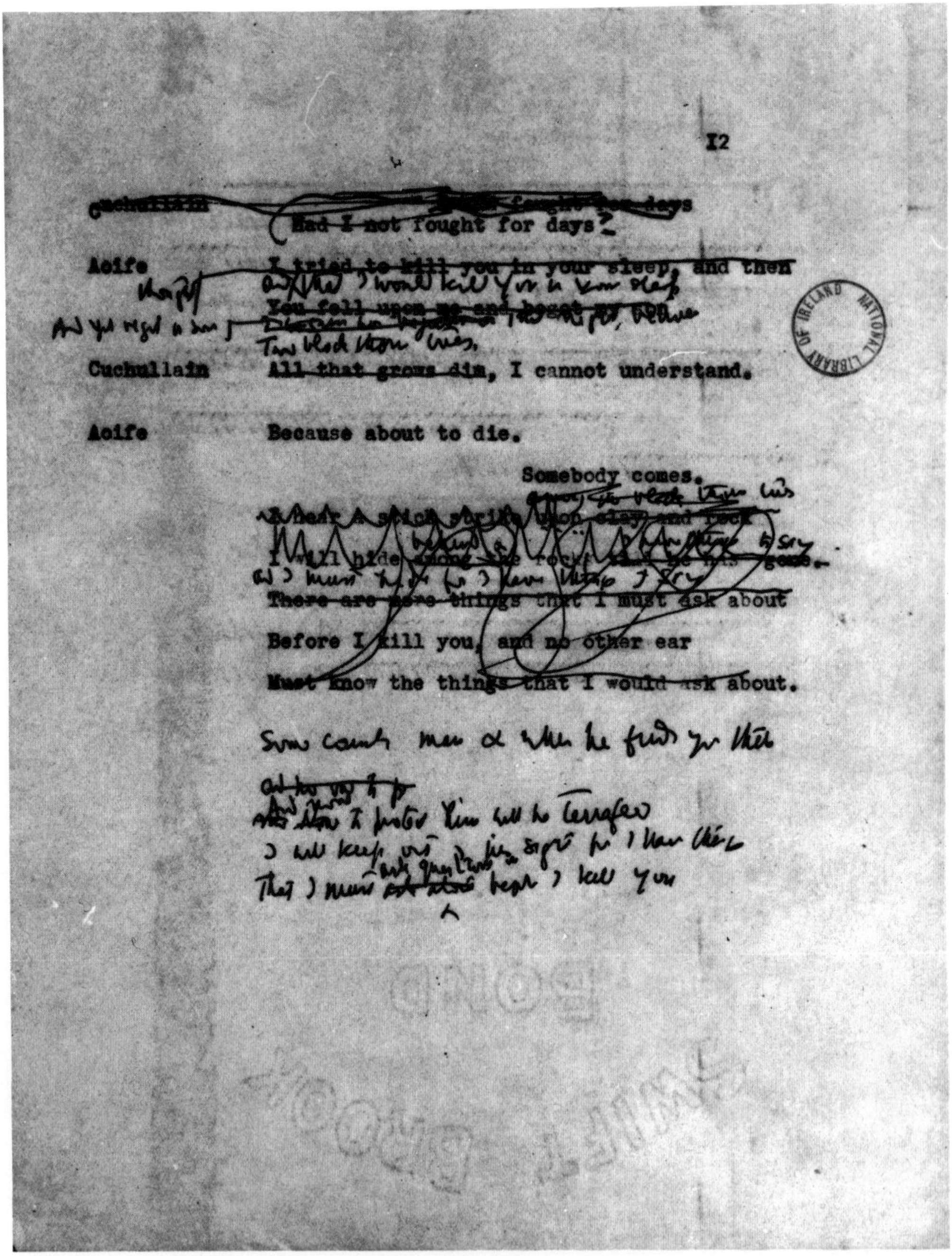

I2

Had I not fought for days?

Acife I tried to kill you in your sleep, and then

You fell upon me and begot my son

Cuchullain All that grows dim, I cannot understand.

Acife Because about to die.

Somebody comes.

There are more things that I must ask about

Before I kill you, and no other ear

Must know the things that I would ask about.

12

~~**Cuchullain I had fought for days.**~~

1 ~~**Had I not fought**~~ **for days**?

2 **Aoife** ~~**I tried to kill you in your sleep, and then**~~

thought [And] that I would kill you in your sleep

3 ~~**You fell upon me and begot my son**~~

[~~?~~] ~~was begotten on~~ that night between

Two black thorn trees.

4 **Cuchullain** ~~**All that grows dim,**~~ **I cannot understand.**

5 **Aoife** **Because about to die.**

Somebody comes.

among the black thorn trees

6 **I hear a stick strike** ~~**upon**~~ ~~**clay and rock**~~

behind a ‾‾‾ I have things to say

7 **I will hide** ~~**among the**~~ **rocks** ~~**till he has gone**~~**.**

And I must hide for I have things to say

8 ~~**There are more things that I must ask about**~~

9 **Before I kill you, and no other ear**

10 **Must know the things that I would ask about.**

11 Some country man & when he finds you there

~~And no one to p~~

And none

12 ~~And~~ ~~None~~ to protect him will be terrafied

13 I will keep out of his sight for I have things

ask questions on

14 That I must ~~ask about~~ before I kill you

^

And yet begot a son

The passage below the rule is from the left margin (revision of l. 3).

1 The question mark after "days" was added in pencil; "I had fought for days" was cancelled in pencil. In going over the typescript, Yeats apparently intended to cancel both line and revision.

7 The period after "gone" was cancelled in ink.

13

(She goes, the Blind Man of"B ile's Strand"comes in)
He moves his stick about unti he finds the standing
stone; he lays his stick down, stoops and touches
Cuchullain's feet. He feels the legs)

Blind Man Ah! Ah!

Cuchullain I think you are a blind old man

Blind Man A blind old beggar man. What is your name?

Cuchullain Cuchullain.

Blind Man I was there when you went mad,
...sea and fought against the waves,
They said that I would find you weak with wounds,
And there is something bound about your hands
So that they cannot move, soft womanish stuff,
I have been fumbling with my stick since the dawn
And then eard many voices. I began to beg.
Somebody said that I was in Maeve's tent,
And somebody else, a big man by his voice,
That if I brought Cuchullain's head in a bag
I would be given twelve pences; I had the bag
To carry what I get at kitchen doors,
And fter that how I could find the way
I thought it would have taken till the nig t
But this has been my lucky day.

[?~~weak w~~]
1 They say that you are weak with wounds
2 I stood between a fool & the sea at Baile s Strand
3 When you went mad. What s bound about your hands
13
4 So that they cannot move — some womanish stuff
~~**(She goes, the Blind Man of "B ile's Strand" comes in)**~~
~~**He moves his stick about unti he finds the standing**~~
~~**stone; he lays his stick down, stoops and touches**~~
~~**Cuchullain's feet, He feels the legs)**~~
5 **Blind Man** **Ah! Ah!**
6 **Cuchullain** **I think you are a blind old man**
7 **Blind Man** **A blind old beggar man. What is your name?**
8 **Cuchullain** **Cuchullain.**
~~I know, I know for I was there~~
I was there when you went mad
Blind M n ~~**I was there when you went mad,**~~
~~When you went mad & killed your son & now~~
9 ~~**Killed your son and fought against the waves,**~~
~~And now they say~~ you are
~~They tell me~~ [?I] ~~shall~~ And now they say that ~~I shall~~
10 ~~**They said that I would find you**~~ **weak with wounds**.
~~But what is~~ ~~What is there~~ bound & wound about your hands
11 ~~**And there is something bound about your hands**~~
12 ~~**So that they cannot move, soft womanish**~~ **stuff,**
13 **I have been fumbling with my stick since the dawn**
14 **And then eard many voices. I began to beg.**
15 **Somebody said that I was in Maeve's tent,**
16 **And somebody else, a big man by his voice,**
17 **That if I brought Cuchullain's head in a bag**
n
18 **I would be given twelve pen|ies;** **I had the bag**
{T
19 **{to carry what I get at kitchen doors,**
Somebody told me how to
20 ~~**And after that how I could**~~ **find the** ~~**way**~~ place
21 **I thought it would have taken till the night**
22 **But this has been my lucky day.**

In the third line of the stage directions, the "w" in "down" was added in ink.

6 The arrow was added in pencil.

10 The typed comma after "wounds" was either converted to a period or cancelled in ink.

18 The second "n" in "pennies" and the following semicolon were added in pencil. The semicolon was written over a typed period.

14

Cuchullain Twelve pennies!

Blind Man I would not promise anything until the woman,
The great queen Maeve herself, repeated the words.

Cuchullain Twelve pennies! What better reason for killing a man?
You have a knife, but have you sharpened it?

Blind Man I keep it sharp because it cuts my food.
(He lays bag on ground and begins feeling Cuchullain's body, his hands mounting upward)

Cuchullain I think that you know everything Blind Man,
My mother or my nurse said that the blind
Know everything.

Blind Man No, but they have good sense.
How could I have got twelve pennies for your head
If I had not good sense?

Cuchullain There floats out there
The shape that I shall take when I am dead,
My soul's first shape, a soft feathery shape,
And is not that a strange shape for a soul
Of a great fighting man?

Blind Man Your shoulder is there,
This is your neck. Ah! Ah! Are you ready Cuchullain?

14

Cuchullain Twelve pennies!
Blind Man I would not promise anything until the woman,
The great queen Maeve herself, repeated the words.
Cuchullain Twelve pennies/! What better reason for killing a man?
You have a knife, but have you sharpened it?
Blind Man I keep it sharp because it cuts my food.
(He lays bag on ground and|begins feeling Cuchullain's body, his hands mounting upward)
Cuchullain I think that you know everything Blind Man,
My mother or my nurse said that the blind
Know everything.
Blind Man No, but they have good sense.
How could I have got twelve pennies for your head
If I had not good sense?
Cuchullain There floats out there
The shape that I shall take when I am dead,
My soul's first shape, a soft feathery shape,
And is not that a strange shape for a soul
Of a great fighting man?
Blind Man ~~Yours~~ Your shoulder is there,
This is your neck. Ah! Ah! Are you ready Cuchullan?

---

3 The exclamation point was cancelled with a typed slash.
In the stage directions, the slash between "and" and "begins" was inserted in pencil.
14 The "s" in "yours" was cancelled in pencil.
15 The "n" in "Cuchullan" was typed over "i"; the question mark following the word was added in pencil.

15

Cuchullain   I say ~~[illegible]~~ it is about to sing.

(The stage darkens)

Blind Man   Ah! Ah!

As the curtain rises upon a bare stage

She is the Morrigu

~~(Music of pipe and drum. [illegible] the music ceases, there is nobody upon the stage except [illegible], a woman with a crow's head. She stands towards the back. She holds a black parallelogram the size of a man's head. There are six other parallelograms near the [illegible] back cloth)~~

Morague   The dead can hear me and to the dead I speak

here is great

This is Cuchullain's ~~head~~ those other six

Gave him six mortal wounds; this man came first,

Youth longer though the years ran on, that season

~~His youth had come to an end, he had that age~~

a woman's love

~~Women have lo~~ved the best, Maeve; ~~for a lover,~~ Cathleen's love

This man had given him the second wound

He had possessed her once, these were her sons

Two valiant men that gave the third and fourth

Th se other men were men of no account

They saw that he was weakening and crept in

And gave him the sixth wound and one the fifth,

Conor avenged him, I arrange the dance.

15

I say
Cuchullain ~~Clear now~~, it is about to sing.
(The stage darkens)
Blind Man Ah! Ah!
(Music of pipe and drum, ~~the curtain falls); it rises,~~ the music ceases, there is nobody upon the stage except ~~the Morague,~~ a woman with a crow's head. She stands towards the back. S he holds a black parallelogram the size of a man's head. There are six other parallelograms near the @@@@@@@ back cloth)
Moragüe The dead can hear me and to the dead I speak
head is great
This ∧ ~~is~~ ∧ Cuchullain's ~~head~~, those other six
Gave him six mortal wounds; this man came first
Youth lingered though the years ran on, that season
~~His youth had come to an end, he had that age~~
~~called him her~~
A woman loves latest lover
~~Women have loved~~ the best, Maeve~~s for ∧ a lover~~;
This man had given him the second wound
He had possessed her once, these were her sons
Two valiant men that gave the third and fourth
These other men were men of no account
They saw that he was weakening and crept in
One gave him the sixth wound and one the fifth,
d
Conor avenged him, I arrange ∧ the dance.

---

as the curtain rises upon
a bare stage

She is the Morrigu

The passages below the rule are from the left margin (revisions of the stage directions).

1 The comma after "now" was cancelled.

In the first line of the stage directions, the typed bracket after "falls" was cancelled and the semicolon added in pencil. In the second line, the commas after "rises" and "ceases" were cancelled in ink. In the third line, the comma after "Morague" was cancelled in ink. In the seventh line, the cancelled word was "curtain."

6 The "s" after "Maeve" was added in ink; the semicolon after "lover" was added in pencil.

13 The "d" in "arranged" was added in ink.

16

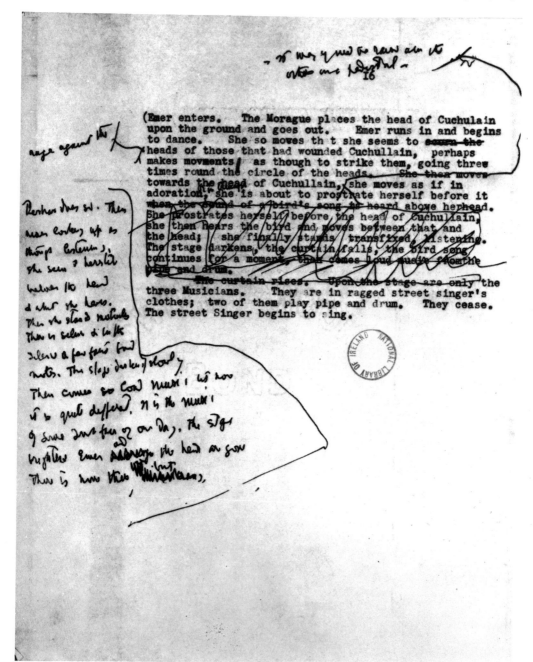

(Emer enters. The Morague places the head of Cuchulain upon the ground and goes out. Emer runs in and begins to dance. She so moves th t she seems to ~~scorn the~~ heads of those that had wounded Cuchullain, perhaps makes movments as though to strike them, going three times round the circle of the heads. ~~She then moves~~ towards the ~~head~~ of Cuchullain, she moves as if in adoration, she is about to prostrate herself before it ~~when the sound of a bird's song is heard above herhead. She prostrates herself before the head of Cuchullain, she then hears the bird and moves between that and the head; she finally stands transfixed listening. The stage darkens, the curtain falls, the bird song continues for a moment, then comes loud music from the pipe and drum.~~

~~The curtain rises. Upon the stage are only~~ the three Musicians. They are in ragged street singer's clothes; two of them play pipe and drum. They cease. The street Singer begins to sing.

— It may if need be raised above the
others on a pedestal —

16

(Emer enters. The Morague places the head of Cuchulain upon the ground and goes out. Emer runs in and begins to dance. She so moves that she seems to ~~scorn the~~ heads of those that had wounded Cuchullain, perhaps makes movments, as though to strike them, going three times round the circle of the heads. She then moves towards the head of Cuchullain, ^ she moves as if in
or in triumph
adoration, ^ she is about to prostrate herself before it when the sound of a bird's song is heard above herhead. She prostrates herself before the head of Cuchullain, she then hears the bird and moves between that and the head; she finally stands transfixed, listening. The stage darkens, the curtain falls, the bird song continues for a moment, then comes loud music fromthe pipe and drum.

The curtain rises. Upon the stage are only the three Musicians. They are in ragged street singer's clothes; two of them play pipe and drum. They cease. The street Singer begins to sing.

---

rage against the

Perhaps does so. Then
rises looking up as
though listening.
She seems to hesitate
between the head
& what she hears.
Then she stands motionless
There is silence & in the
silence a few faint bird
notes. The stage darkens slowly
Then comes ~~so~~ loud music but now
it's quite different. It is the music
of some Irish fair of our day. The stage
and
brightens Emer[?~~Morrigu~~] the heads are gone
[?~~but~~] but
There is none there ~~musicians~~.

The passages below the rule are from the left margin (revisions of the stage directions).
In the fifth line of the stage directions, the comma after "movments" was cancelled in pencil.

17

Singer The harlot sang to the beggarman.
I meet them face to face
Meet Conal, Cuchullain, and Usna's boys
All that most ancient race;
Maeve had three in an hour they say;
Adore those clever eyes
Those muscular bodies but can get
No grip upon their thighs
~~(Pipe and drum music)~~
I meet those long pale faces
Hear their great horses, then
Recall what centuries have passed
Since they were living men
That there are still some living
That do my limbs unclothe
But that the flesh my flesh has gripped
I both adore and loathe

(Pipe and drum music)

~~3~~
17

<u>Singer</u> The harlot sang to the beggarman.
I meet them face to face
~~Carnac~~
~~Meet~~ Conal, Cuchullain, ~~and~~ Usna's boys
All that most ancient race;
had
Maeve ~~used up~~ three in an hour they say;
I ∧ Adore those clever eyes
Those muscular bodies but can get
No grip upon their thighs
~~(Pipe and drum music)~~
I meet those long pale faces
Hear their great horses, then
Recall what centuries have passed
Since they were living men
That there are still some living
That do my limbs unclothe
But that the flesh my flesh has gripped
I both adore and loathe
<u>(Pipe and drum music)</u>

This leaf was originally numbered "3," and may have been taken from an earlier typescript; see the headnote to this section, p. 126.

3 The comma after "Cuchullain" was added in ink.

18

Singer Are these things that men adore and loathe
Their sole reality?
What stood in the Post Office
With Pearse and Connolly?
What comes out of the mountain
Where ~~men first~~ shed their blood?
Who ~~has dreamed~~ thought Cuchullain till it seemed
He stood where they had stood.

No body like ~~this~~ his body
Has modern woman borne,
But an old man looking back on life
Imagines it in scorn
A statue's there to mark the place
By Oliver Sheppard done
So ends the tale ~~of~~ that the harlot
Sang to the baggarman.

<u>(Music from pipe and drum)</u>

The curtain falls

18

o that
Singer **Are th|se things men adore and loathe**
/
Their sole reality?
What shood in the Post Office
With Pearse and Connolly?
What comes out of the mountain
Where men first shed their blood?
thought
Who ~~has dreamed~~ Cuchullain till it seemed
^
He stood where they had stood.

his
No body like ~~this~~ body
Has modern woman borne,
But an old man looking back on life
Imagines it in scorn
A statue's there to mark the place
By Oliver Sheppard done
that
So ends the tale ~~of~~ the harlot
Sang to the baggarman.
(Music from pipe and drum)
The curtain falls

1 The "o" in "those" was added in pencil.
6 The question mark after "blood" was added in ink.
15 "of" was cancelled in pencil.

6 Copies Corrected Jan 22. 1939

THE DEATH OF CUCHULLAIN

(A bare stage of any period. A very old man looking like something out of mythology)

Old Man I have been asked to produce a play called "The Death of Cuchullain". It is the last of a series of plays which has for theme ~~the~~ his life and death ~~of a legendary Irish figure~~. I have been selected because I am out of fashion and out of date like the antiquated romantic stuff the thing~~s~~ is made of. I am so old that I have forgotten the name of my father and mother, unless indeed I am, as I affirm, the son of Talma, and he was so old that ~~men~~ his friends and acquaintances still read Virgil and Homer. When they told me that I could have my own way I wrote certain guiding principles on a bit of newspaper. I wanted an audience of fifty or a hundred, and if there are more I beg them not to shuffle their feet or talk when the actors are speaking. I am sure that as I am producing a play for people I like it is not ~~likely~~ probable in this vile age that they will be more in number ~~numerous~~ than those who listened to the first performance of Milton's "Comus". On the present occasion they must know the old epics and Mr. Yeats' plays about them; such people however poor have libraries of their own. ~~they know the old epics and Mr. Yeats' plays and though they are poor men have their own libraries.~~ If there are more than a hundred I wont be able to escape people who

Evolution of the Text from TS6 to the Printed Versions

Typescript No. 7, on which Mrs. Yeats wrote out (possibly from Yeats's dictation) the revised version of TS6, is marked "corrected Jan 22 · 1939"; thus it predates her husband's death and its divergences from TS6 could have received authorial sanction.

According to Dorothy Wellesley, Yeats gave his wife corrections for the play on January 26. The extant documents do not clearly corroborate this story, as none of the substantive variants between the two typescripts show definite signs of having been introduced *after* the initial correction of TS7 by the twenty-second. On the cover of National Library of Ireland folder MS 8772#1, in Mrs. Yeats's hand, is a note saying, "Typescripts are corrected by WBY also corrections (*dictated*) by G.Y—". This may be a reference to the task completed by the twenty-second, but it is also possible that Mrs. Yeats copied *most* of the changes and that "dictated" refers only to the corrections Dorothy Wellesley says Yeats gave his wife on the twenty-sixth. If Dorothy Wellesley's account *was* accurate, Yeats's last thoughts about the play would almost certainly still be found in TS7, for the earliest of the typescripts postdating No. 7 was clearly posthumous. National Library of Ireland MS 8772#3 is marked "Uncorrected typescript / Place names etc have not been corrected / This version not to be lent. G. Y. [that is, George Yeats] 18·2·39." (See further pp. 181–182.) NLI MS 8772#4 is a carbon of TS3, as is the typescript in Senator Yeats's collection. All three of these contain corrections in the hand of F. R. Higgins. MS 8772#5 seems to be even later than these. All published versions of the play were of course also posthumous; Yeats never saw proofs even of the version in *Last Poems and Two Plays* (at least one set of which was corrected by Mrs. Yeats and Higgins).

Some of the differences between TS6 and TS7 are clearly improvements; others are questionable and may in fact represent errors. Yeats routinely allowed his wife and his editors (especially Elizabeth Yeats for the Cuala Press and Thomas Mark for Macmillan) to suggest corrections of his texts and changes in spelling and punctuation—though he often went over the suggestions carefully and did not always accept them. In the case of *The Death of Cuchulain* that process had only begun when he died, and thus there was no opportunity for him to "authorize" printed versions.

The text given below, though not a "reading text," may help the reader who wishes to avoid the complexities of the literatim transcription in the preceding section. Its primary purpose, however, is to show how much the play changed as that process developed. The basic text is that of TS6 in its final, revised form. All variant readings from TS7 are given in the apparatus; the degree of "authority" of each of these is uncertain, and may vary from one instance to the next. For example, it seems likely that Mrs. Yeats would have felt more free to alter punctuation than wording, and that Yeats would have been less likely to notice such changes; and some of the "substantive" alterations may have been errors that Yeats simply overlooked. Dictation could easily have led to confusion and errors, and Yeats might also have made changes as he was reading the text to her or even misread his own text. The apparatus also includes all variants between the basic text and the earliest and "final" printed texts, *Last Poems and Two Plays* and *Collected Plays*.

In the basic text, certain types of mechanical errors have been silently corrected and variants from their original forms have not been recorded: (a) errors involving spacing of letters, words, or lines; (b) typing errors, including the striking of one letter for another and the omission of letters; (c) errors in the closing of brackets; (d) errors in the uniform use of italics (as represented by underscoring) in stage directions; (e) errors involving the absence of an initial capital immediately following a full stop or at the beginning of a new line of verse. Yeats's frequent ampersands have been expanded.

The same principles have been applied to TS7.

Variant practices in the use of brackets to enclose stage directions have not been recorded.

The following abbreviations are used in the variants:

TS7 NLI MS 8772#7
LP *Last Poems and Two Plays by William Butler Yeats* (Dublin: The Cuala Press, 1939).
CP *The Collected Plays of W. B. Yeats* (London: Macmillan, 1952).

The spelling of proper names varies in the later versions as follows:

TS7	*LP, CP*
Cuchullain, Cuchulain	Cuchulain
Ethne, Eithne	Eithne
Conal Caernach	Conall Caernach
Morrague, Morague	Morrigu
Concubar	Conchubar
Maeve	Maeve

THE DEATH OF CUCHULLAIN

(*A bare stage of any period. A very old man looking like something out of mythology*)

Old Man I have been asked to produce a play called "The Death of Cuchullain". It is the last of a series of plays which has for theme his life and death. I have been selected because I am out of fashion and out of date like the antiquated romantic stuff the thing is made of. I am so old that I have forgotten the name of my father and mother, unless indeed I am, as I affirm, the son of Talma, and he was so old that his friends and acquaintances still read Virgil and Homer. When they told me that I could have my own way I wrote certain guiding principles on a bit of newspaper. I wanted an audience of fifty or a hundred, and if there are more I beg them not to shuffle their feet or talk when the actors are speaking. I am sure that as I am producing a play for people I like it is not probable in this vile age that they will be more in number than those who listened to the first performance of Milton s Comus On the present occasion they must know the old epics and Mr Yeats' plays about them. Such people however poor have libraries of their own If there are more than a hundred I wont be able to escape people who are educating themselves out of the book societies, book clubs and the like, sciolists all, pickpockets and opinionated bitches. Why pickpockets? I will explain that, I will make it all quite clear.

(*drum and pipe behind the scene, then silence*)

Directions before a Scene.—*A bare CP* *mythology. LP, CP*
b *The Death of Cuchulain CP*
i aquaintances *TS7*
j that I could] I could *LP* way, *LP, CP*
m more, *CP*
o like, *CP*
p probable, *CP* age, *LP, CP*
r Milton's *Comus*. On *TS7, LP, CP*
s Mr Yeats' *TS7* Mr. Yeats' *LP, CP*
t them; such people however poor have *TS7, LP* them; such people, however poor, have *CP*
u own. *TS7, LP, CP*
v won't *CP*
w book societies and *TS7, LP* Book Societies and *CP*
Directions after z *Drum LP, CP* *silence. LP, CP*

aa That's from the musicians; I asked them to do that
bb if I was getting excited. If you were as old you would
cc find it easy to get excited. Before the night ends you
dd will meet the music. There is a singer, a piper and a
ee drummer. I have picked them up here and there about
ff the streets, and I will teach them, if I live, the music
gg of the beggarman, Homer's music. I promise a
hh dance. I wanted a dance because where there are no
ii words there is less to spoil. Emer must dance, there
jj must be severed heads—I am old, I belong to mythology—
kk severed heads for her to dance before. I had
ll thought to have had those heads carved, but no, if the
mm dancer can dance properly no woodcarver can look
nn as well as a parallelogram of painted wood. But I was
oo at my wit's end to find a good dancer; I could have
pp got such a dancer once, but she has gone; the tragi-comedian
qq dancer, the tragic dancer, upon the same
rr neck love and loathing, life and death. I spit three
ss times. I spit upon the dancers painted by Degas.
tt I spit upon their short bodices, their stiff stays,
uu their toes whereon they spin like peg-tops, above
vv all upon that chambermaid face. They might have
ww looked timeless Rameses the Great, but not the
xx chambermaid, that old maid history! I spit! I spit!
yy I spit!

(*The stage is darkened, the curtain falls. Pipe and drum begin and continue until the curtain rises again on a bare stage half a minute later. Eithne Inguba enters.*)

1 Ethne Cuchullain! Cuchullain!

(*Cuchullain enters from back*)

I am Emer's messenger,
2 I am your wife's messenger, she has bid me say
3 You must not linger here in sloth for Maeve
4 With all those Connacht ruffians at her back
5 Burns barns and houses up at Emain Macha:
6 Your house at Muirthemne already burns.

---

dd piper, *CP*
gg beggar-man *CP* music. ¶I *LP*
mm wood-carving *LP, CP*
ww timeless, *TS7, LP, CP*
xx history. *TS7, LP, CP*
Directions after yy *continue, LP rises on TS7, LP, CP stage; Half a minute later. Eithne TS7 stage. Half a minute later Eithne LP, CP enters.*] *enters TS7*
3 sloth, *CP*

No matter what's the odds, no matter though
Your death may come of it, ride out and fight.
The scene is set and you must out and fight.

Cuchullain — You have told me nothing. I am already armed
I have sent a messenger to gather men,
And wait for his return. What have you there?

Eithne — I have nothing

Cuchullain — There is something in your hand.

Eithne — No.

Cuchullain — Have you not a letter in your hand?

Eithne — I do not know how it got into my hand.
I am straight from Emer. We were in some place.
She spoke. She saw.

Cuchullain — This letter is from Emer.
It tells a different story. I am not to move
Until tomorrow morning, for, if now,
I must face odds no man can face and live.
Tomorrow morning Conal Caernach comes
With a great host.

Eithne — I do not understand.
Who can have put that letter in my hand?

Cuchullain — And there is something more to make it certain
I shall not stir till morning; you are sent
To be my bedfellow, but have no fear
All that is written but I much prefer
Your own unwritten words. I am for the fight
I and my handful are set upon the fight
We have faced great odds before, a straw decided.
(*The Morrague enters and stands between them*)

Eithne — I know that somebody or something is there
Yet nobody that I can see.

Cuchullain — There is nobody.

---

10 armed, *CP*
13 nothing. *LP, CP*
14 you a *LP, CP*
17 Emer, *LP, CP*
19 to-morrow *LP, CP*
21 To-morrow *LP, CP*
26 fear, *LP, CP*
27 written, *CP*
28 fight, *CP*
29 fight, *LP* fight; *CP*
Directions after 30 *them. TS7, LP*
31 there, *CP*

33 Eithne — Who among the gods of the air and the upper air
34 — Has a birds head
Cuchullain — Morrague is headed like a crow.
35 Eithne — (*Dazed*) Morrague, war goddess, stands between.
36 — Her black wing touched me upon the shoulder, and now
The Morrague goes out
37 — All is is intelligable. Mave put me into a trance
38 — Though when Cuchulain slept with her as a boy
39 — She seemed as pretty as a bird she has changed
40 — She has an eye in the middle of her for head.
41 Cuchullain — A woman that has an an eye in the middle of her forehead
42 — A woman that is headed like a crow,
43 — But she that put those words into your mouth
44 — Had nothing monstrous; you put them there yourself.
45 — You need a younger man, a friendlier man,
46 — But fearing what my violence might do
47 — Thought out those words to send me to my death,
48 — And were in such excitement you forgot
49 — The letter in your hand.
Eithne — Now that I wake
50 — I say that Maeve did nothing out of error
51 — What mouth could you beleve if not my mouth.
52 Cuchulain — When I went mad at my son s death and drew
53 — My sword against the sea it was my wife
54 — That brought me back
Eithne — Better women than I

---

33 and the upper] and upper *LP, CP*
34 bird's head? *TS7, LP, CP*
35 *dazed TS7, LP dazed*]. *CP*
36 and now] and *CP*
Directions after 36 *The Morrague*] *Morrague TS7 Morrigu LP* *out. LP, CP* (Direction moved to 1.37 in TS7, *LP, CP*)
37 is is intelligable] is intelligible. *TS7, LP, CP* into] in *LP, CP* trance, *LP* trance. *CP*
39 bird, *TS7, LP, CP* changed, *LP, CP*
40 forehead *TS7* forehead. *LP, CP*
41 has an eye *TS7, LP, CP* forehead! *LP, CP*
42 crow! *LP, CP*
44 yourself, *LP* yourself; *CP*
46 But, *CP* do, *CP*
47 those] these *LP, CP*
49 hand.] hand. O Eithne, Eithne *TS7*
50 error] reason; *TS7, LP, CP*
51 believe *TS7, LP, CP* mouth.] mouth? *TS7, LP, CP*
52 son's *TS7, LP, CP*
53 sea, *TS7, LP, CP*
54 back. *TS7, LP, CP*

Have served you well but t'was to me you turned
Cuchulain You thought that if you changed I'd kill you for it
When everything subliminal must change
And if I have not changed that goes to prove
That I am monstrous
Eithne You re not the man I loved
That violent man forgave no treachery
If thinking what you think you can forgive
It is because you are about to die.
Cuchulain Spoken too loudly and too near the door
Speak low if you would speak about my death
Or not in that strange voice exulting in it
Who knows what ears listen behind the dor
Eithne Some that would not forgive a traitor, some
That have the passion necessary to life,
Some not about to die. When you are gone
I shall denounce myself to all your cooks,
Scullions, armourers, bed-makers and messengers,
Until they hammer me with a ladle, cut me with a knife
Impale me upon a spit, put me to death
By what foul way best please their fancy,
So that my shade can stand among the shades
And greet your shade and prove it is no traitor.
Cuchulain Women have spoken so plotting man's death
(*Enter a servant*)
Servant Your great horse is bitted. All wait the word.
Cuchullain I come to give it, but must ask a question.
This woman, wild with grief, declares that she
Out of pure treachery has told me lies
That should have brought my death. What can I do?

---

55 well, *TS7, LP, CP* 'tws *TS7* 'twas *LP, CP* turned. *TS7, LP, CP*
56 it, *CP*
57 subliminal] sublunary *TS7, LP, CP* change, *TS7, LP, CP*
59 montstrous. *TS7* monstrous. *LP, CP* You are *TS7* You're *LP, CP* loved, *TS7, LP, CP*
60 treachery. *TS7, LP, CP*
61 If, *CP* think, *CP* forgive, *CP*
63 door; *TS7, LP, CP*
64 death, *TS7, LP, CP*
65 it. *LP, CP*
66 door *TS7* door? *LP, CP*
70 cooks. *LP*
71 bed-makers, *LP*
72 knife, *TS7, LP, CP*
74 fancy,] fancy *TS7*
77 so, *LP, CP* plotting man's] plotting a man's *TS7, LP, CP* death. *LP, CP*
Directions after 77 *Servant CP*
80 woman,] woman *LP*

83 How can I save her from her own wild words?
84 Servant Is her confession true?
Cuchullain I make the truth
85 I say she brings a message from my wife.
86 Servant What if I make her swallow poppy juice.
87 Cuchullain What herbs seem suitable but protect her life
88 As it were your own and should I not return
89 Give her to Conal Caernach because the women
90 Have called him a good lover
Eithne I might have peace that know
91 The Morrigue, the woman like a crow,
92 Stands to my defence and cannot lie
93 But that Cuchulain is about to die.
Pipe and Drum. The stage is dark for a moment
When it lights up again it is empty. Cuchulain
enters wounded. He tries to fasten himself to the stage
with his belt. Aoife enters
94 Aoife Am I recognised, Cuchullain?
Cuchullain You fought with a sword,
95 It seemed that we should kill each other; then
96 Your body wearied and I took your sword.
97 Aoife But look again, Cuchulain look again!
98 Cuchullain Your hair is white.
Aoife That time was long ago
99 And now it is my time, I have come to kill you.
100 Cuchullain Where am I? Why am I here?
Aoife You asked their leave
101 When certain that you had six mortal wounds
102 To drink out of the pool.

---

84 truth, *TS7* truth! *LP, CP*
86 poppy juice? *TS7, LP* poppy-juice? *CP*
87 suitable, *LP, CP*
88 As it] As if it *TS7, LP, CP* own, *LP, CP*
90 lover. *TS7, LP, CP*
91 crow,] crow *LP*
92 lie, *TS7, LP, CP*
Directions after 93 *drum. TS7, LP, CP stage is dark*] *stage grows dark TS7, LP, CP moment. TS7, LP, CP again, LP, CP empty.*] *empty TS7 to the stage with*] *to a pillarstone with TS7 to a pillar-stone with LP, CP Aoife, an erect white-haird woman, enters. TS7 Aoife, an erect white-haired woman enters. LP Aoife, an erect white-haired woman, enters. CP*
95 other, *LP, CP*
97 Cuchulain! Look *TS7, LP, CP*
98 ago, *TS7, CP*
99 time. *TS7, LP, CP*
100 leave, *TS7, LP, CP*
101 wounds, *TS7, LP, CP*
102 pool.] pool *TS7*

Cuchullain — I have put my belt
About this stone and want to fasten it
And die upon my feet, but am too weak.
Fasten this belt.
(*she helps him to do so*)
And now I know your name,
Aoife the mother of my son, we met
At the Hawks Well under the withered trees
I killed him upon Baile's Strand, that is why
Maeve parted ranks that she might let you through.
You have a right to kill me.

Aoife — Though I have
Her army did not part to let me through.
The grey of Macha that great horse of yours
Killed in the battle, came out of the pool
As though it were alive, and went three times
In a great circle round you and that stone
Then leaped into the pool and not a man
Of all that terrified army dare approach
But I approach.

Cuchullain — Because you have the right.

Aoife — But I am an old woman now and that
Your strength may not sart up when the time comes
I wind my veil about this ancient stone
And fasten down your hands.

Cuchullain — But do not spoil your veil
Your veils are beautiful, some with threads of gold

Aoife — I am too old to care for such things now.
(*she has wound the veil about him*)

Cuchullain — There was no reason so to spoil your veil
I am weak from loss of blood.

---

105 belt.] belt *TS7, LP* *She LP, CP* *so. CP*
106 Aoife, *LP, CP* son. We *LP, CP*
107 Hawk's *TS7, LP, CP* trees. *CP*
109 through.] through *TS7*
110 I have] I have, *LP, CP*
111 through.] through *TS7*
112 Macha, *LP, CP*
115 stone, *LP, CP*
116 pool; *CP*
117 approach; *LP* approach, *CP*
119 now, *LP, CP*
120 start *TS7, LP, CP*
122 down your hands.] you to it. *LP, CP* veil. *LP, CP*
123 gold. *LP, CP*
Directions after 124 (*She LP, CP* *him. CP*
125 veil: *CP*

Aoife — I was afraid,
But now that I have wound you in the veil
I am not afraid. Our son—how did he fight.
Cuchullain — Age makes more skilful but not better men.
Aoife — I have been told you did not know his name,
And wanted, because he had a look of me,
To be his friend, but Concubar forbade it.
Cuchullain — Forbade it and commanded me to fight;
That very day I had sworn to do his will,
Yet I refused him and spoke about a look,
But somebody spoke of witchcraft and I said
Witchcraft had made the look and fought and killed him
Then I went mad, I fought with the rich vague sea.
Aoife — I seemed invulnerable; you took my sword
You threw me on the ground and left me there.
I searched the mountain for your sleeping place
And laid my virgin body at your side,
And yet because you had left me hated you
And thought that I would kill you in your sleep
And yet begot a son that night between
Two black thorn trees.
Cuchullain — I cannot understand.
Aoife — Because about to die.
Somebody comes.
Some country man and when he finds you there
And none to protect him will be terrafied
I will keep out of his sight for I have things
That I must ask questions on before I kill you

---

127 veil, *LP*
128 afraid. Our son—how did he fight? *TS7* afraid. But how did my son fight? *LP* afraid. But—how did my son fight? *CP*
130 name,] name *CP*
135 Yet I refused] Yet refused *LP, CP* him, *LP, CP* look; *TS7, LP, CP*
137 look, *TS7, LP, CP* him. *LP, CP*
138 with the rich vague sea.] against the sea. *TS7, LP, CP*
139 sword, *LP, CP*
141 sleeping-place *CP*
143 yet, *TS7, CP* me, *TS7, LP, CP* hated you. *LP* hated you, *CP*
After 143 Cuchullain [speaker] Had I not fought for days? *TS7*
144 sleep, *TS7, CP*
146 thorn-trees. *CP*
147 die! *LP, CP* comes, *CP*
148 countryman, *TS7, CP* countryman; *LP* you there, *TS7* you here *LP* you here, *CP*
149 him, *TS7, LP, CP* terrified. *TS7, LP, CP*
150 sight, *CP*
151 you. *TS7, LP, CP*

(*She goes, the Blind Man of "Baile's Strand" comes in He moves his stick about until he finds the standing stone; he lays his stick down, stoops and touches Cuchullain's feet, He feels the legs*)

152 Blind Man — Ah! Ah!
Cuchullain — I think you are a blind old man
153 Blind Man — A blind old beggar man. What is your name?
154 Cuchullain — Cuchullain.
Blind Man — They say that you are weak with wounds
155 I stood between a fool and the sea at Baile s Strand
156 When you went mad. What s bound about your hands
157 So that they cannot move—some womanish stuff
158 I have been fumbling with my stick since the dawn
159 And then heard many voices. I began to beg.
160 Somebody said that I was in Maeve's tent,
161 And somebody else, a big man by his voice,
162 That if I brought Cuchullain's head in a bag
163 I would be given twelve pennies; I had the bag
164 To carry what I get at kitchen doors,
165 Somebody told me how to find the place
166 I thought it would have taken till the night
167 But this has been my lucky day.
Cuchullain — Twelve pennies!
168 Blind Man — I would not promise anything until the woman,
169 The great queen Maeve herself, repeated the words.
170 Cuchullain — Twelve pennies. What better reason for killing a man?
171 You have a knife, but have you sharpened it?
172 Blind Man — I keep it sharp because it cuts my food.
(*He lays bag on ground and begins feeling Cuchullain's body, his hands mounting upward*)
173 Cuchullain — I think that you know everything Blind Man,

Directions after 151 *goes. The CP* *Baile's Strand LP* *'On Baile's Strand' CP* *in. LP, CP* *feet. LP, CP* *legs. LP, CP*
152 man. *LP, CP*
153 beggar-man. *CP*
154 wounds. *TS7, LP, CP*
155 Fool *LP, CP* Baile's *TS7, LP, CP*
156 What's *TS7, LP, CP*
157 move? Some *TS7, LP, CP* stuff. *TS7, LP, CP*
158 since the dawn] since dawn *LP, CP*
165 place; *LP, CP*
166 night, *CP*
169 Queen *CP*
170 pennies! *LP, CP*
Directions after 172 *upward. LP, CP*
173 everything, *CP* Man,] Man. *LP, CP*

174 My mother or my nurse said that the blind
175 Know everything.
Blind Man — No, but they have good sense.
176 How could I have got twelve pennies for your head
177 If I had not good sense?
Cuchullain — There floats out there
178 The shape that I shall take when I am dead,
179 My soul's first shape, a soft feathery shape,
180 And is not that a strange shape for a soul
181 Of a great fighting man?
Blind Man — Your shoulder is there,
182 This is your neck. Ah! Ah! Are you ready Cuchullain?
183 Cuchullain — I say it is about to sing.
(*The stage darkens*)
Blind Man — Ah! Ah!
(*Music of pipe and drum, the music ceases as the curtain rises upon a bare stage there is nobody upon the stage except a woman with a crow's head. She is the Morrigu She stands towards the back. She holds a black parallelogram the size of a man's head. There are six other parallelograms near the back cloth*)
184 Moraigue — The dead can hear me and to the dead I speak
185 This head is great Cuchullain's, those other six
186 Gave him six mortal wounds; this man came first,
187 Youth lingered though the years ran on, that season
188 A woman loves the best, Maeve s latest lover;
189 This man had given him the second wound
190 He had possessed her once, these were her sons
191 Two valiant men that gave the third and fourth
192 These other men were men of no account
193 They saw that he was weakening and crept in

---

180 for a soul] for the soul *CP*
181 fighting-man? *CP*
182 ready, *CP* Cuchulain! *CP*
183 say, *LP* *darkens. CP*
Directions after 183 *drum, the curtain falls, the music TS7 drum, the curtain falls. The music LP, CP stage. There TS7, LP, CP Morrigu. LP, CP parallelogram, LP, CP back cloth. LP backcloth. CP*
184 me, *CP* speak. *LP, CP*
186 wounds. This *CP* first,] first; *CP*
188 best. *LP, CP* Maeve's *TS7, LP, CP* lover;] lover, *LP, CP*
189 man, *LP, CP* wound, *LP, CP*
190 once,] once; *LP, CP* sons, *LP, CP*
191 fourth; *LP* fourth: *CP*
192 account, *LP, CP*
193 in; *CP*

194 One gave him the sixth wound and one the fifth,
195 Conor avenged him, I arranged the dance.

(Emer enters. The Morague places the head of Cuchulain upon the ground and goes out. Emer runs in and begins to dance. She so moves that she seems to rage against the heads of those that had wounded Cuchullain, perhaps makes movements as though to strike them, going three times round the circle of the heads. She then moves towards the head of Cuchullain, — It may if need be raised above the others on a pedestal — she moves as if in adoration or in triumph, she is about to prostrate herself before it Perhaps does so. Then rises looking up as though listening. She seems to hesitate between the head and what she hears. Then she stands motionless There is silence and in the silence a few faint bird notes. The stage darkens slowly Then comes loud music but now it's quite different. It is the music of some Irish fair of our day. The stage brightens Emer and the heads are gone There is none there but the three Musicians. They are in ragged street singer's clothes; two of them play pipe and drum. They cease. The street Singer begins to sing.)

196 Singer The harlot sang to the beggarman.
197 I meet them face to face
198 Conal, Cuchullain, Usna's boys
199 All that most ancient race;
200 Maeve had three in an hour they say;

---

194 fifth,] fifth; *LP*, *CP*
195 Conor] Conall *LP*, *CP* him,] him. *LP*, *CP*
Directions after 195 [Ellipses indicate identity with the basic text.]

... *may, if need be, raised* ... *listening; she* ... *motionless. There* ... *slowly. Then* ... *music, but now it is quite* ... *head* ... *gone. There* ... *TS7*

... *of Cuchulain, it may, if need be, raised* ... *pedestal. She* ... *triumph. She* ... *before it. Perhaps* ... *rises, looking* ... *listening; she* ... *motionless. There* ... *slowly. Then* ... *music, but now it is quite* ... *Fair* ... *brightens. Emer* ... *head* ... *gone. There* ... *musicians* ... *singers' clothing; two* ... *them begin to play the pipe* ... *singer* ... *LP*

... *of Cuchulain; it may, if need be, be raised* ... *pedestal. She* ... *or triumph. She* ... *before it, perhaps* ... *so, then rises, looking* ... *as if listening; she* ... *motionless. There* ... *silence, and* ... ¶ ... *slowly. Then* ... *music, but now it is quite* ... *Fair* ... *brightens. Emer* ... *head* ... *gone*. ... *There is no one there* ... *musicians* ... *street-singers'* ... *them begin to pipe* ... *Street-Singer* ... *CP*

196 beggar-man. *CP*
197 face to face, *CP*
198 boys, *TS7*, *LP*, *CP*
200 hour, *CP* say;] say. *LP*, *CP*

I Adore those clever eyes
Those muscular bodies but can get
No grip upon their thighs
I meet those long pale faces
Hear their great horses, then
Recall what centuries have passed
Since they were living men
That there are still some living
That do my limbs unclothe
But that the flesh my flesh has gripped
I both adore and loathe
(*Pipe and drum music*)
Are those things that men adore and loathe
Their sole reality?
What stood in the Post Office
With Pearse and Connolly?
What comes out of the mountain
Where men first shed their blood?
Who thought Cuchullain till it seemed
He stood where they had stood.

No body like his body
Has modern woman borne,
But an old man looking back on life
Imagines it in scorn
A statue's there to mark the place
By Oliver Sheppard done
So ends the tale that the harlot
Sang to the beggarman.
(*Music from pipe and drum*)
The curtain falls

---

201 adore *LP, CP* eyes, *LP, CP*
202 bodies, *LP, CP*
203 thighs. *LP, CP*
204 faces, *CP*
207 men. *LP, CP*
209 unclothe, *LP, CP*
211 loathe. *LP, CP*
Directions after 211 *music. CP*
217 blood?] blood, *LP*
219 stood.] stood? *LP, CP*
221 borne,] borne. *LP*
223 scorn. *TS7, LP, CP*
224 place, *CP*
225 done. *TS7, CP* done, *LP*
227 beggar-man. *CP*
Directions after 227 *drum. CP*
THE CURTAIN FALLS *LP* THE END *CP*

Notes on Textual Problems

u The period in TS6 may have been cancelled unintentionally.

mm–nn TSS 6 and 7 have "no woodcarver can look as well," but "look" was a revision of "do" and both Yeats and Mrs. Yeats failed to see that this change necessitated a corresponding alteration from "woodcarver" to "wood-carving." The change was first made in the later typescripts.

14 TSS 6 and 7 both read "Have you not a letter in your hand?" The "not" was omitted in typing the later typescripts, probably by accident.

33 TSS 6 and 7 were both corrected to read "of the air and the upper air." The second "the" was omitted in typing the later typescripts, probably by accident.

35–43 Among the typescripts is a leaf (numbered "5") containing a version of a passage much altered by Yeats in the correction of TS6:

EITHNE Morrague War Goddess stands between,
Her black wing touched me upon the shoulder and now
All is intelligible.
(*Morrague goes out*)
Maeve put me in a trance,
Though when Cuchullain slept with her as a boy
She seemed as pretty as a bird, she has changed,
She has an eye in the middle of her forehead.

CUCHULLAIN A woman that has an eye in the middle of her forehead
A woman that is headed like a crow
But she that put those words into your mouth
etc

It was probably typed to facilitate the reading of a passage revised so extensively that it had become difficult to follow, but does not seem to have been used in preparing the later typescripts.

36 TSS 6 and 7 (and the later TS5) read "and now"; in TSS 3 and 4 the "now" was omitted during the typing process, probably by accident.

47 TSS 6 and 7 read "those" but the "o" in TS7 (a carbon at this point) was faint and led to the reading "these" in later typescripts and in the printed texts.

Directions after 93 The corrected TS6 read "*stage is dark.*" The corresponding page of TS7 was taken from an earlier typescript (now lost), and it read "*stage grows dark.*" In altering the page to bring it into line with TS6, Mrs. Yeats may have overlooked the discrepancy. On the other hand the TS6 version, a holograph insertion, shows clear evidence of haste; and it is conceivable that the more precise "*grows*" was intentionally allowed to stand. A problem of the same sort occurs in the last sentence. In TS6 Yeats wrote only "*Aoife enters.*" The earlier typescript contained the phrase "*an erect white-haird woman,*" and Mrs. Yeats did not cancel it.

122 TS6 read "And fasten you to it"; Yeats corrected this to "And fasten down your hands." Mrs. Yeats made the same change in TS7, and it was incorporated into the later typescripts. The change back to "you to it" was made during correction of the proofs of *LP* and adopted by all the printed versions.

128 TS6 read "But how did my son fight?" Yeats corrected to "Oúr son—how did he fight." The correction was followed in TS7 and the later typescripts. The return to the uncorrected TS6 version was made during correction of the proofs of *LP*; that reading was followed by all the printed texts.

135 TSS 6 and 7 were both corrected to read "Yet I refused." The "I" was omitted in typing TSS 3 and 4, probably by accident.

143 The comma after "yet" in TS7 is uncertain.

188–189 In correcting TS6 Yeats wrote "best, Maeves latest lover;" and Mrs. Yeats altered TS7 appropriately. TSS 3, 4, and 5 replaced the semicolon with a period, but still clearly applied the phrase to the warrior who gave Cuchulain the *first* wound. By changing the comma after "best" to a period, ending the line with a comma, and introducing a second comma between "man" and "had" in line 189, the corrected proofs of *LP* transferred the phrase to the second warrior.

195 TSS 6 and 7 both had "Conor" instead of "Conall." The manuscript version was definitely "Conal." "Conall" was a change made in the correction of TSS 3 and 4.

222 *The Variorum Edition* erroneously omits "back."

225 The TS7 reading could be a comma.